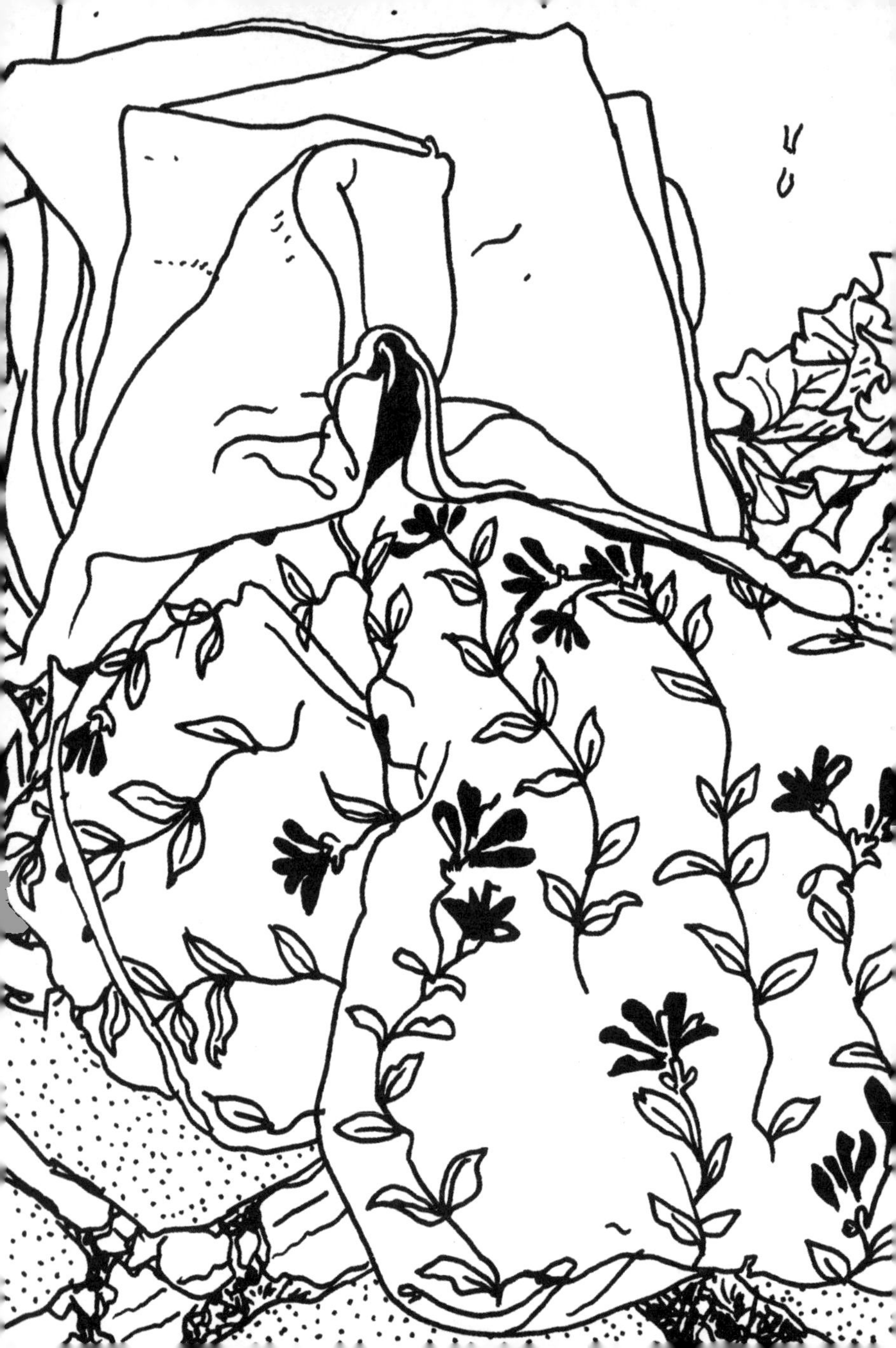

Ingo Giezendanner
Sloppy Sleep

GRR89

GRR89
Sloppy Sleep

Drawings, Scans, Layout & Production
Ingo Giezendanner www.grrrr.net

Conceived during a residency at Cité Internationale des Arts Paris
Kindly supported by Präsidialabteilung Stadt Zürich and Franziska & Bruno

First Edition

Published by Nieves
www.nievesbooks.com

ISBN 978-3-907179-23-9

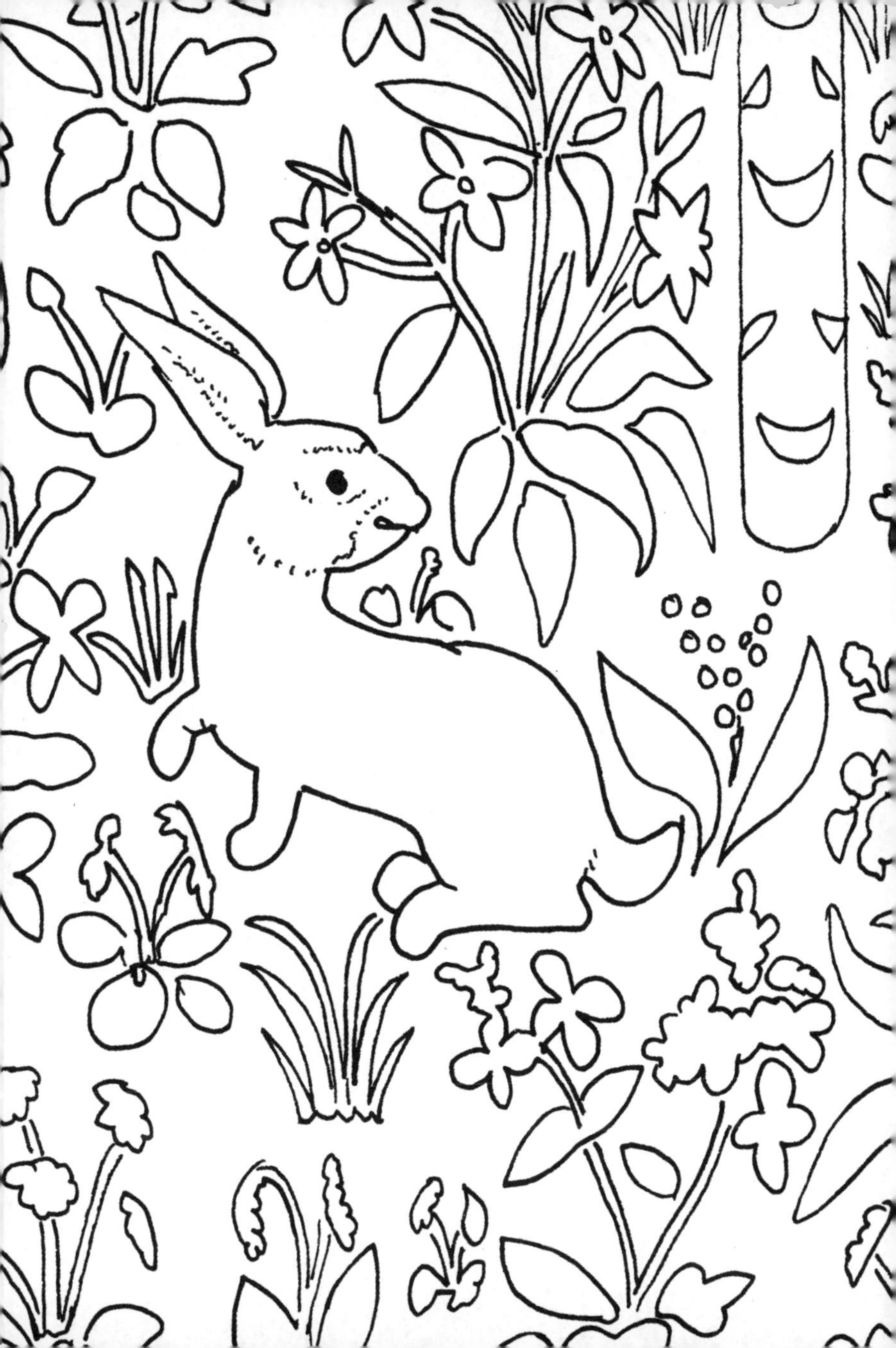

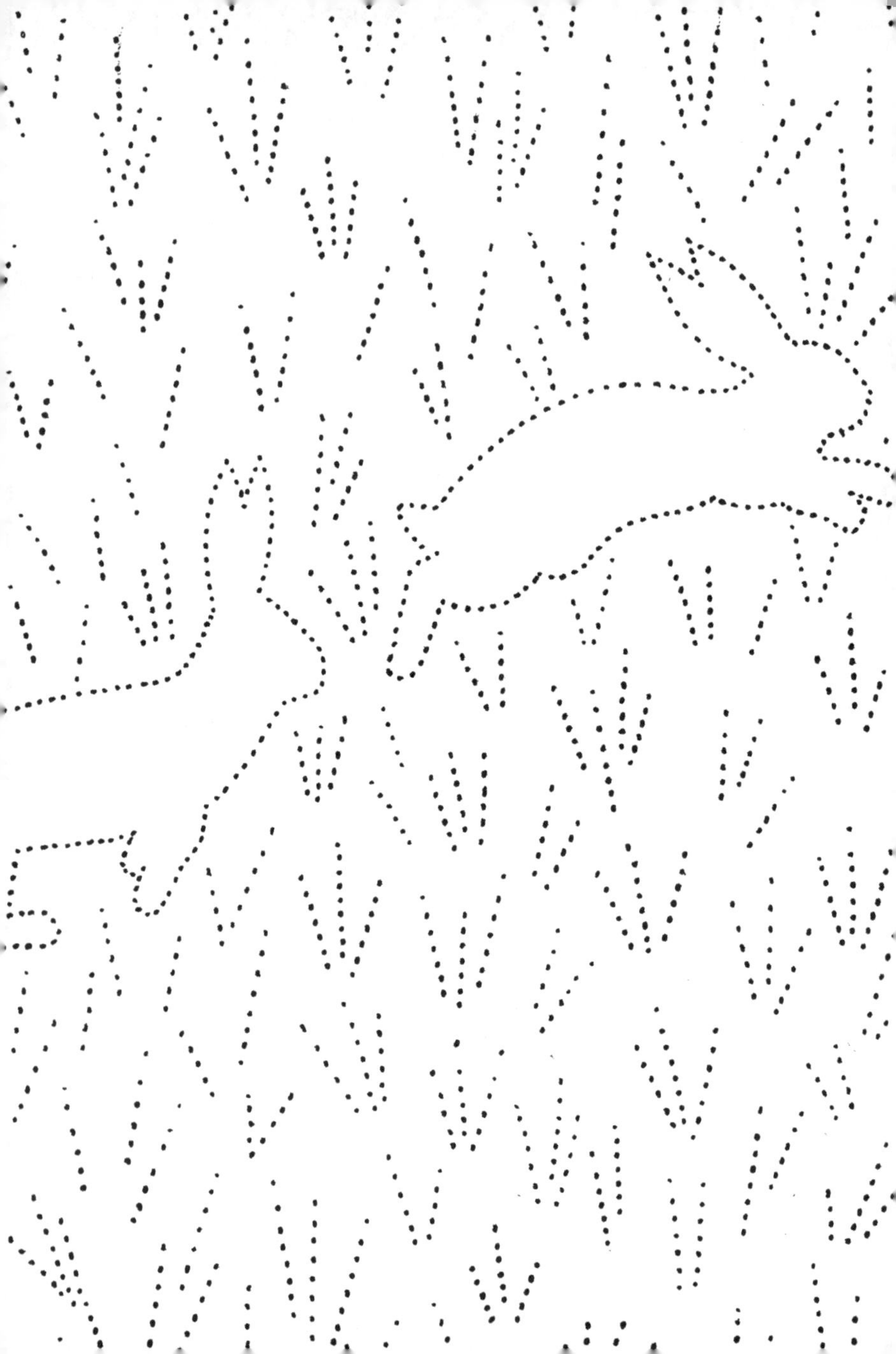

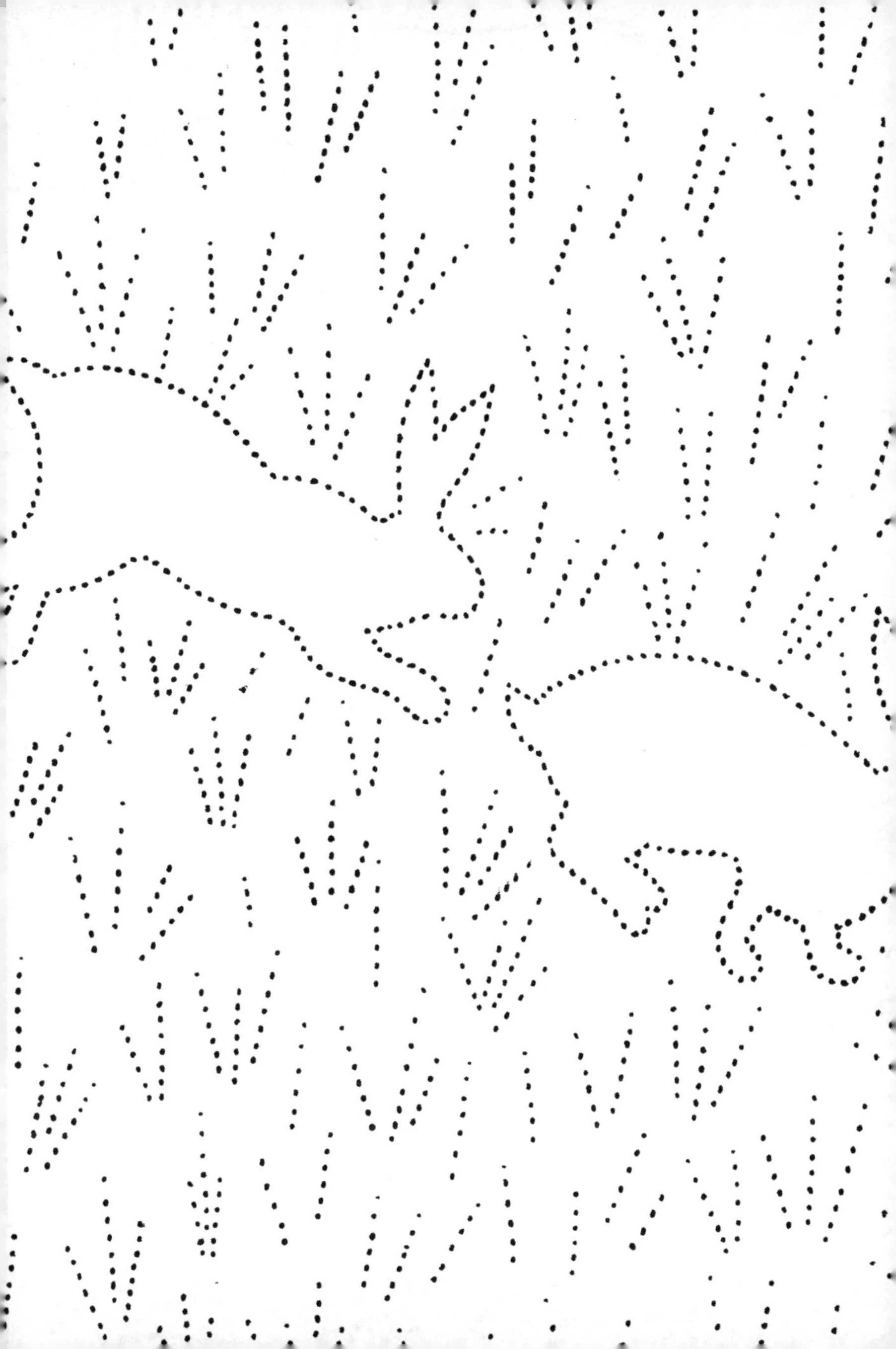

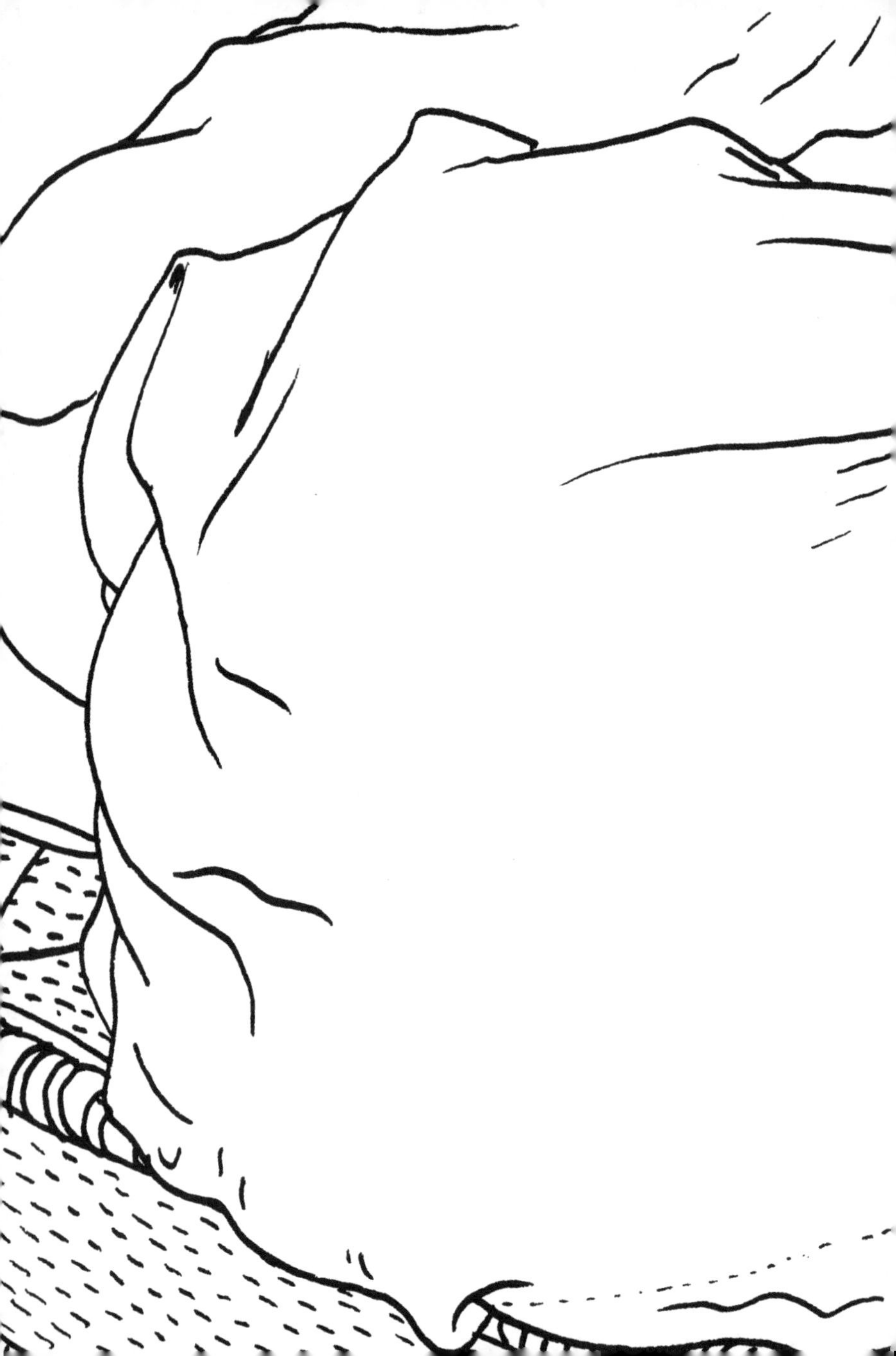

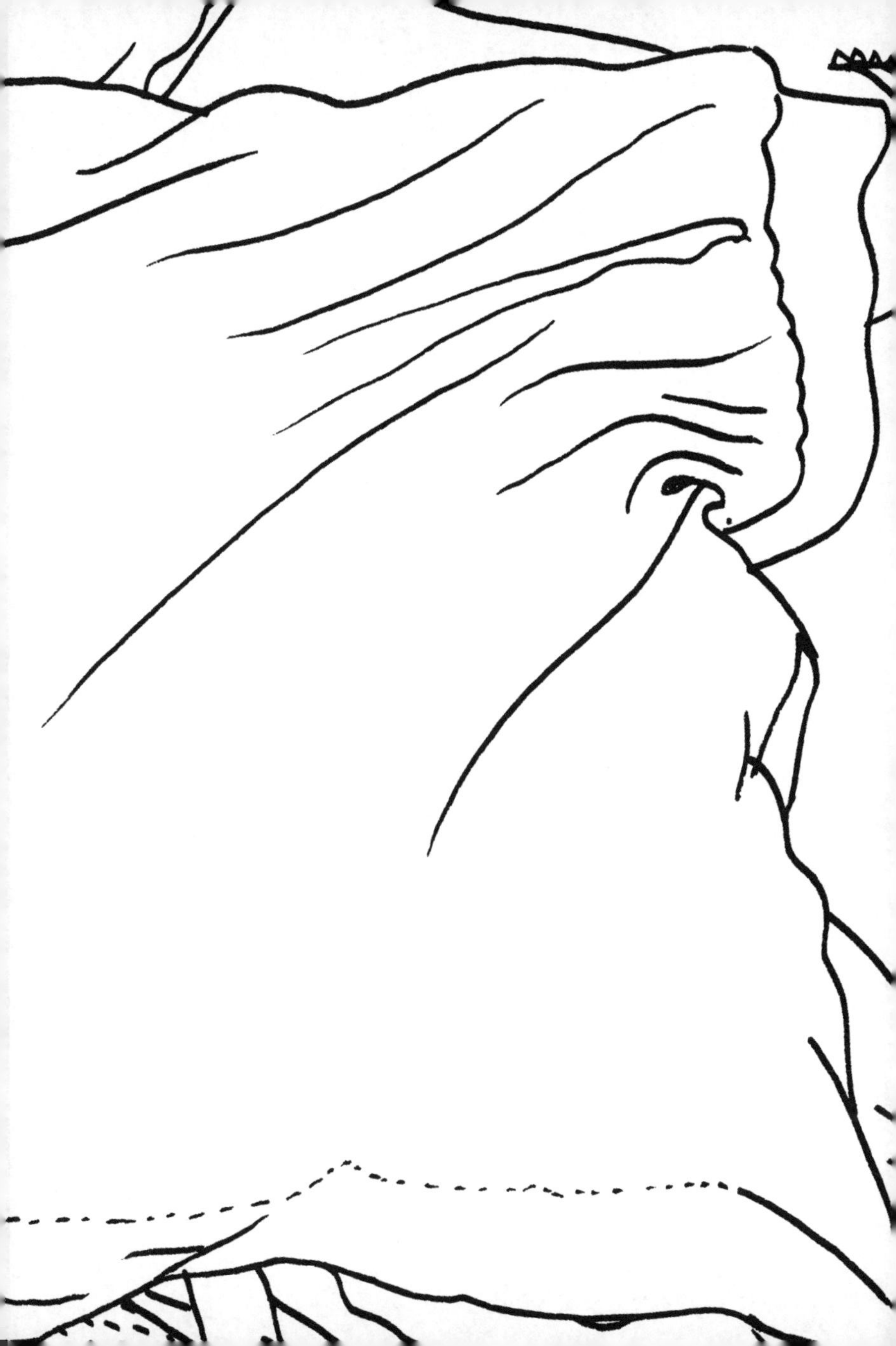

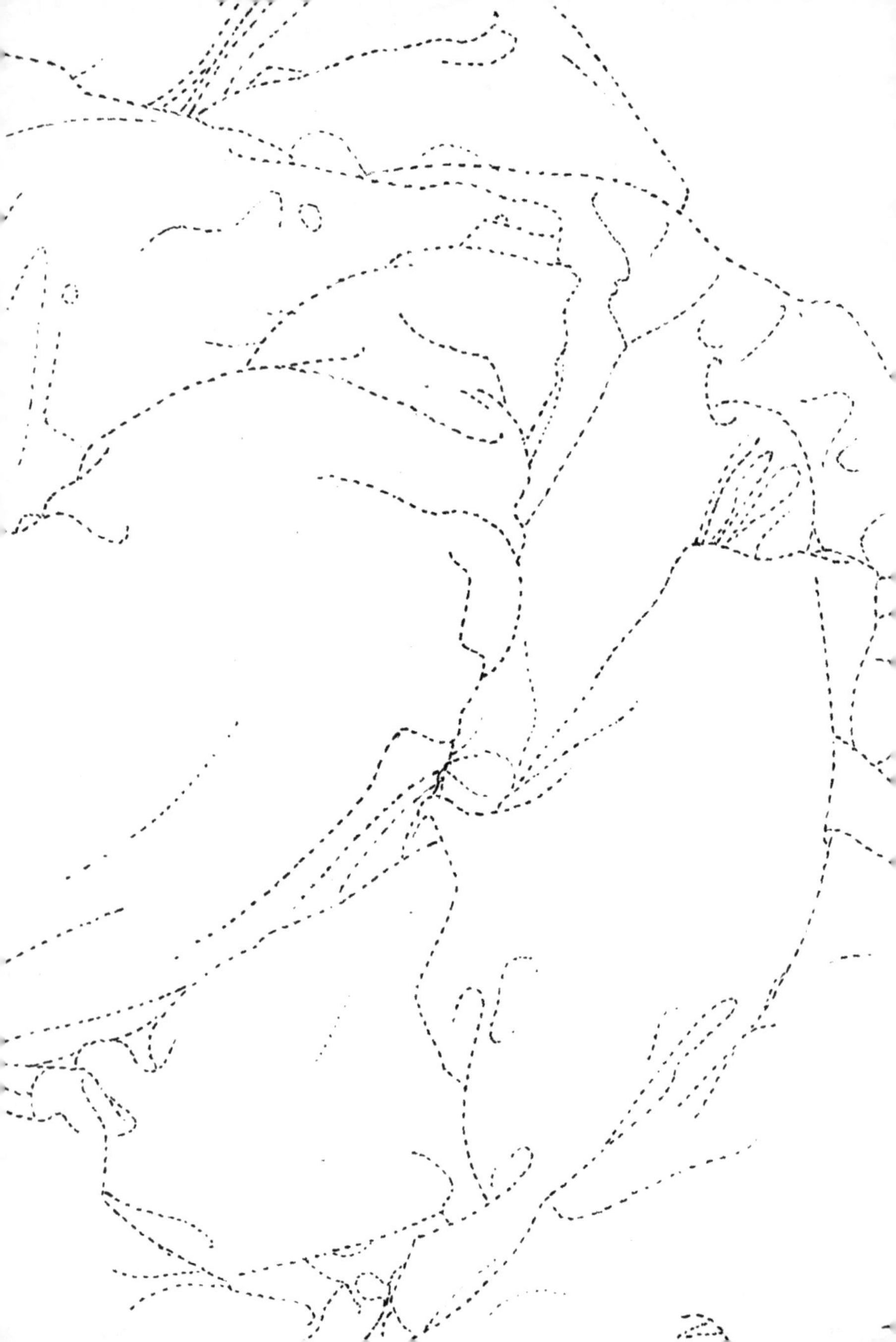

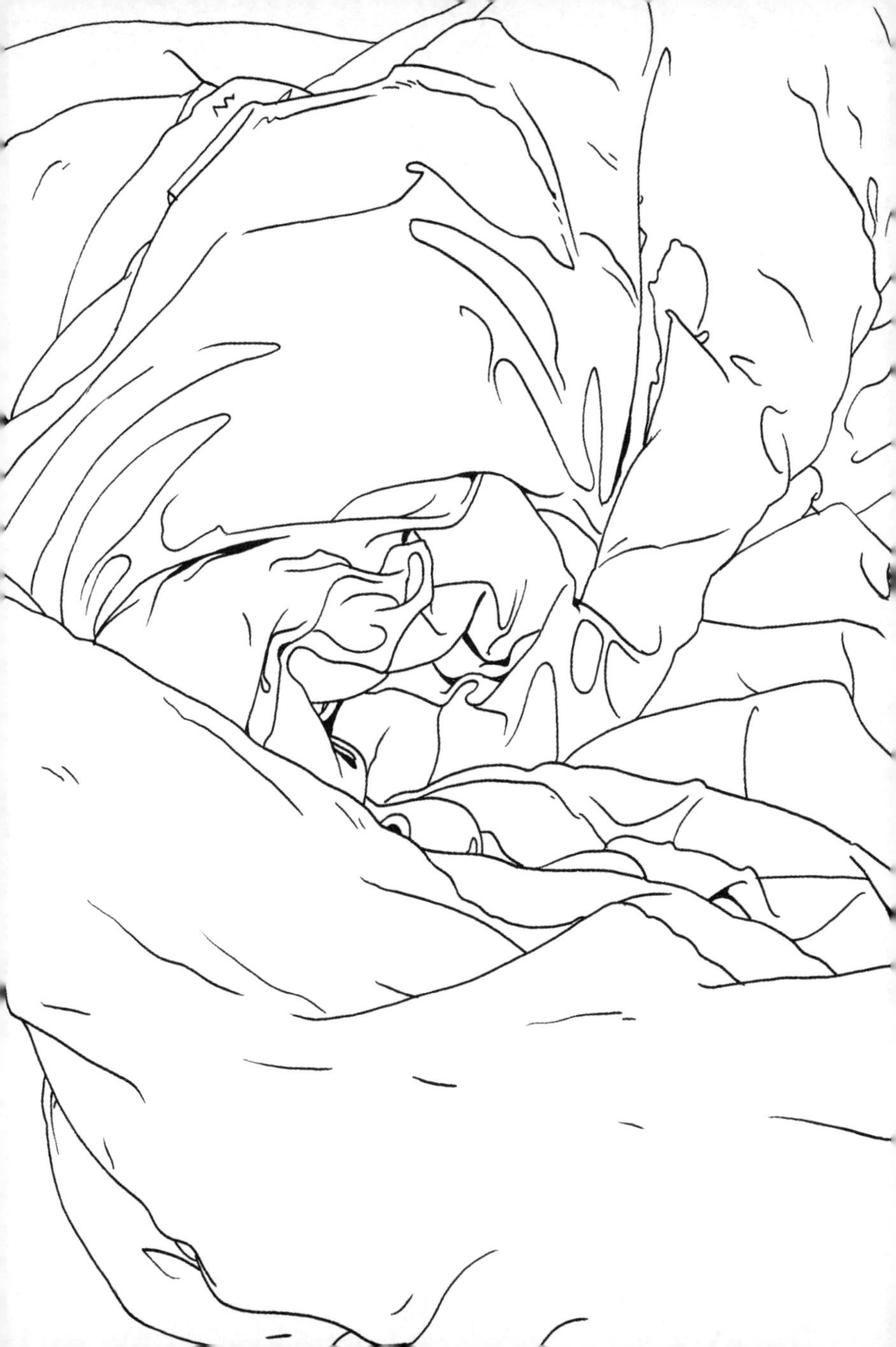

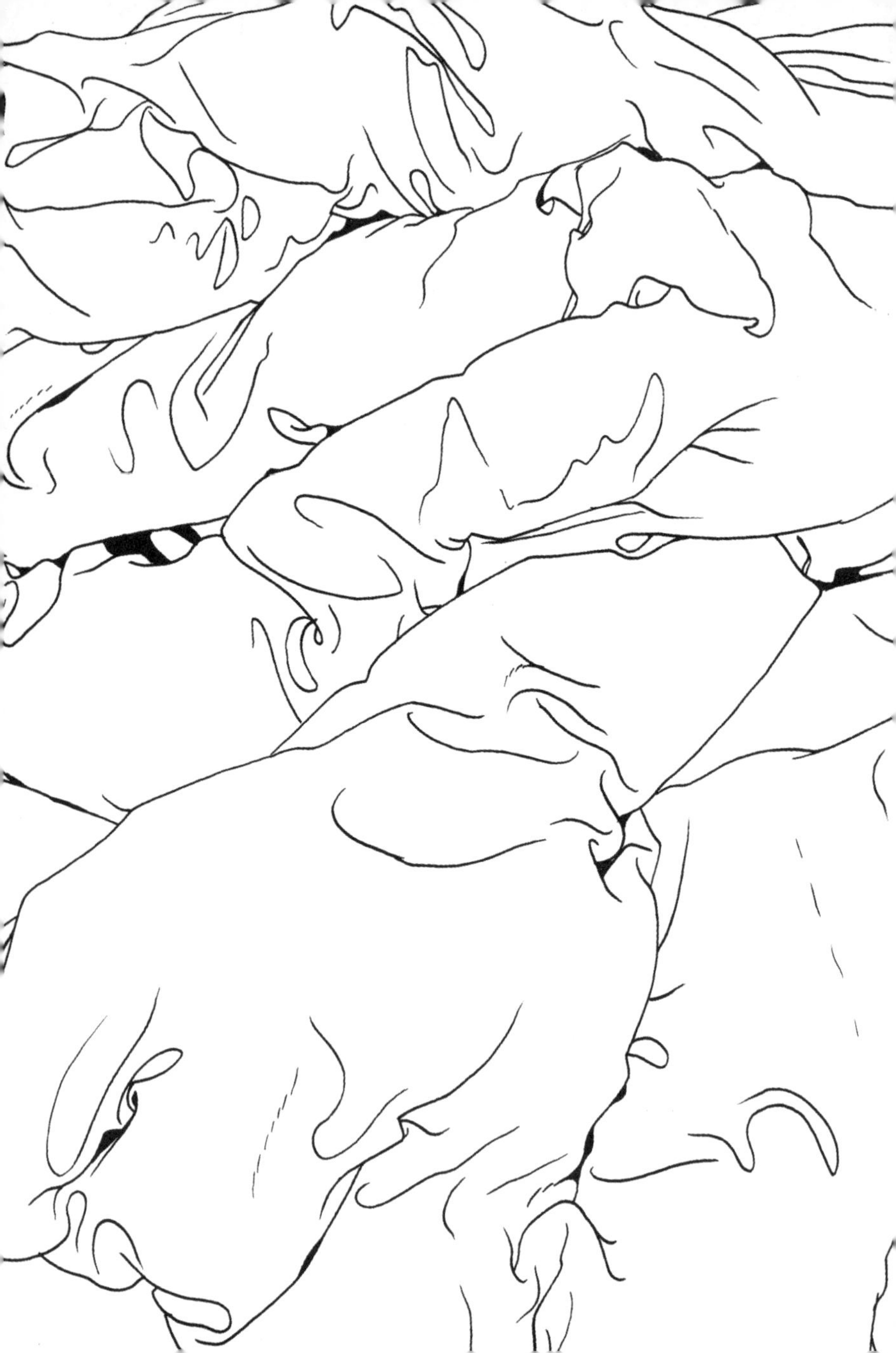

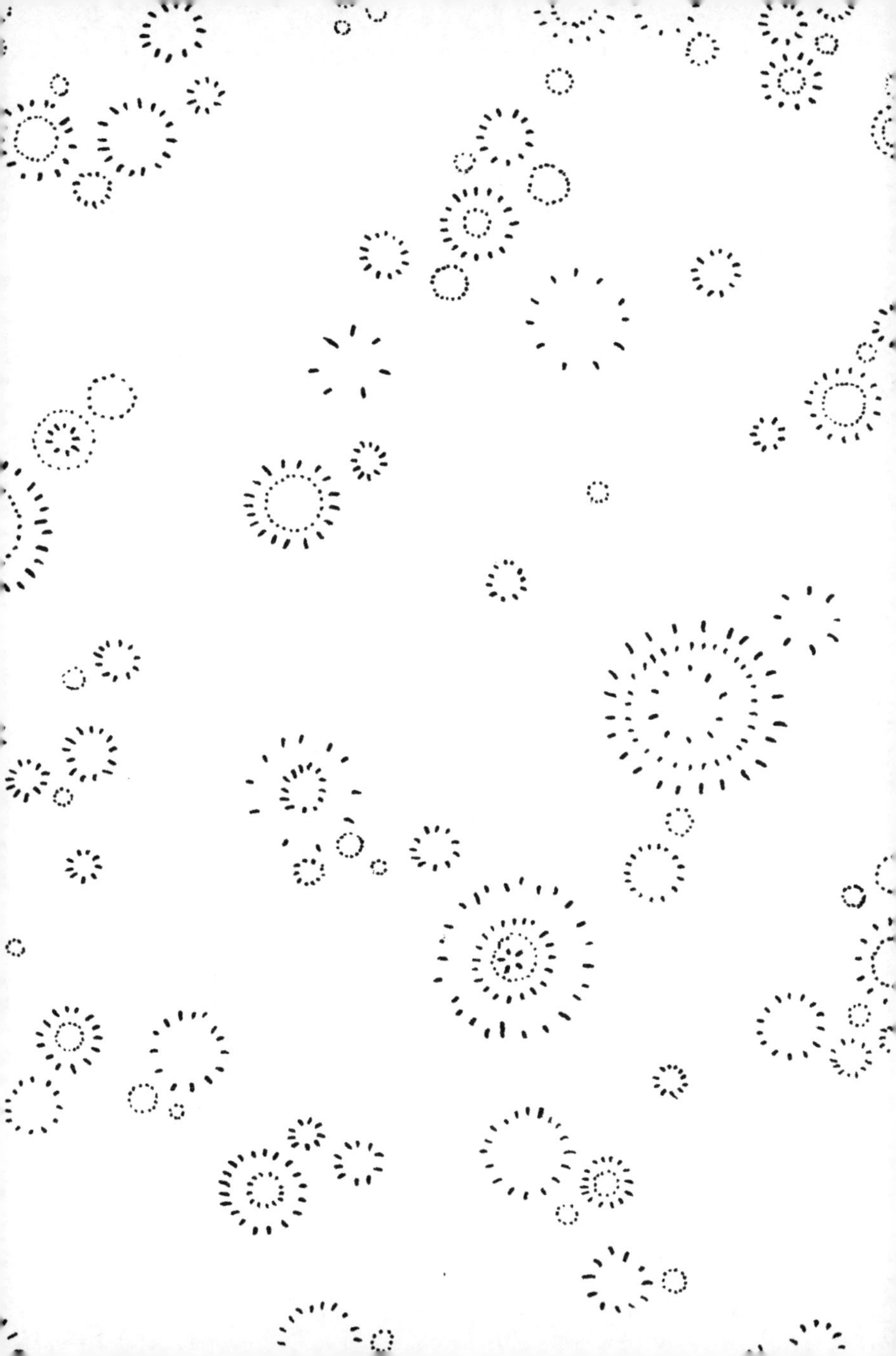

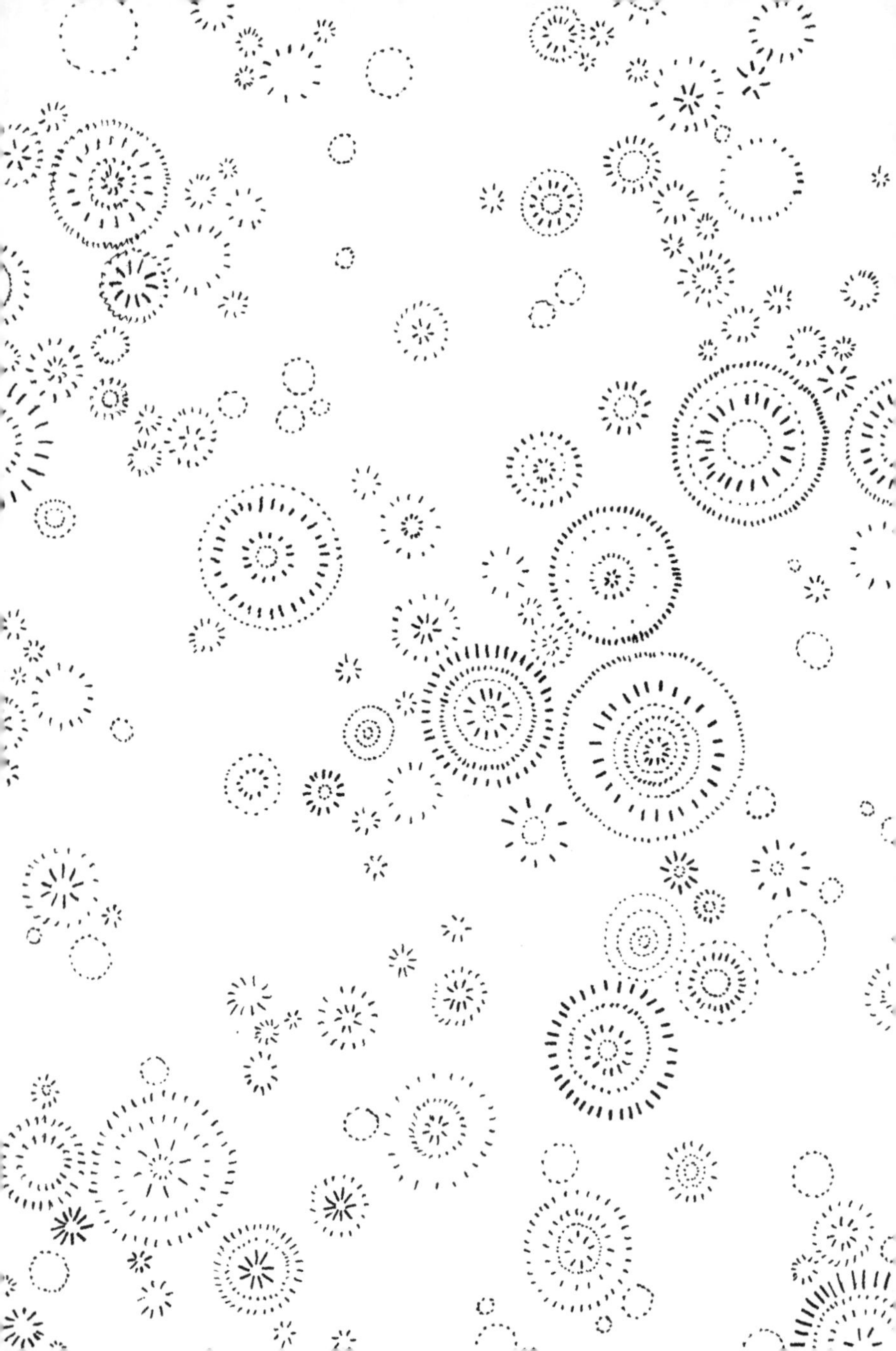

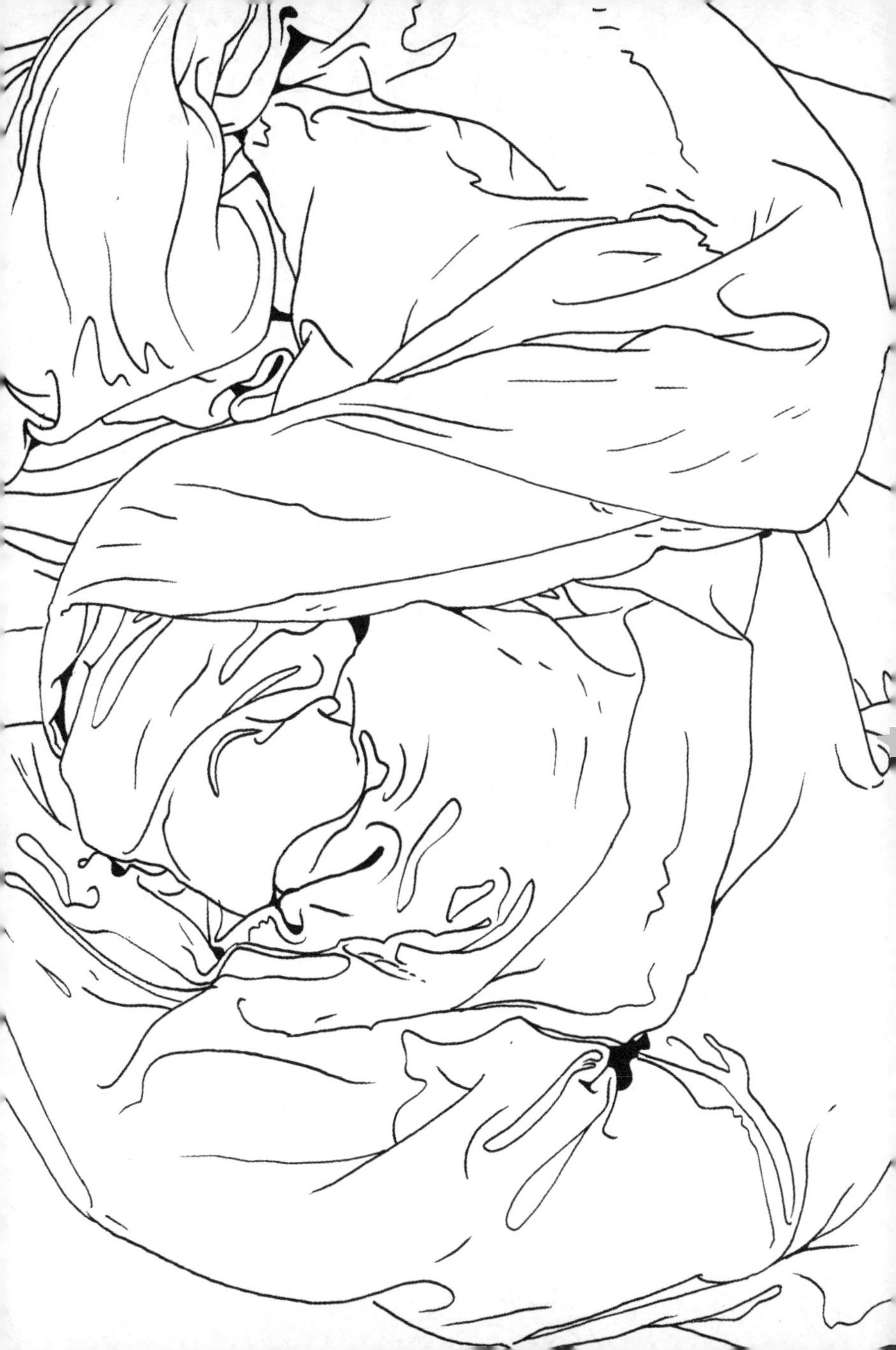

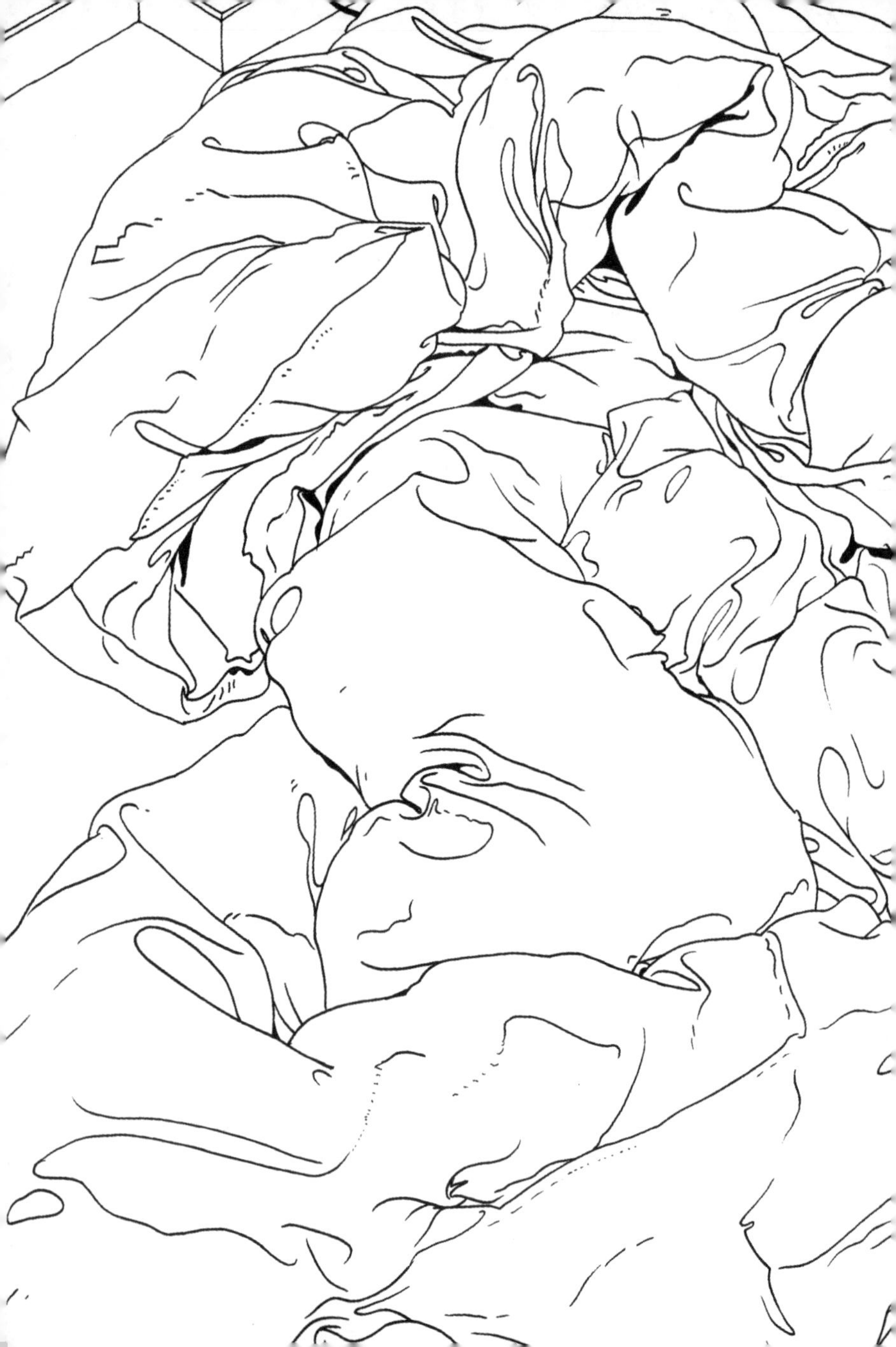

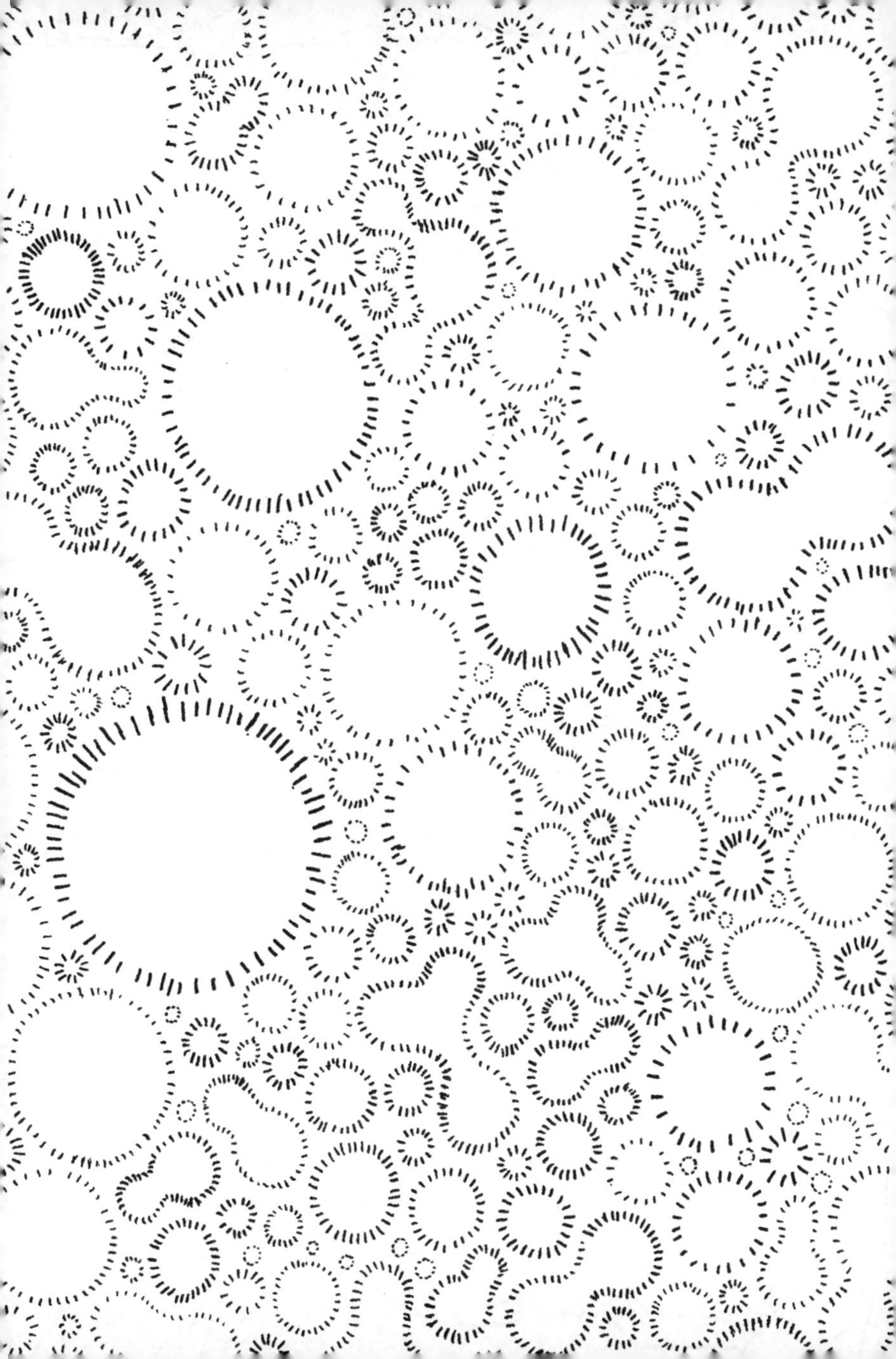

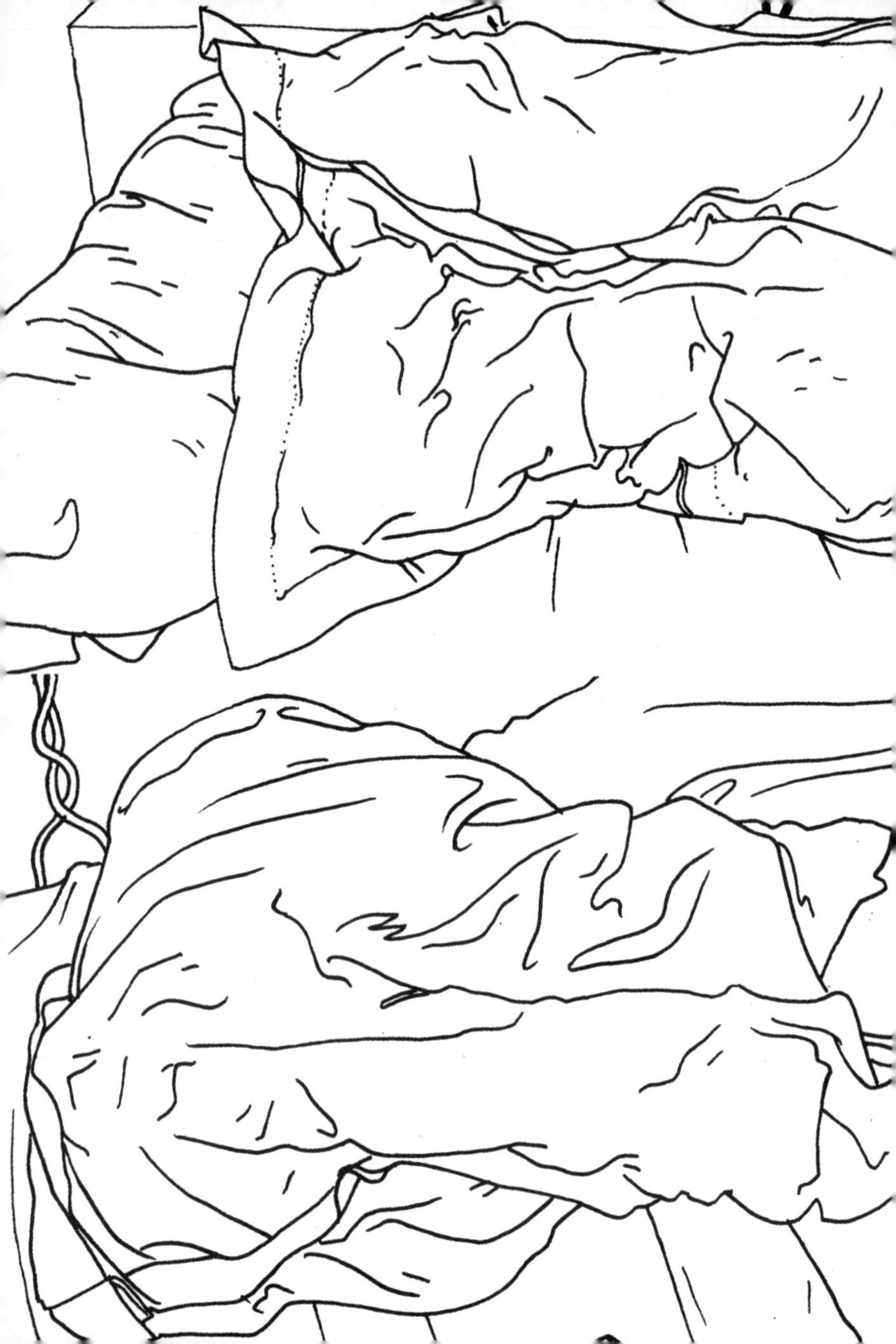

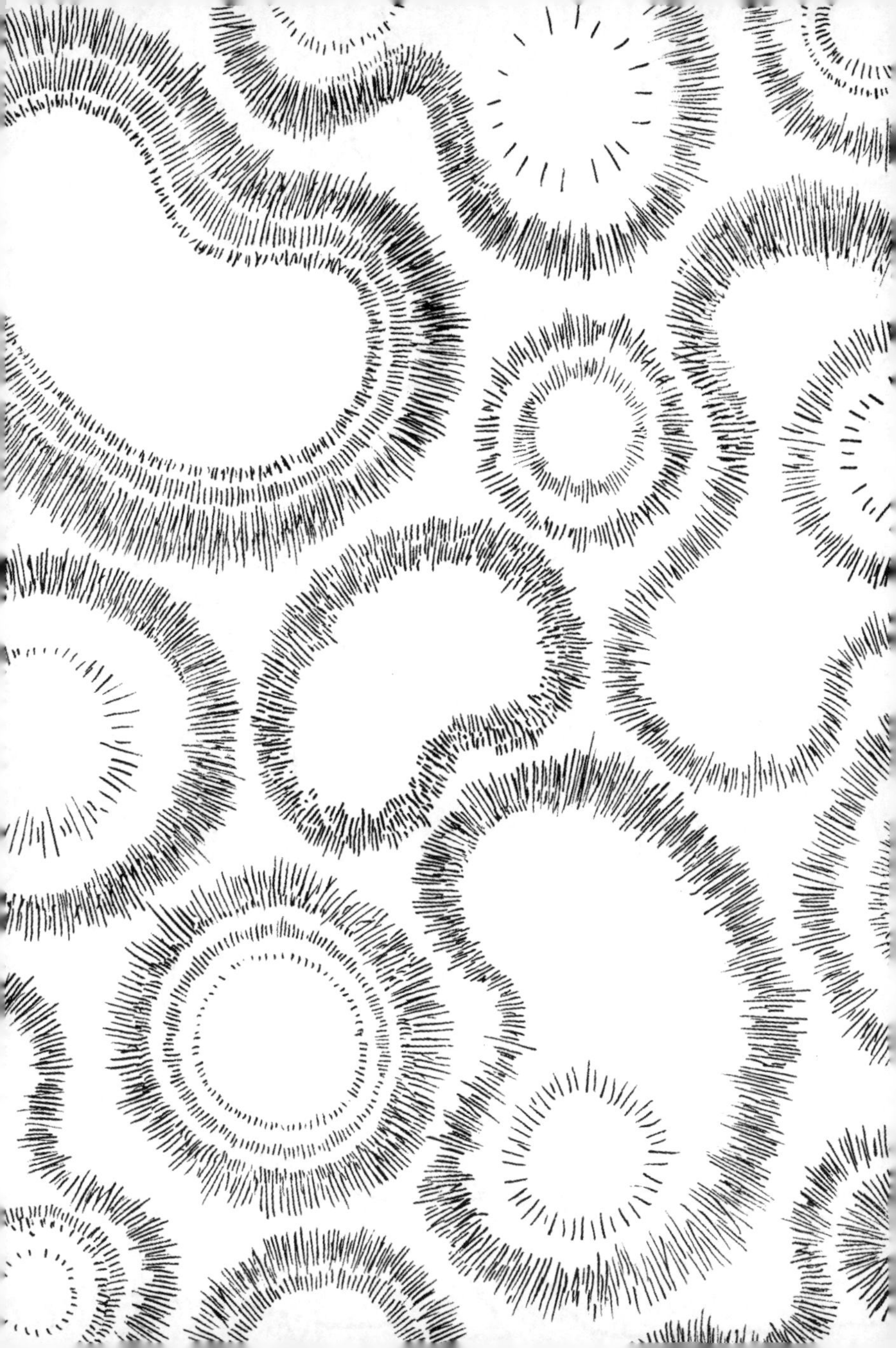

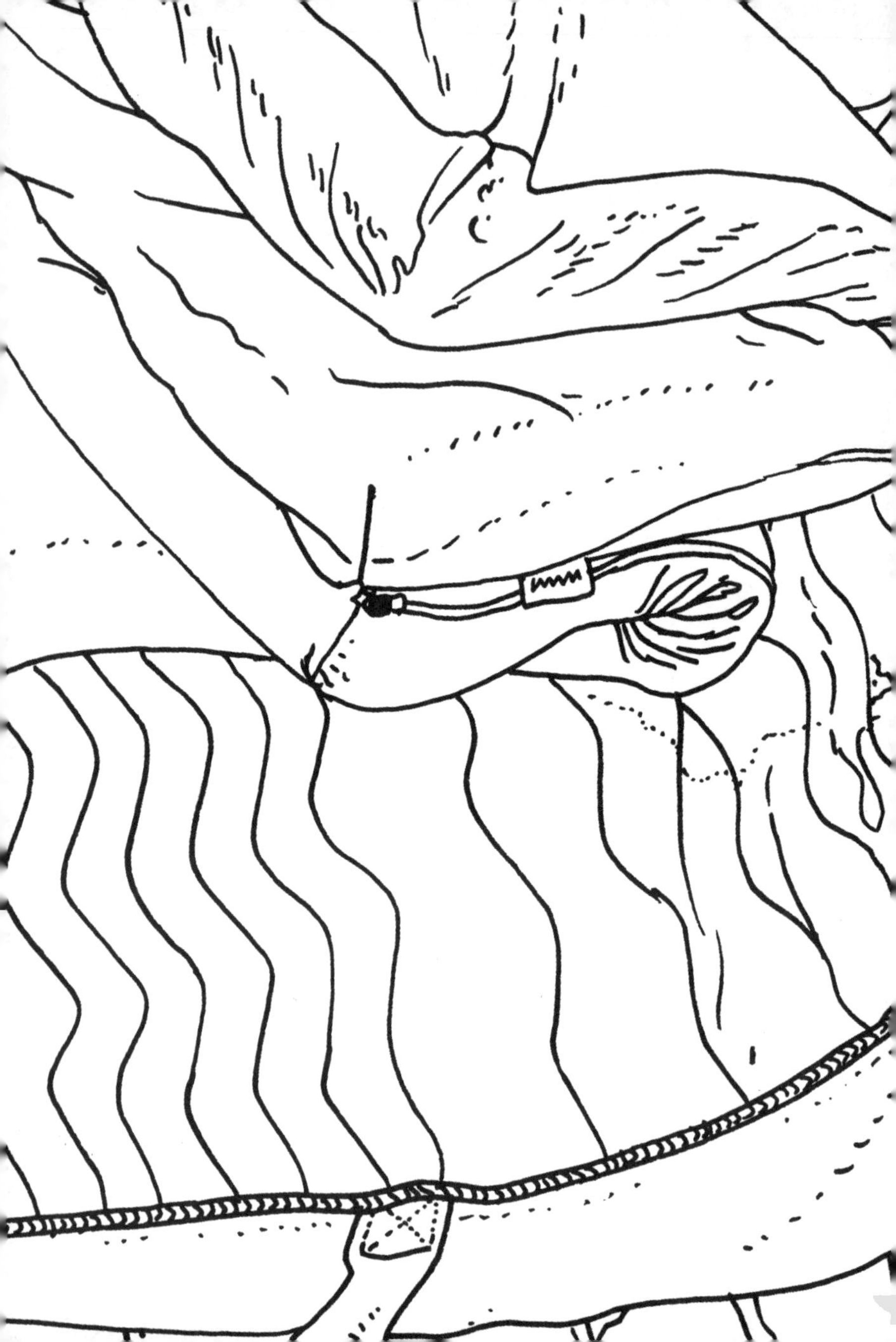

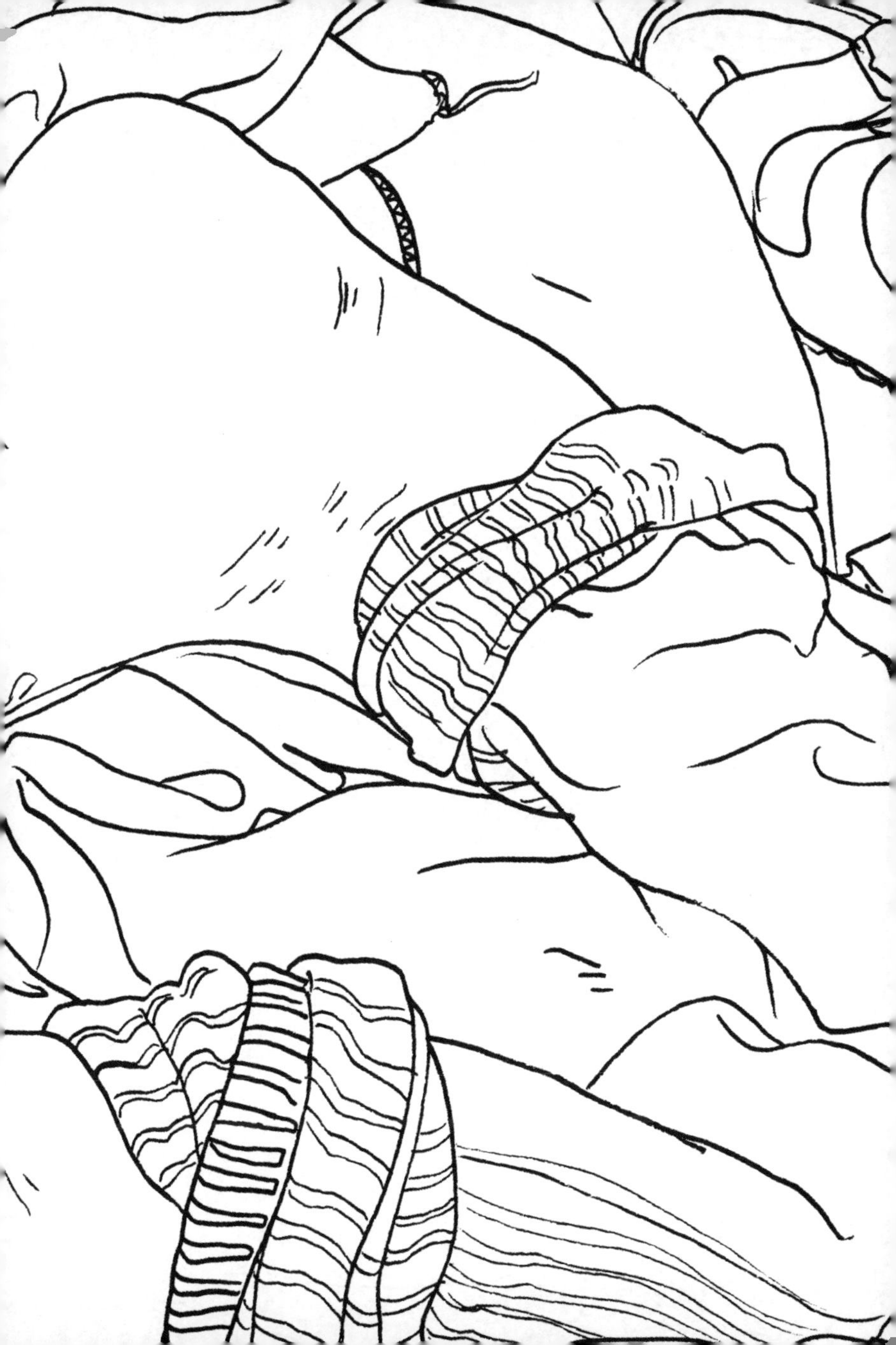

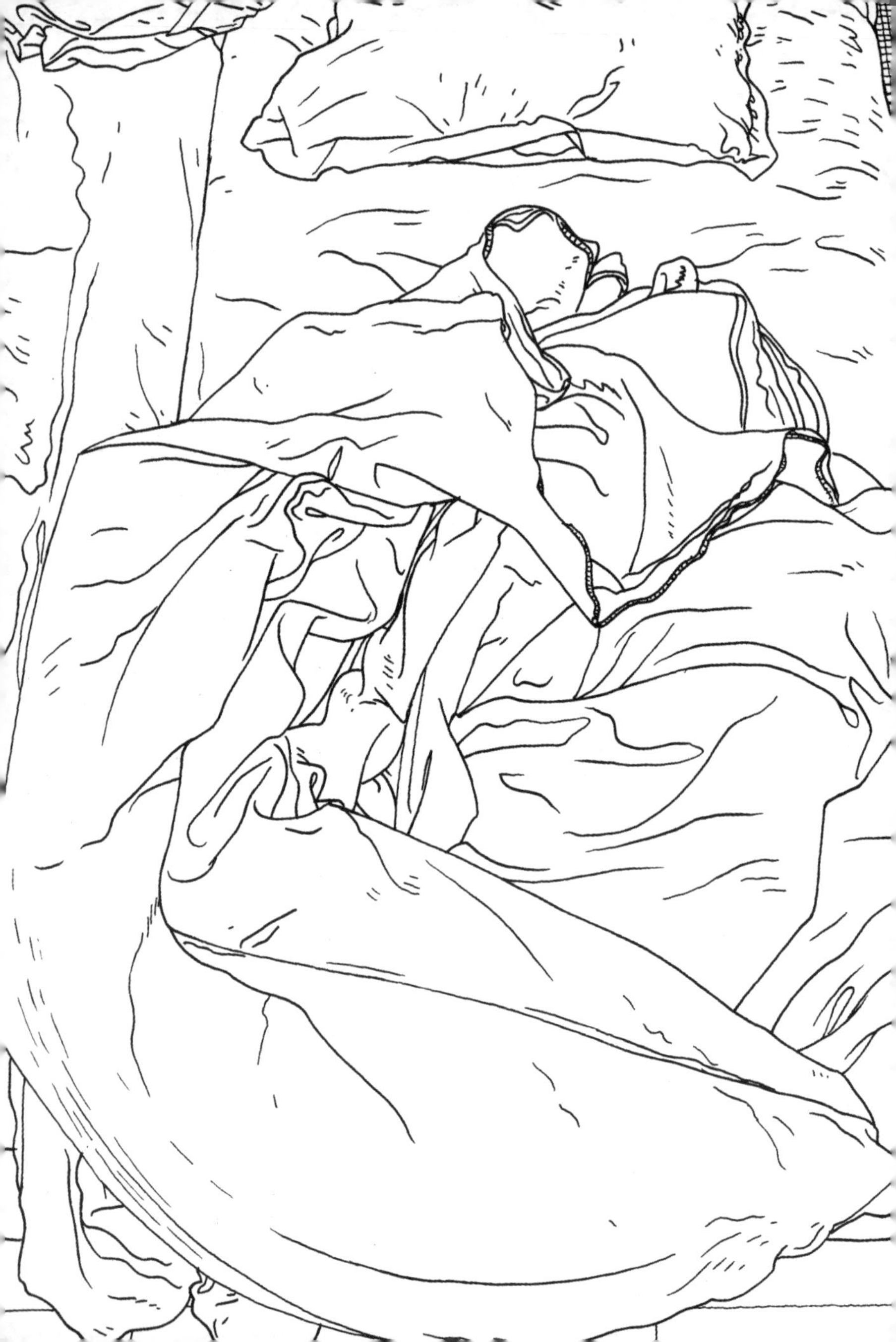

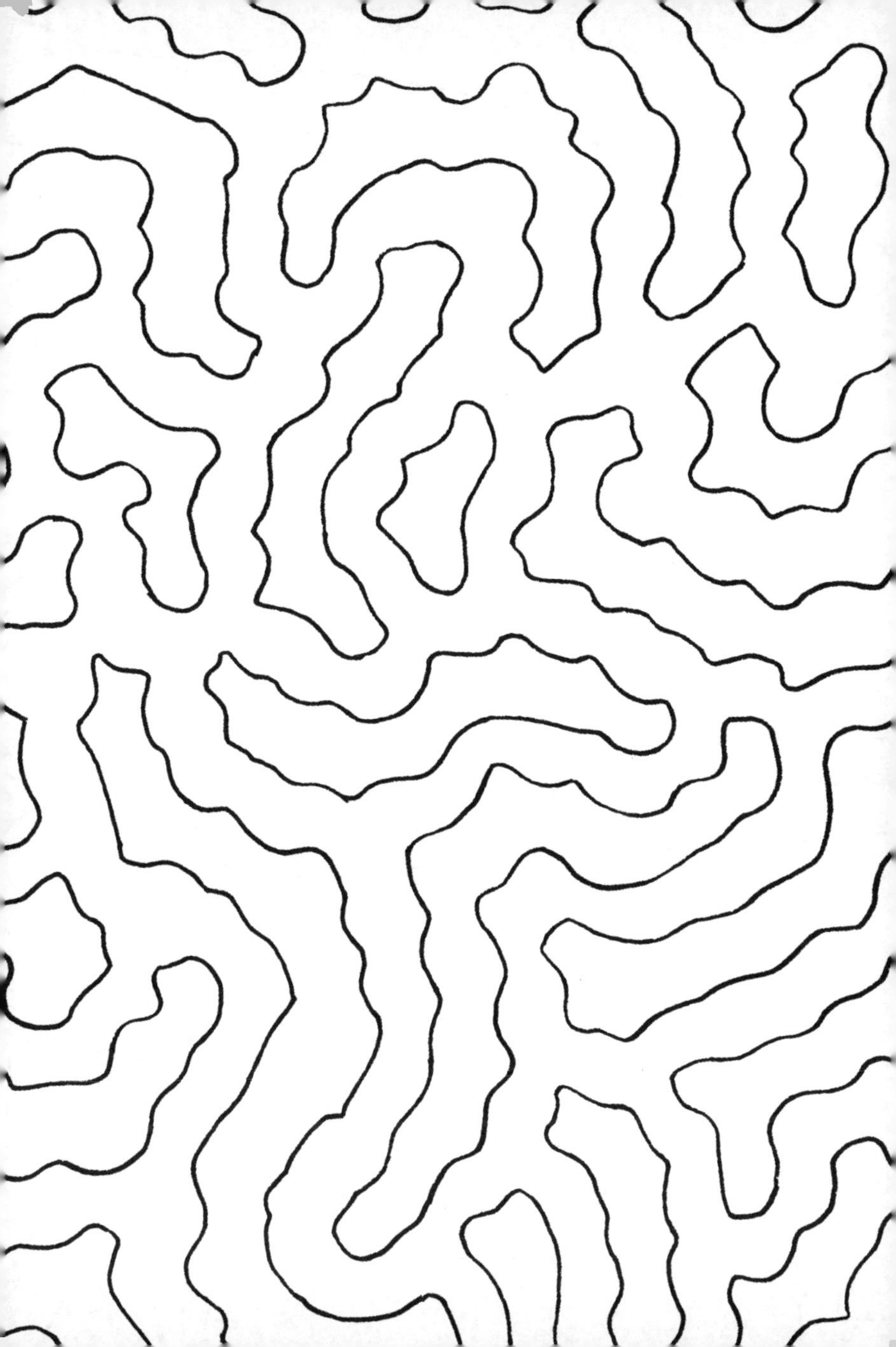

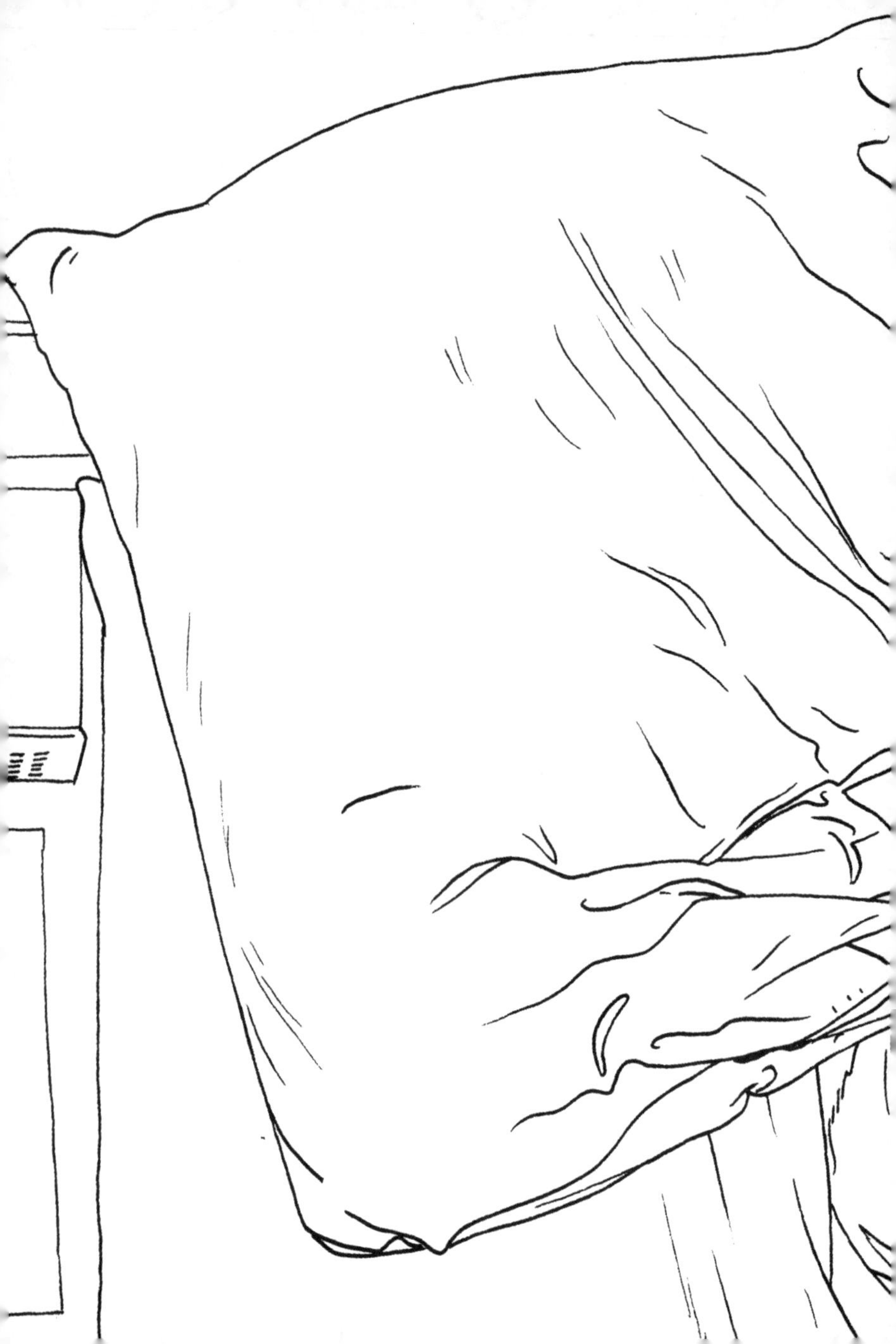

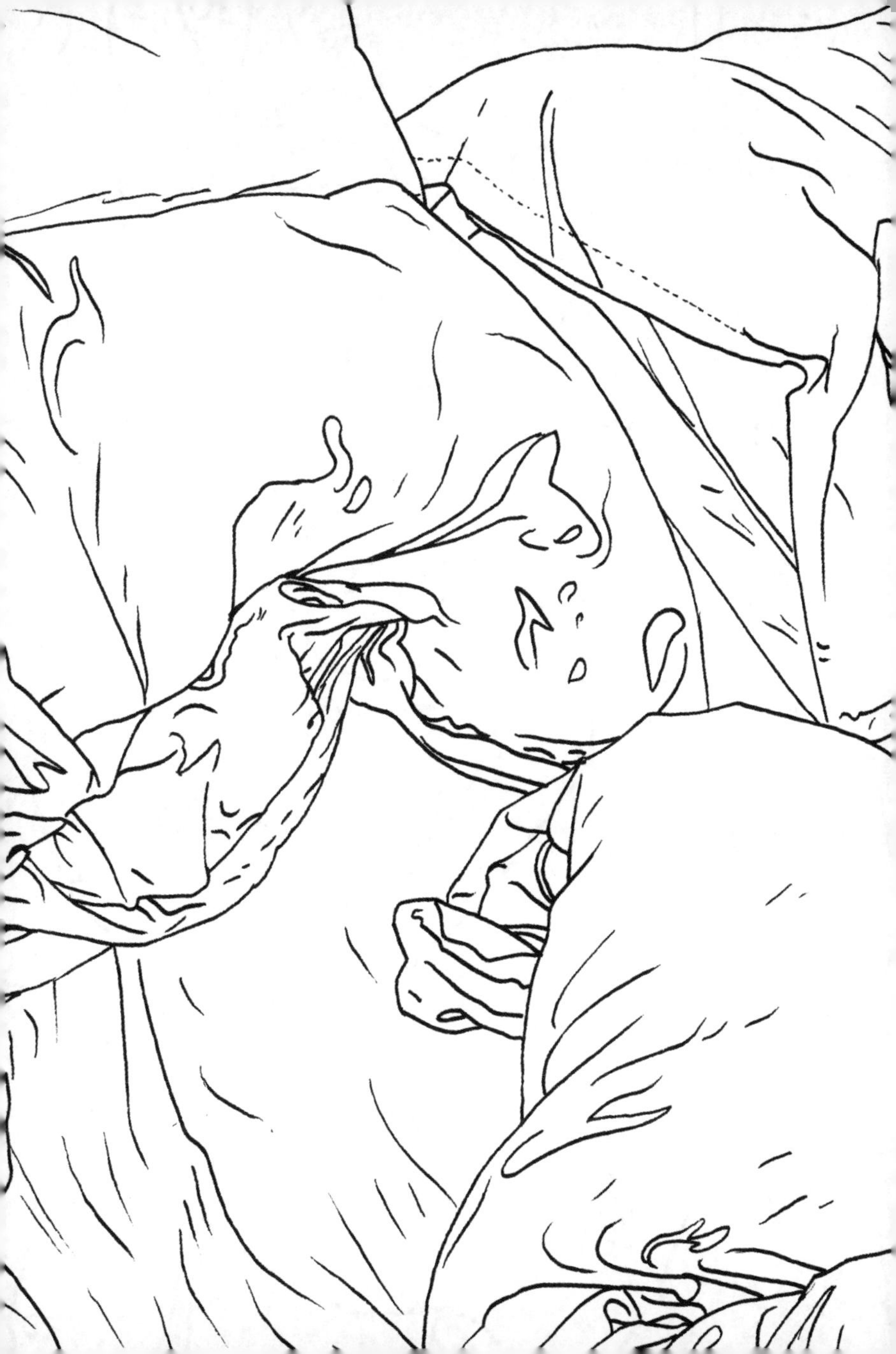

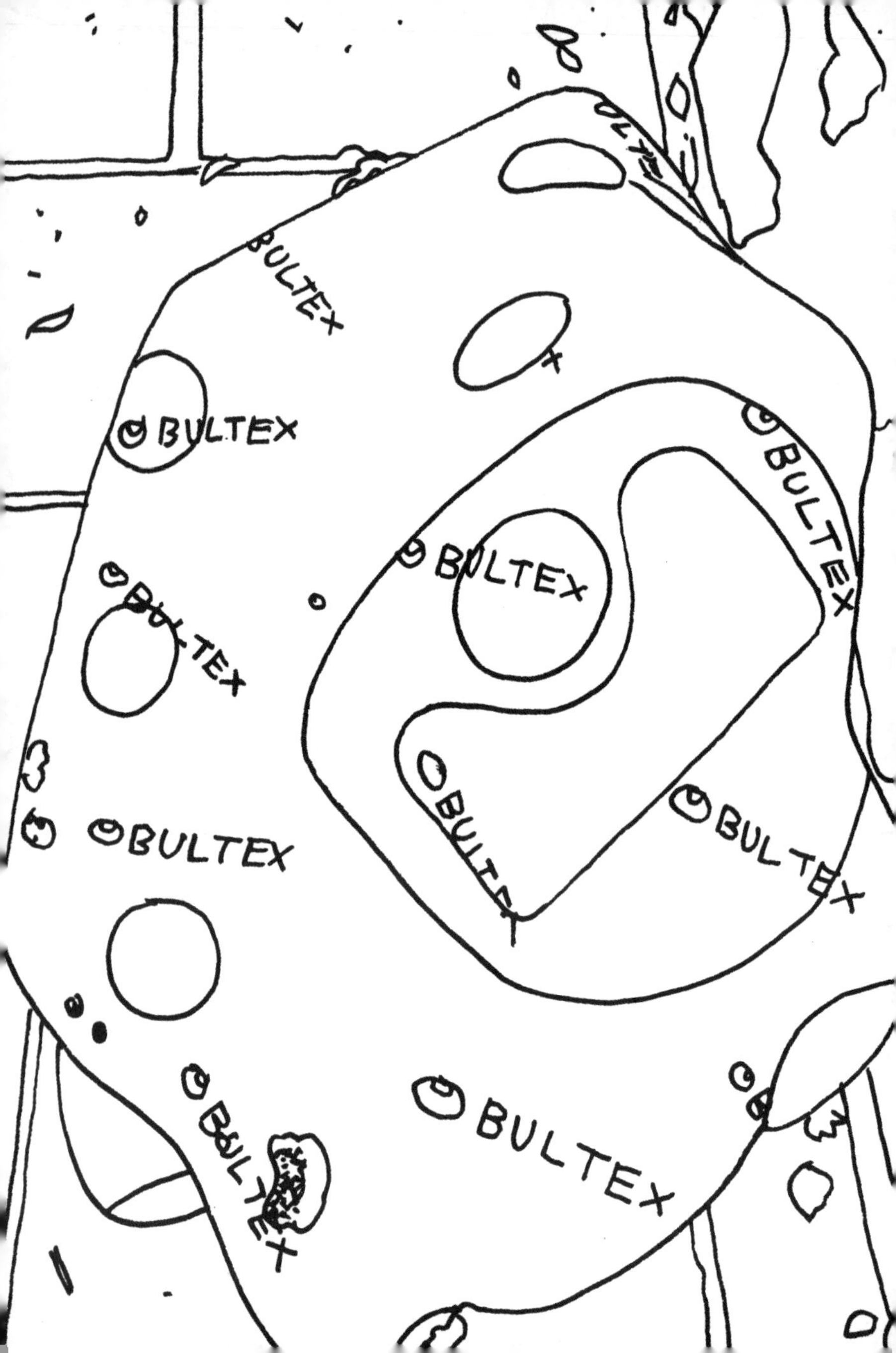
BULTEX
BULTEX
BULTEX
BULTEX
BULTEX
BULTEX
BULTEX
BULTEX

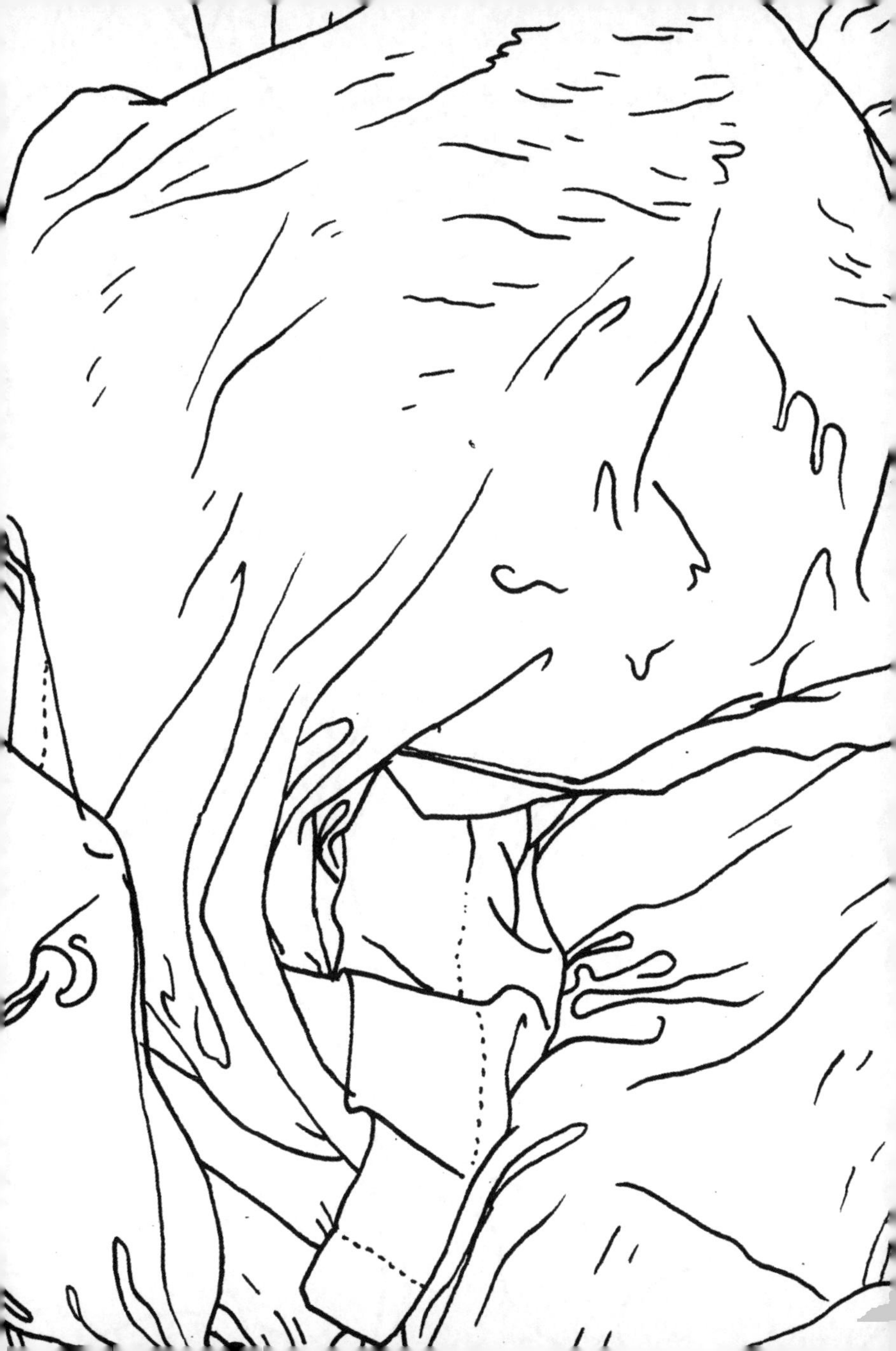

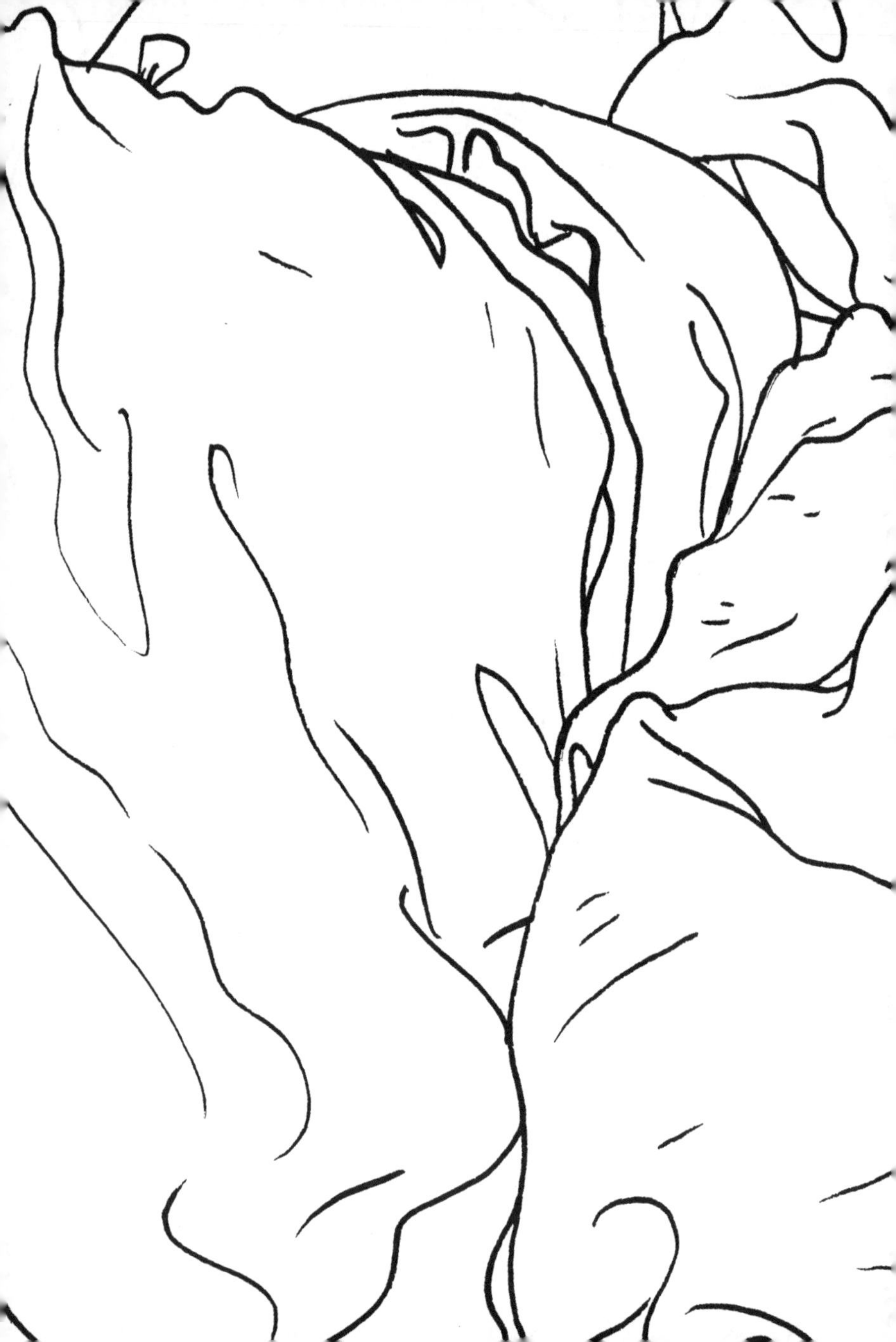

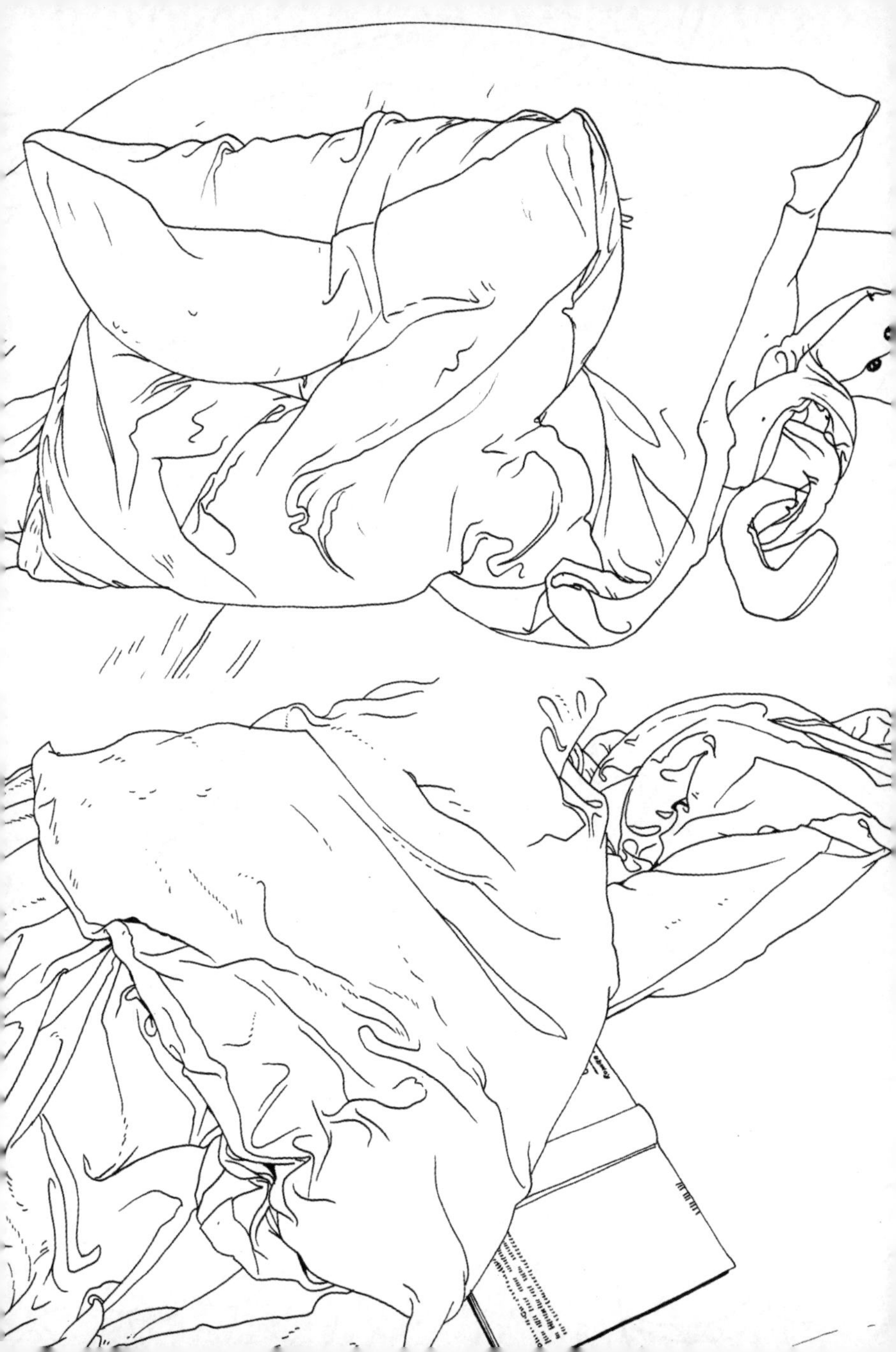

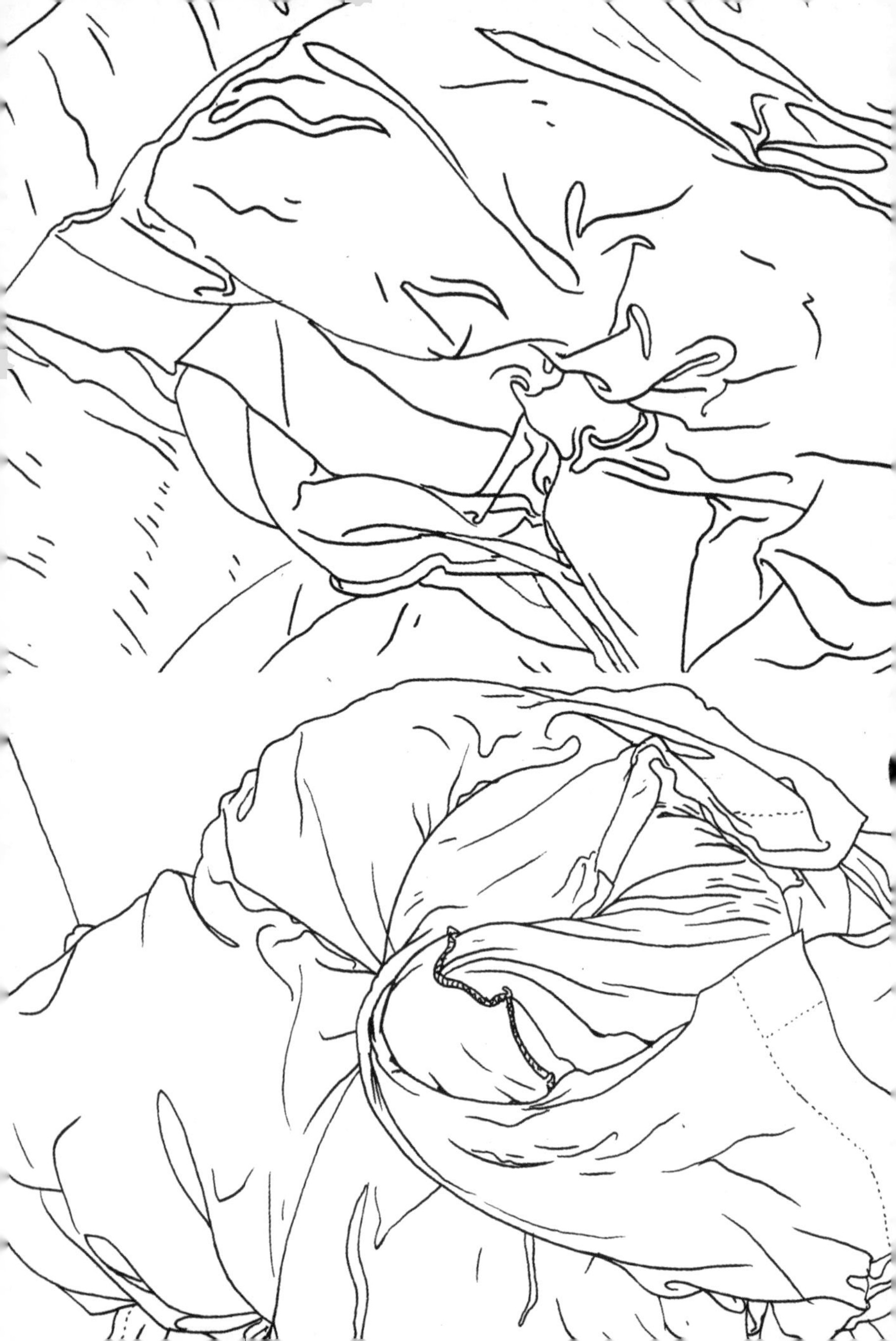

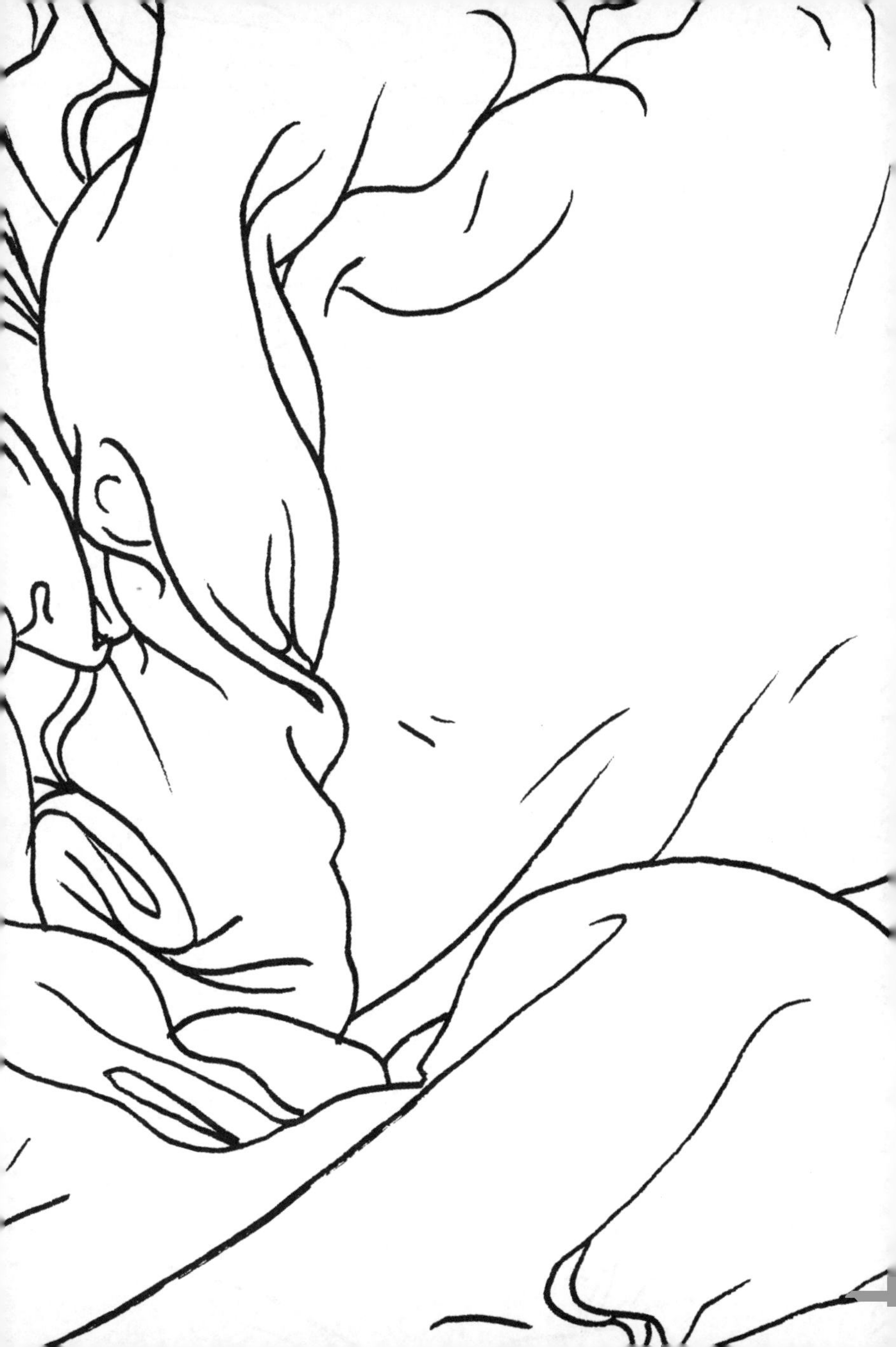

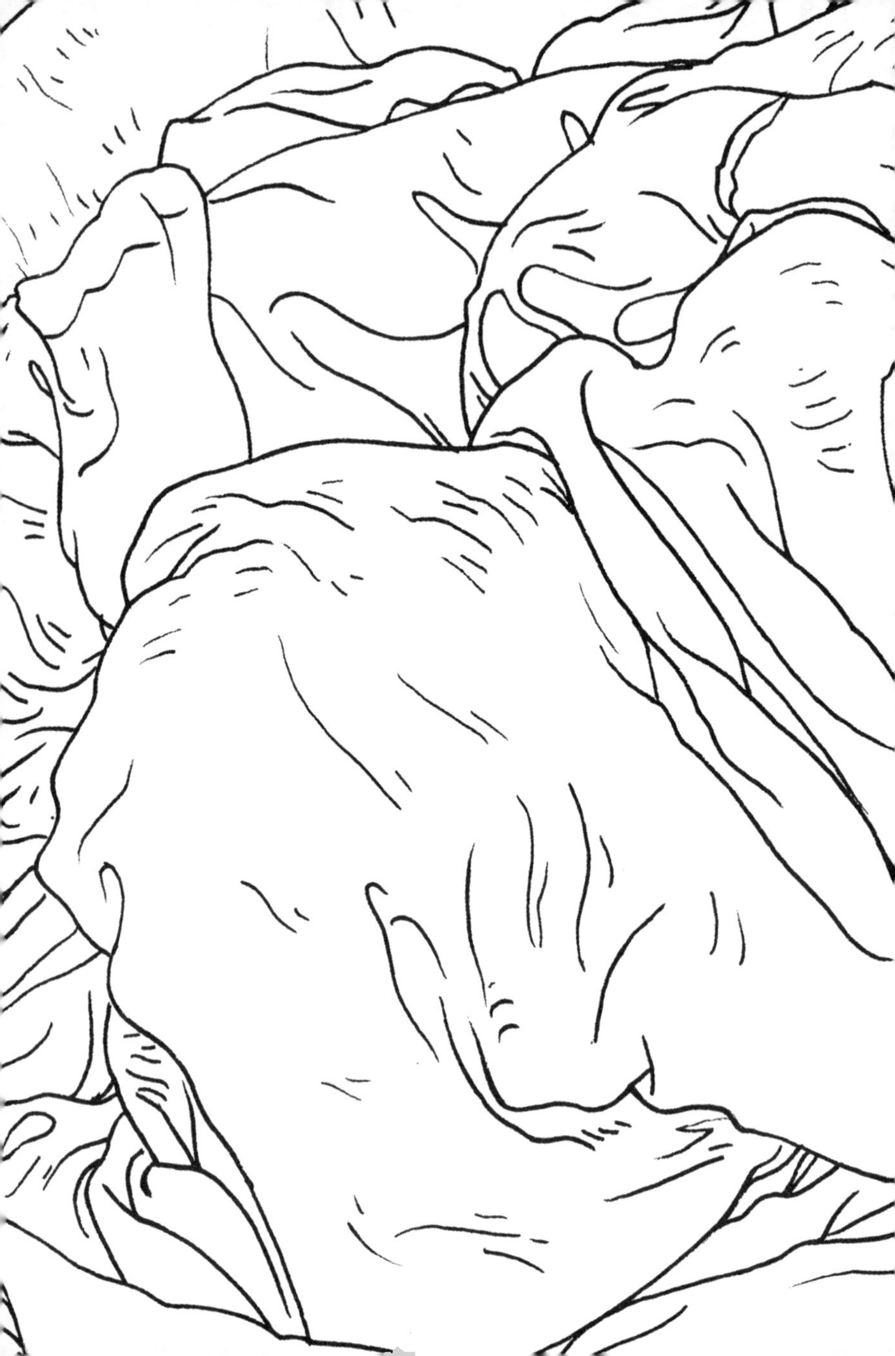

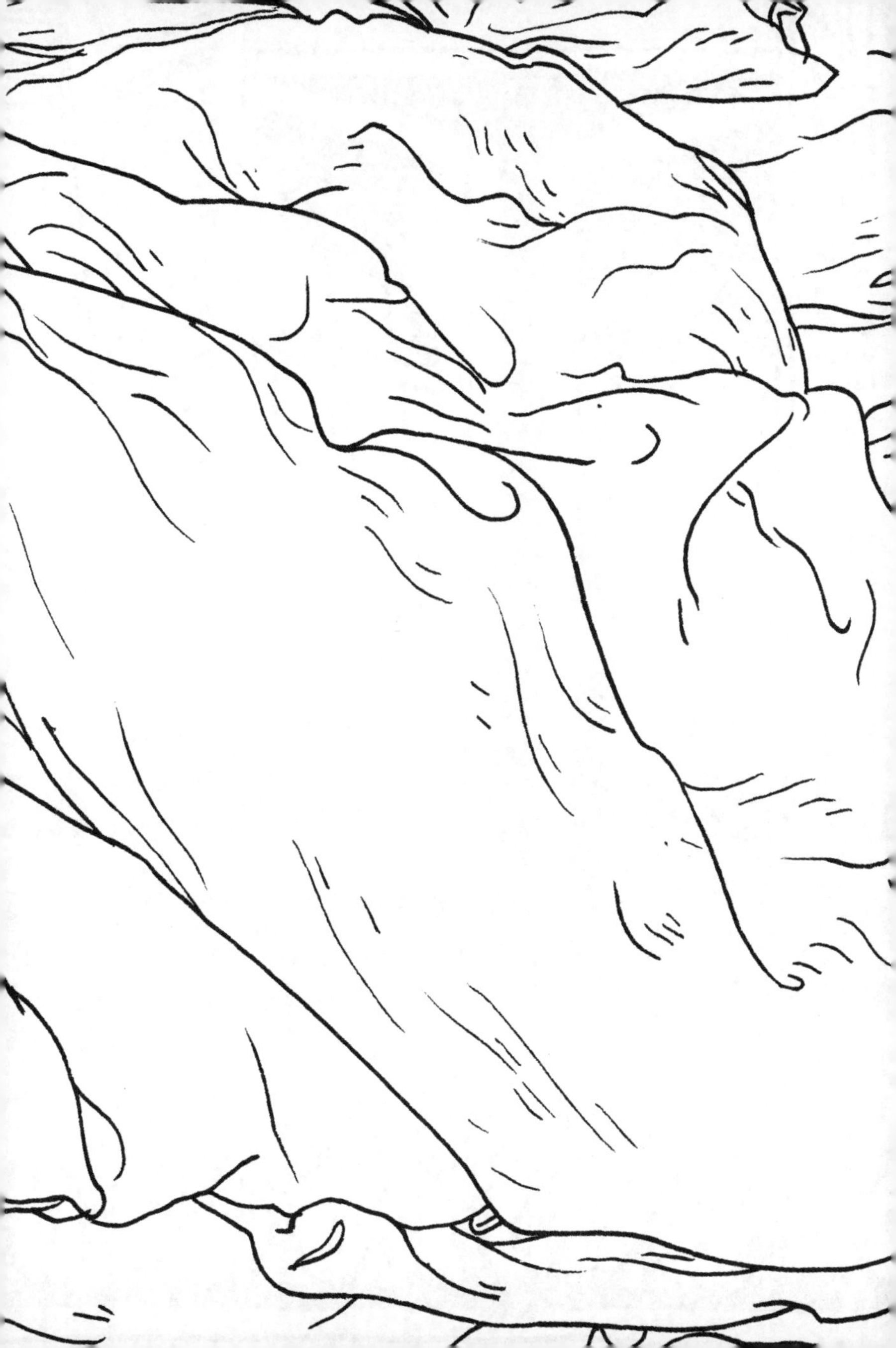

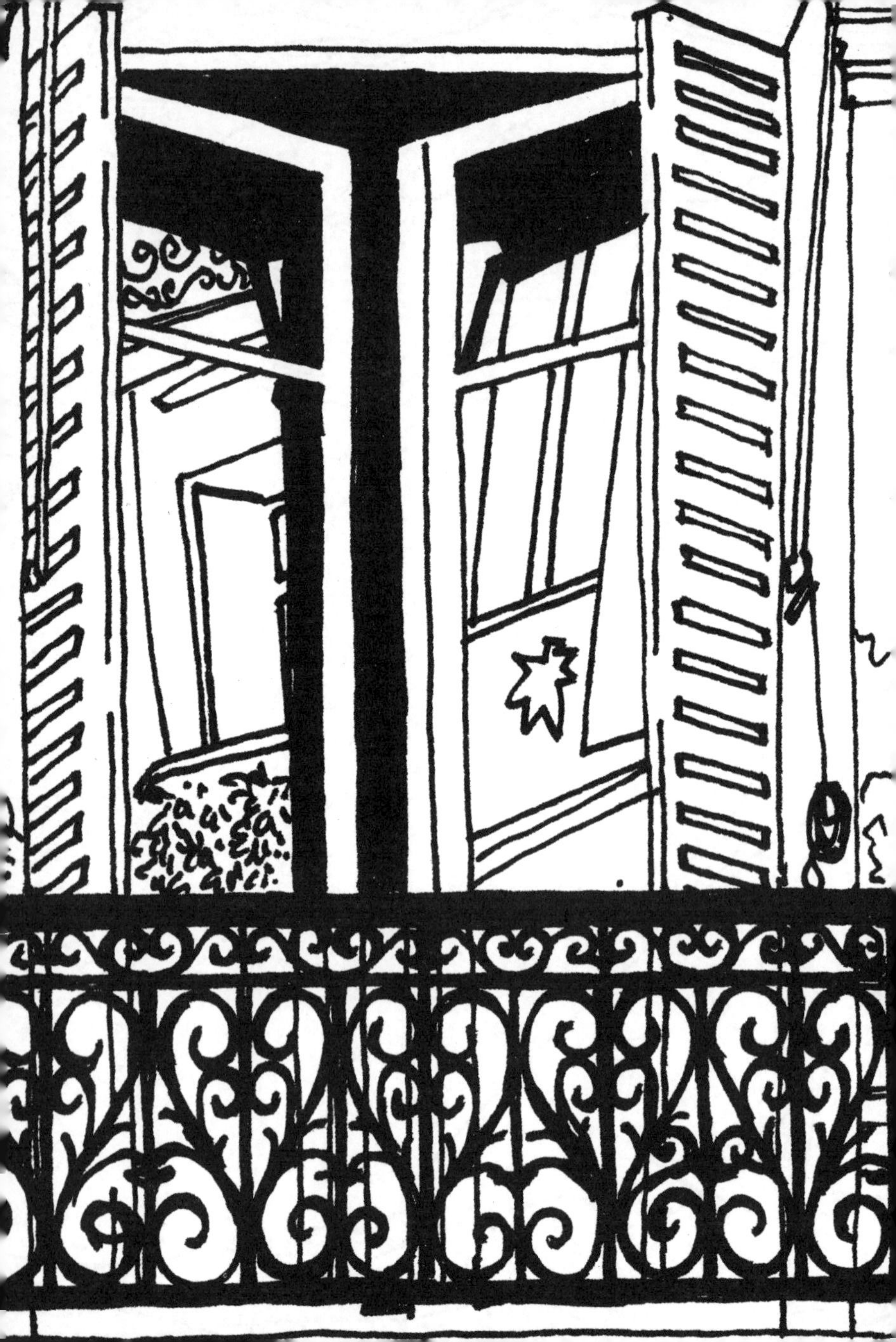

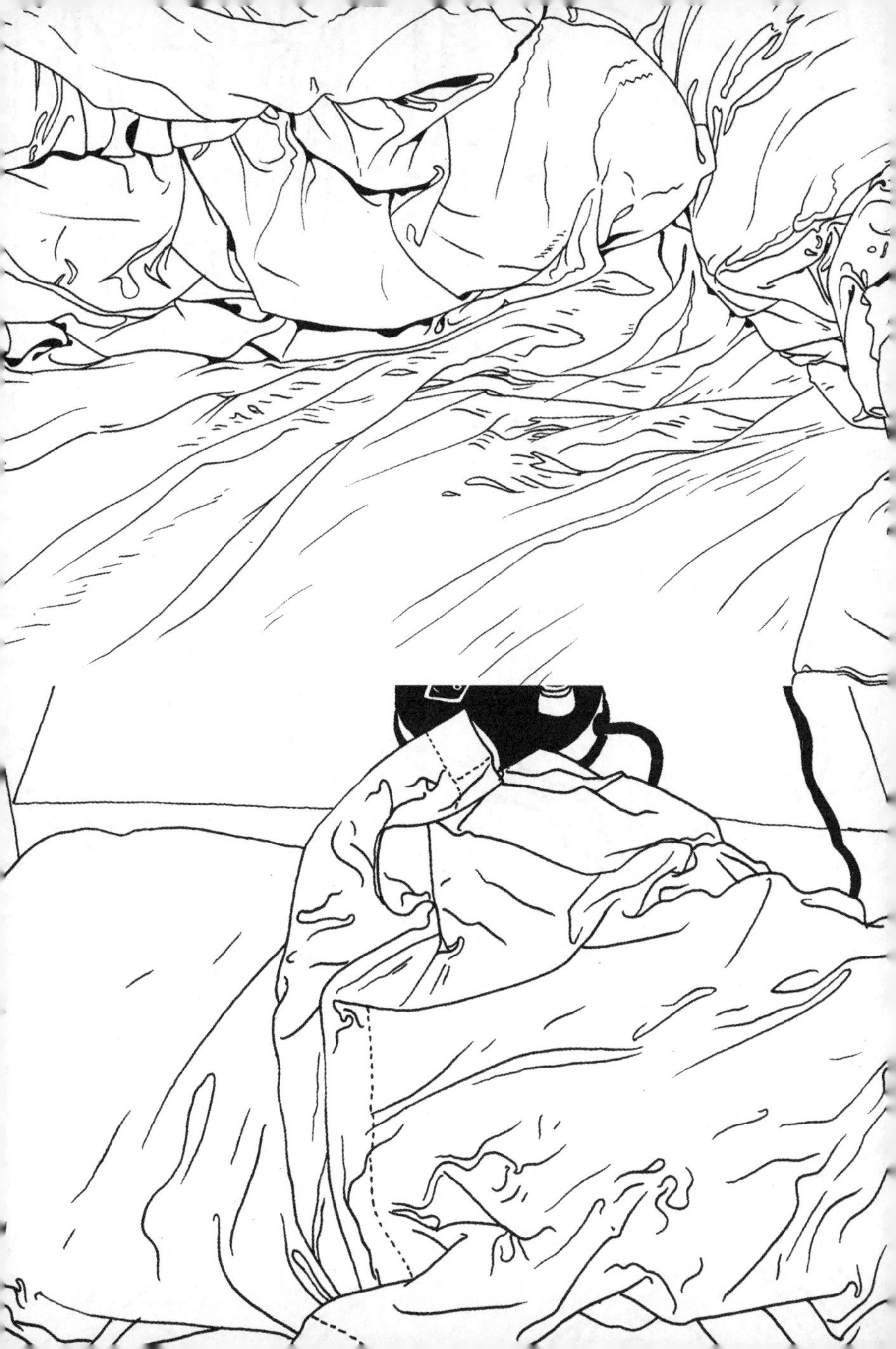

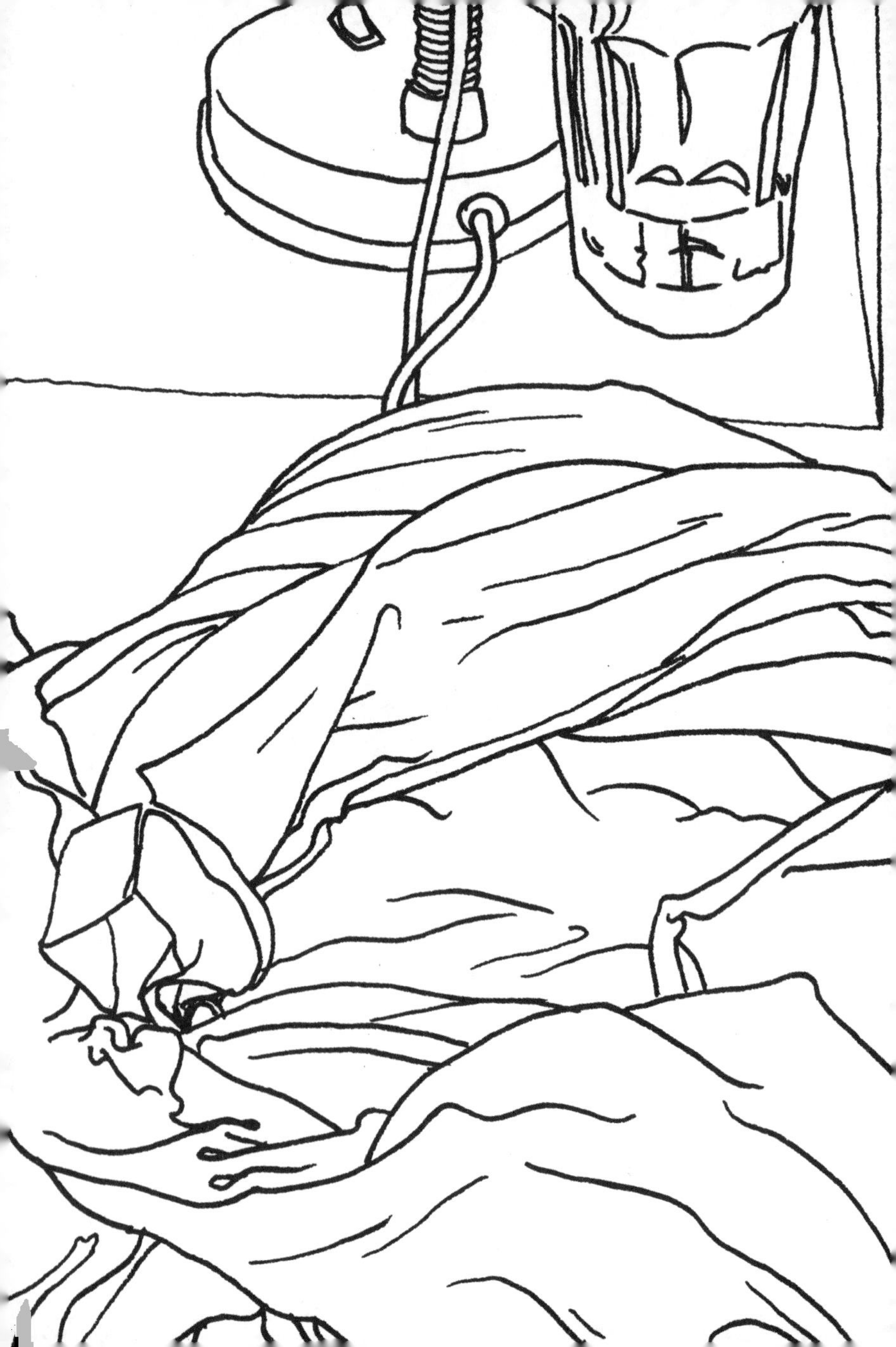

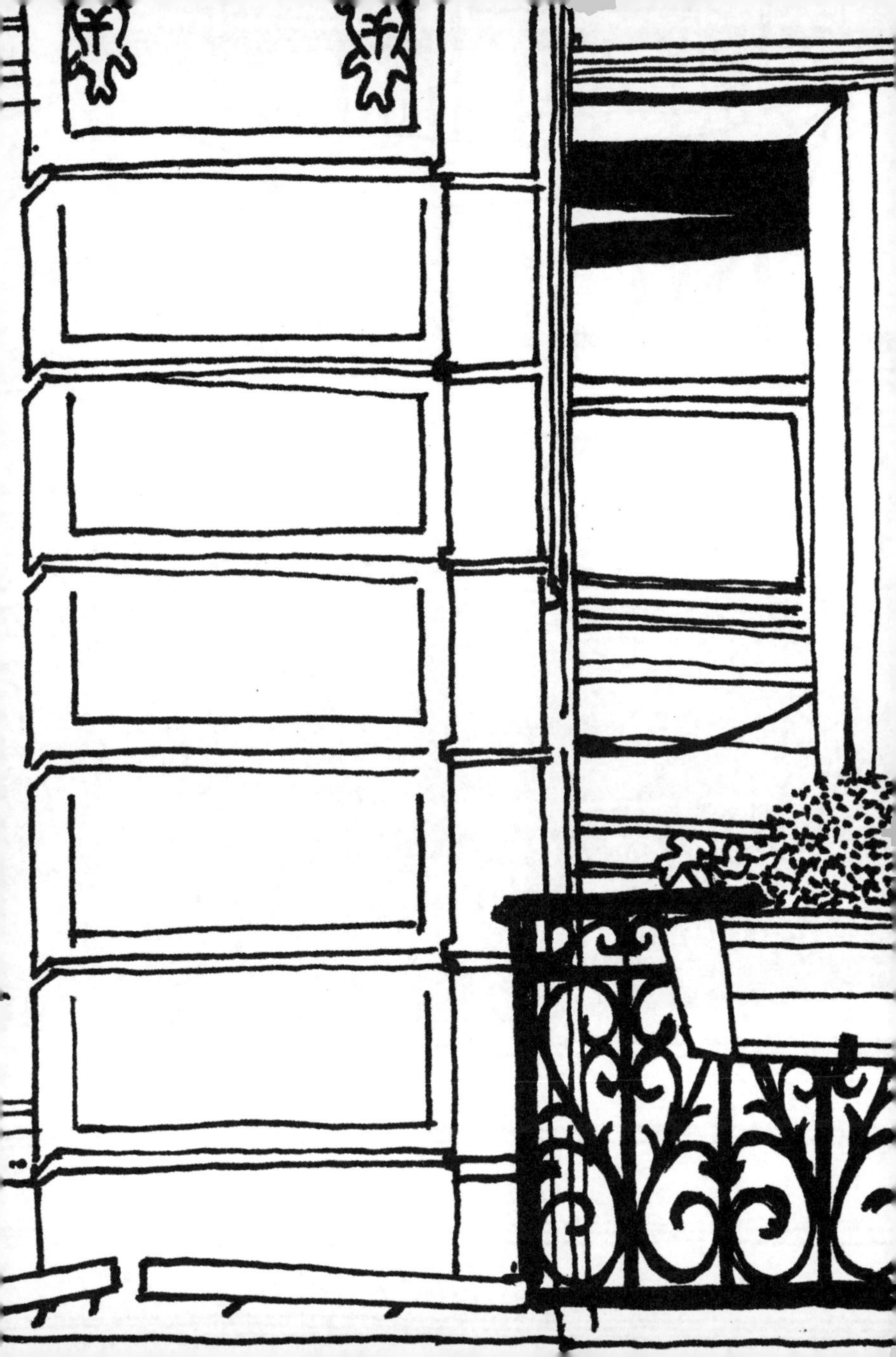

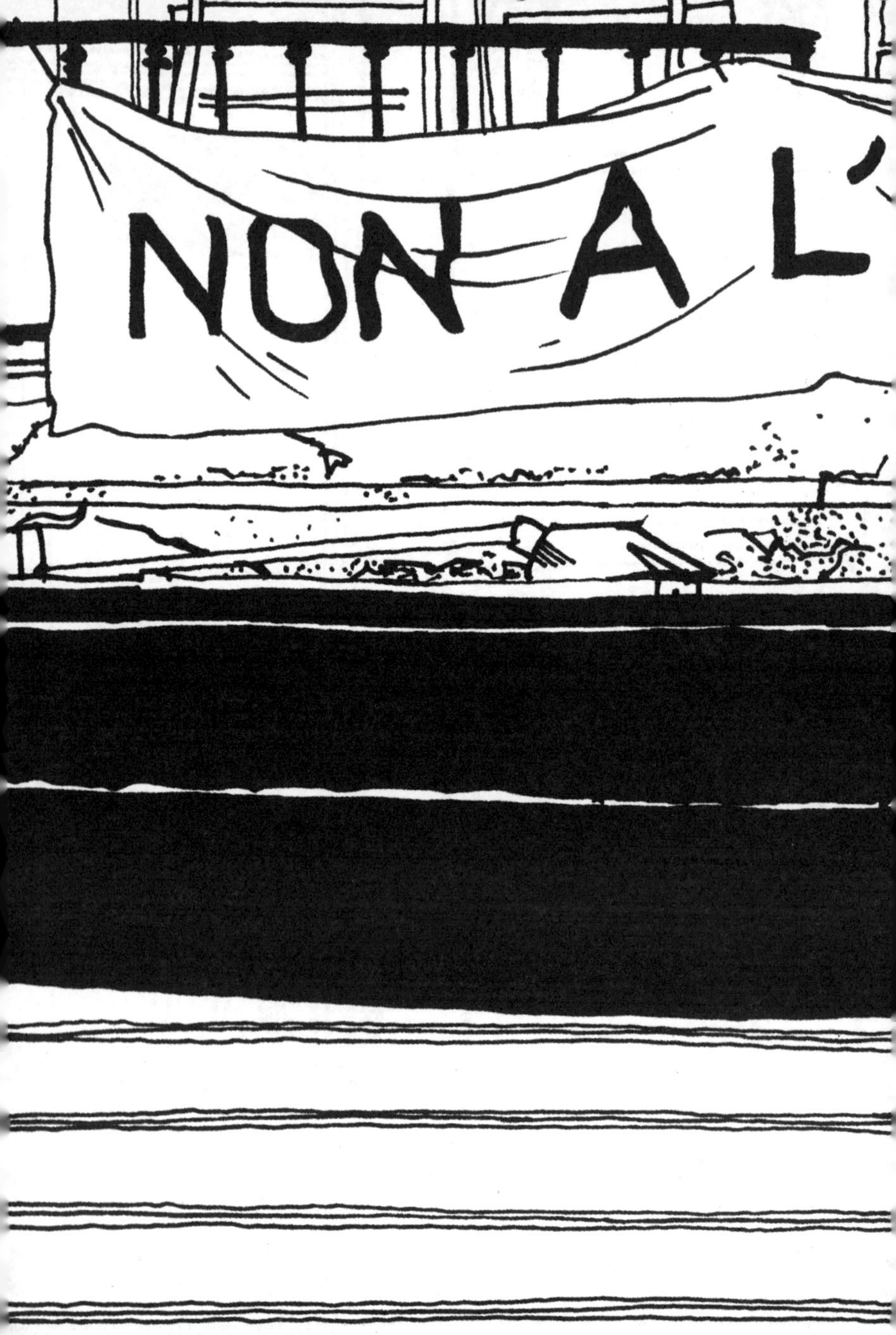
NON A L'

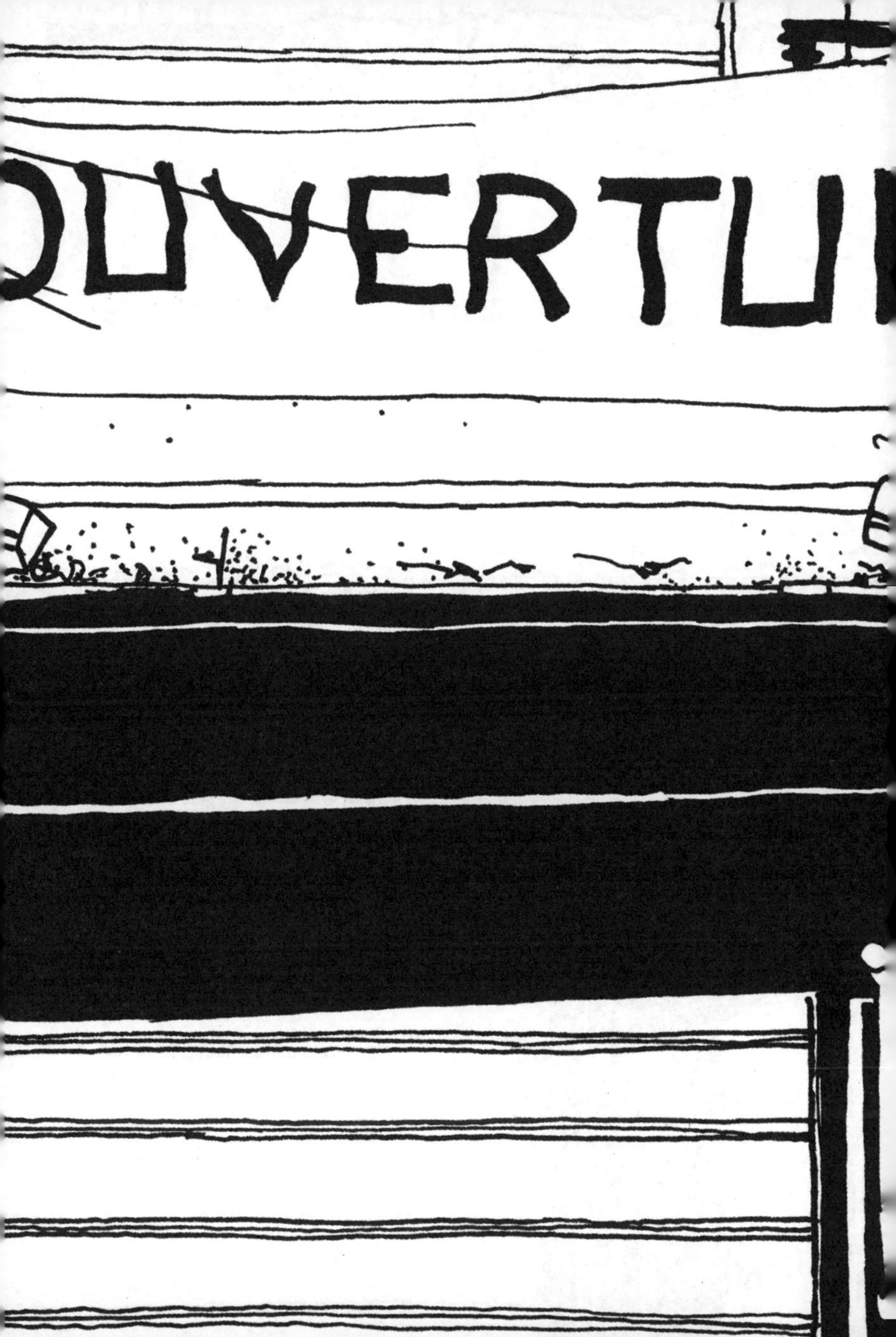
OUVERTU

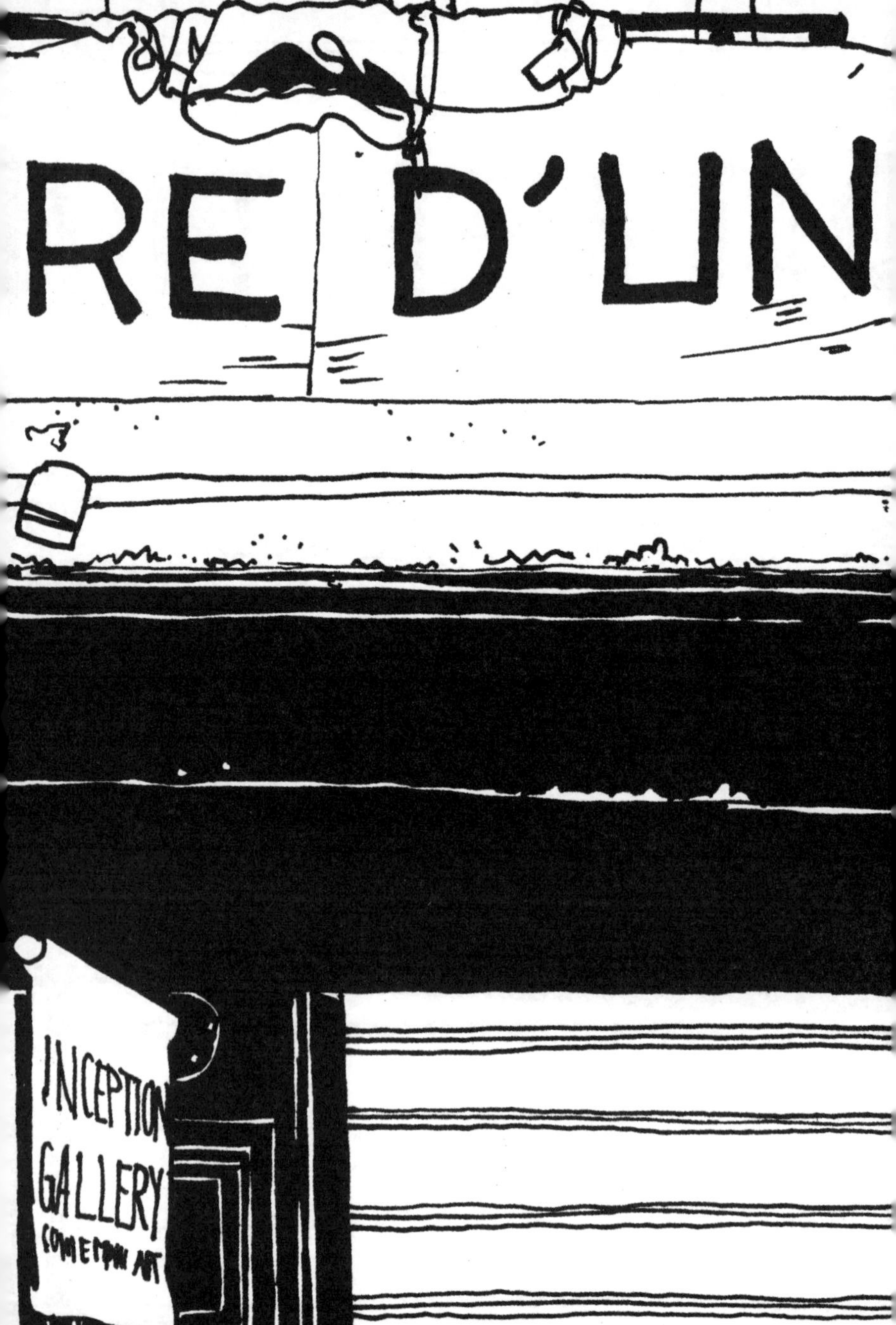
RE D'UN
INCEPTION
GALLERY

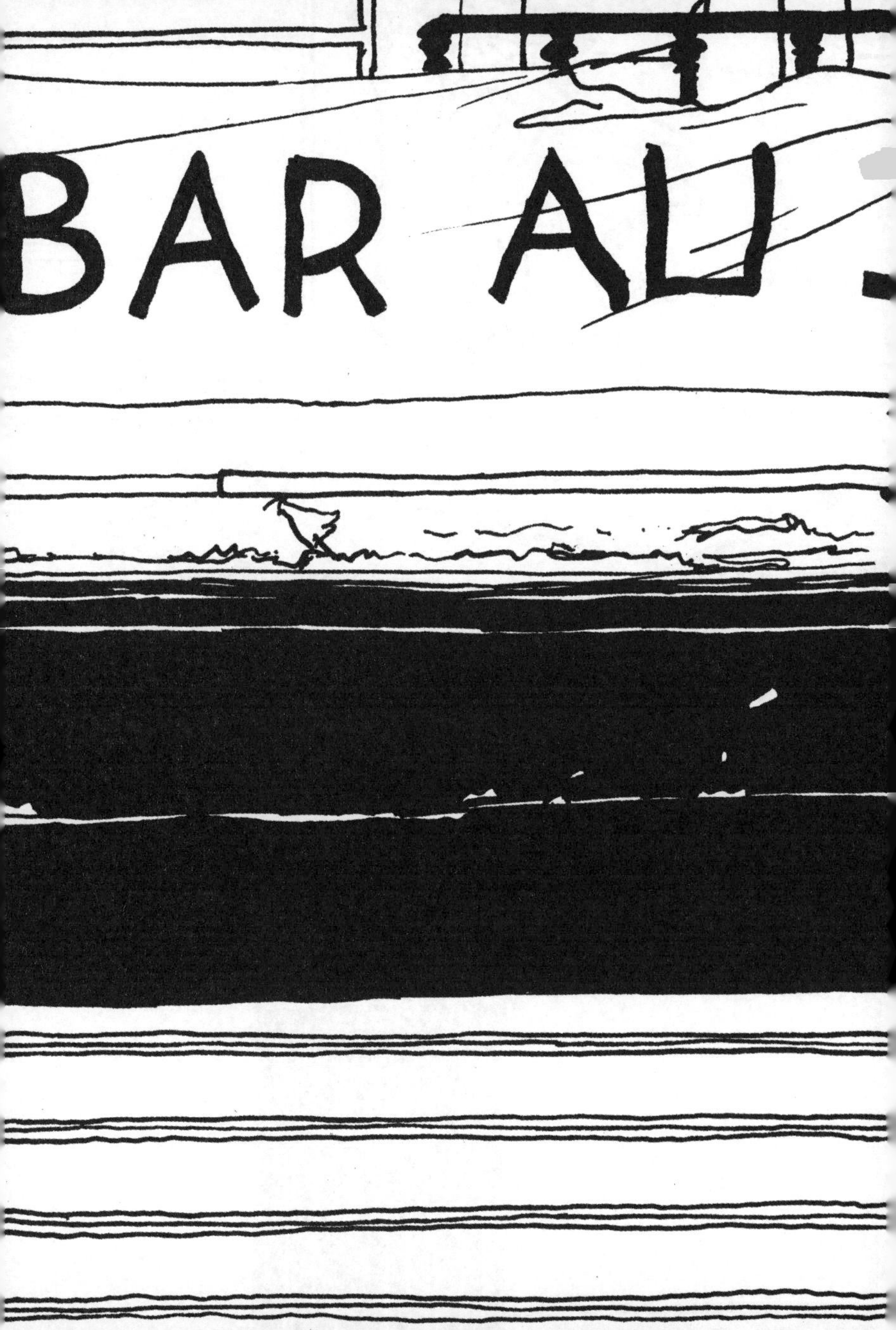
BAR AU

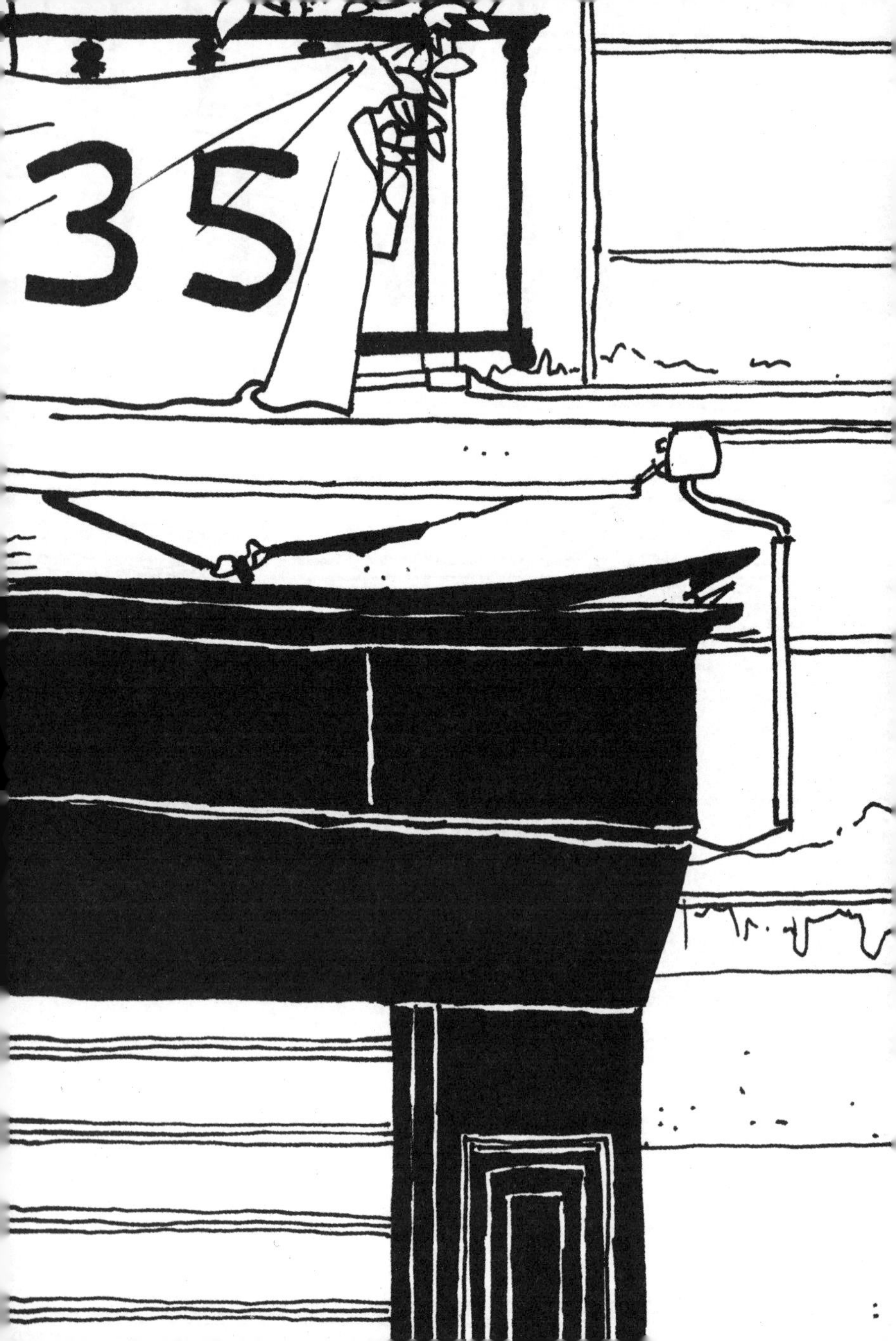
35

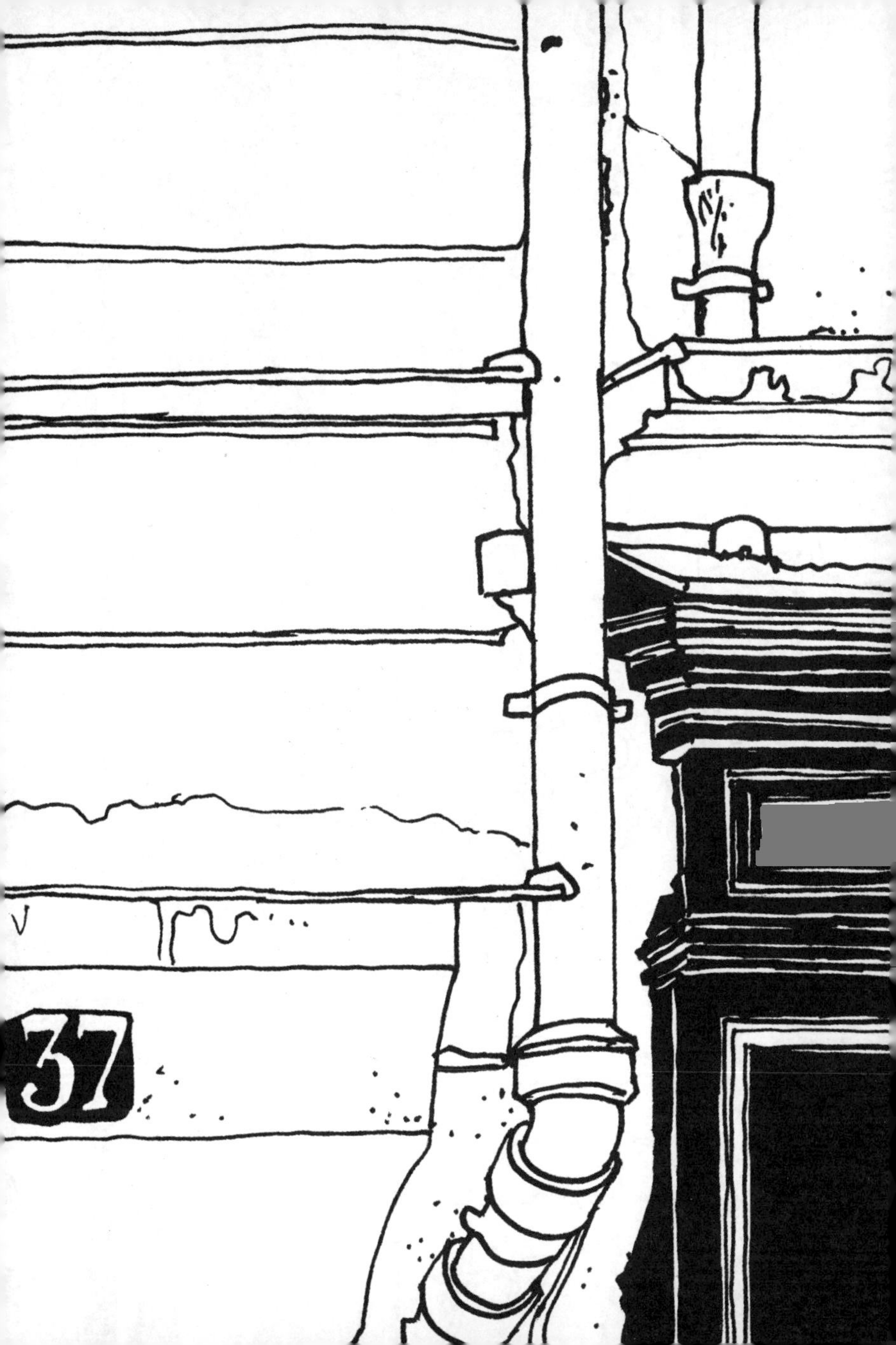
37

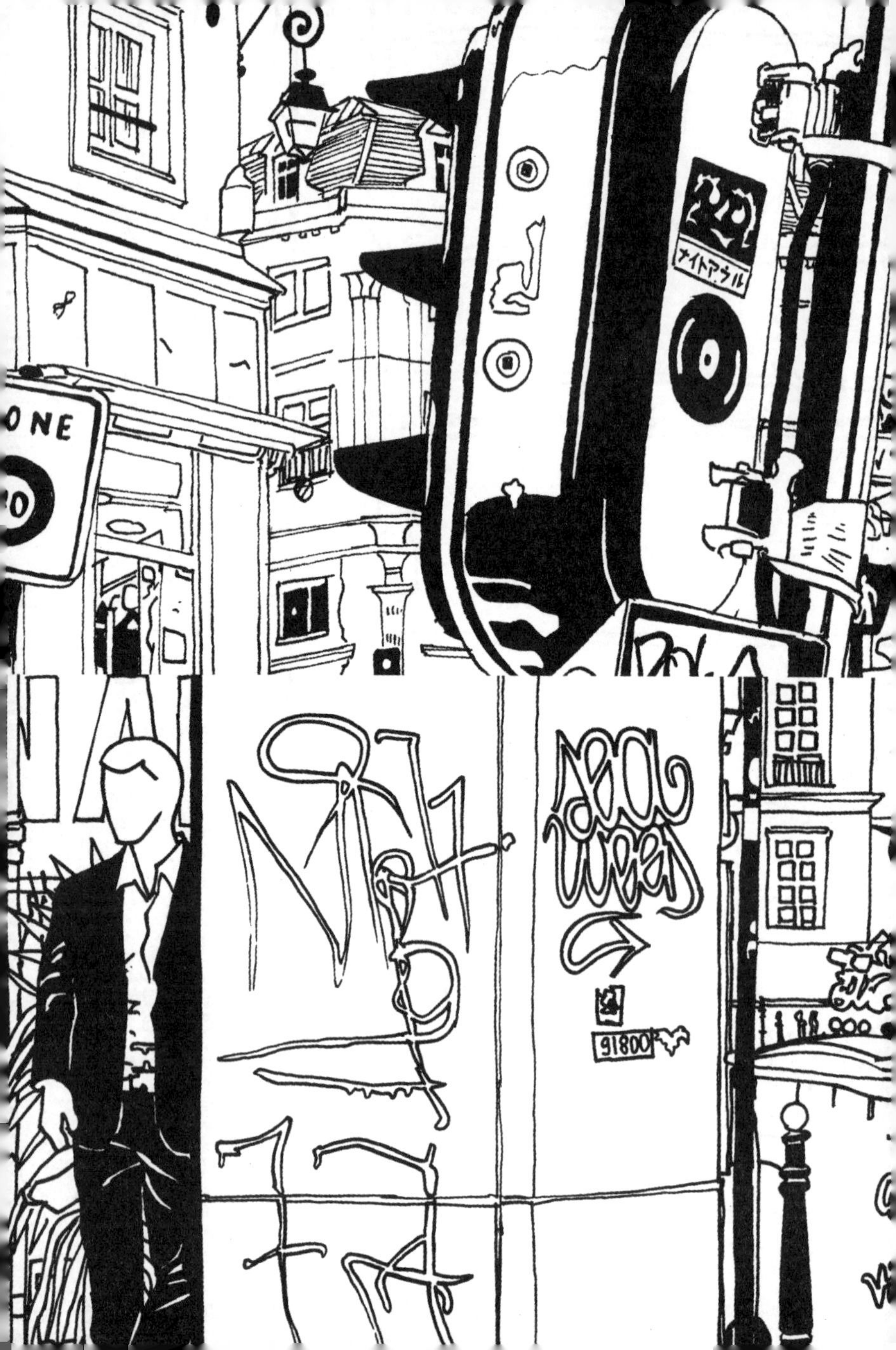
ONE
ナイトアウル
91800

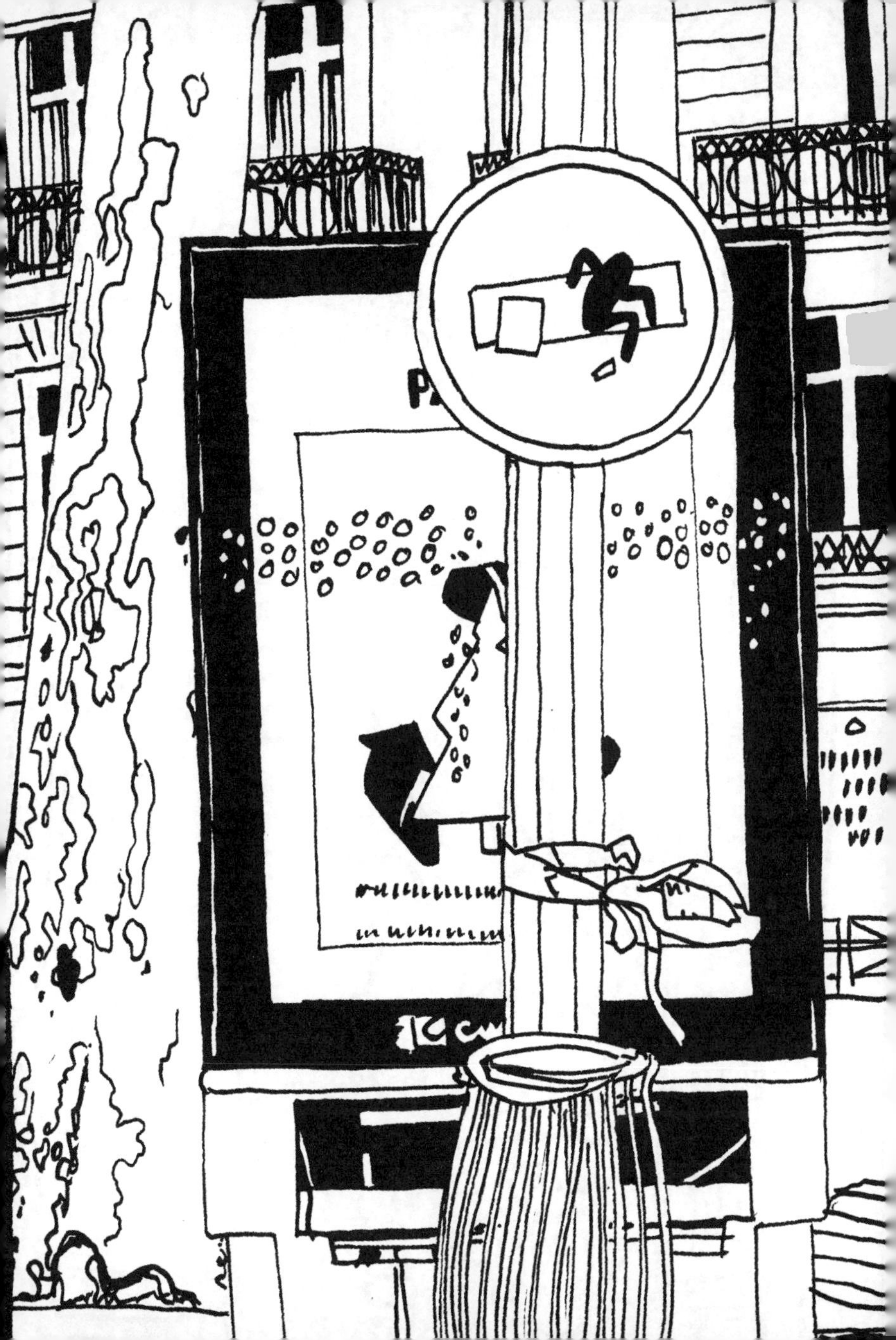

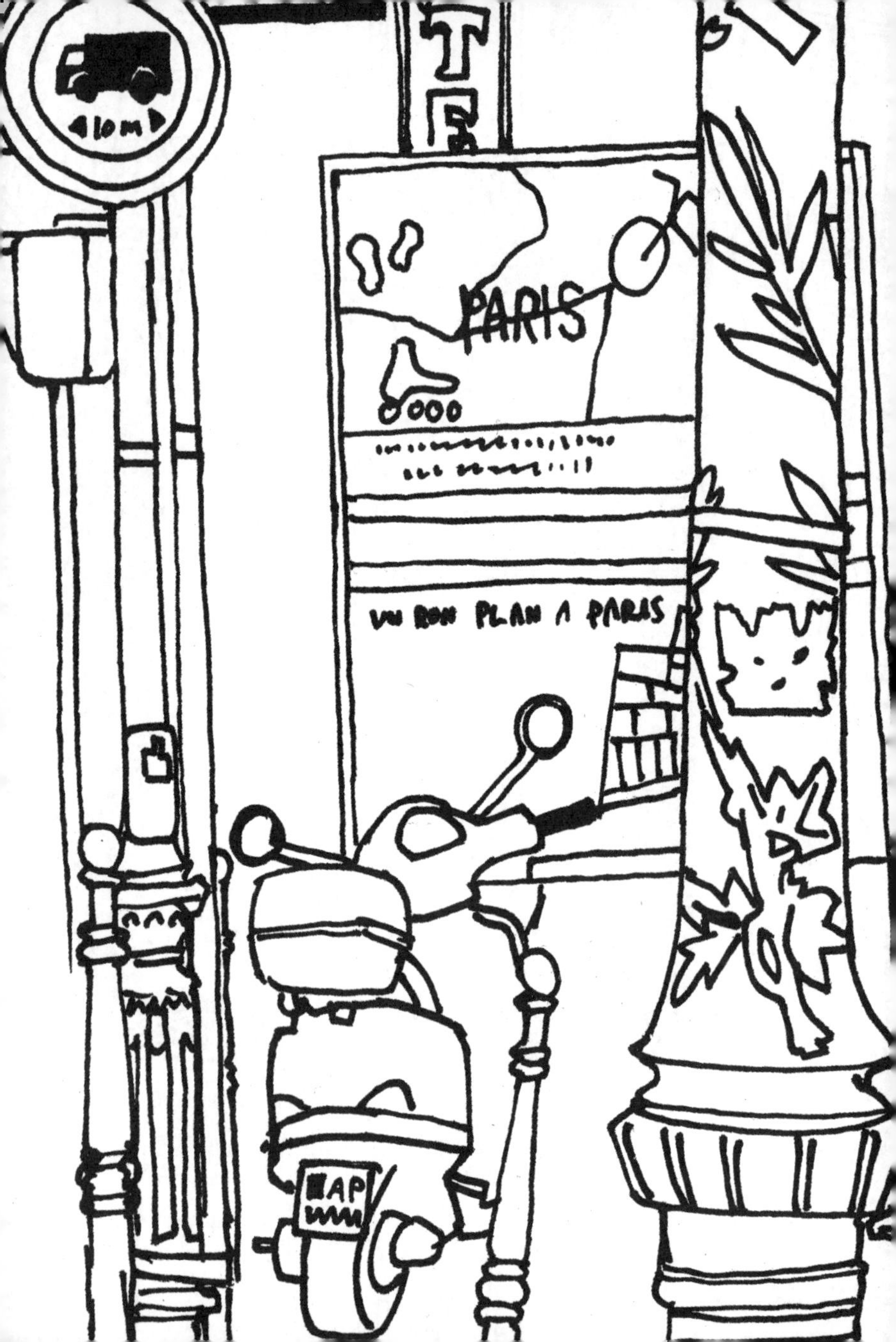
10m
PARIS
UN BON PLAN A PARIS

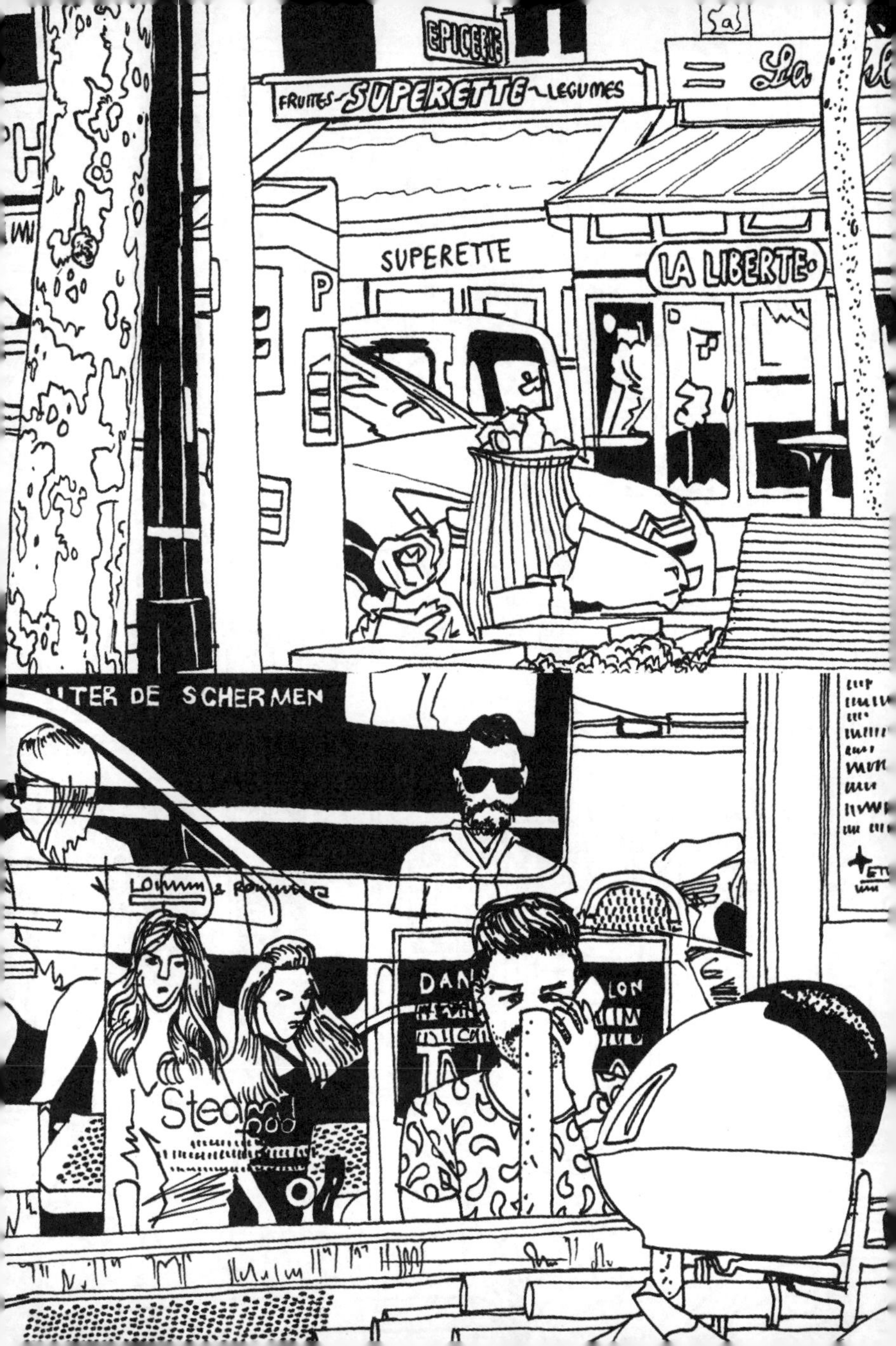
EPICERIE
FRUITES SUPERETTE LEGUMES
SUPERETTE
P
LA LIBERTE
TER DE SCHERMEN
DAN
LON

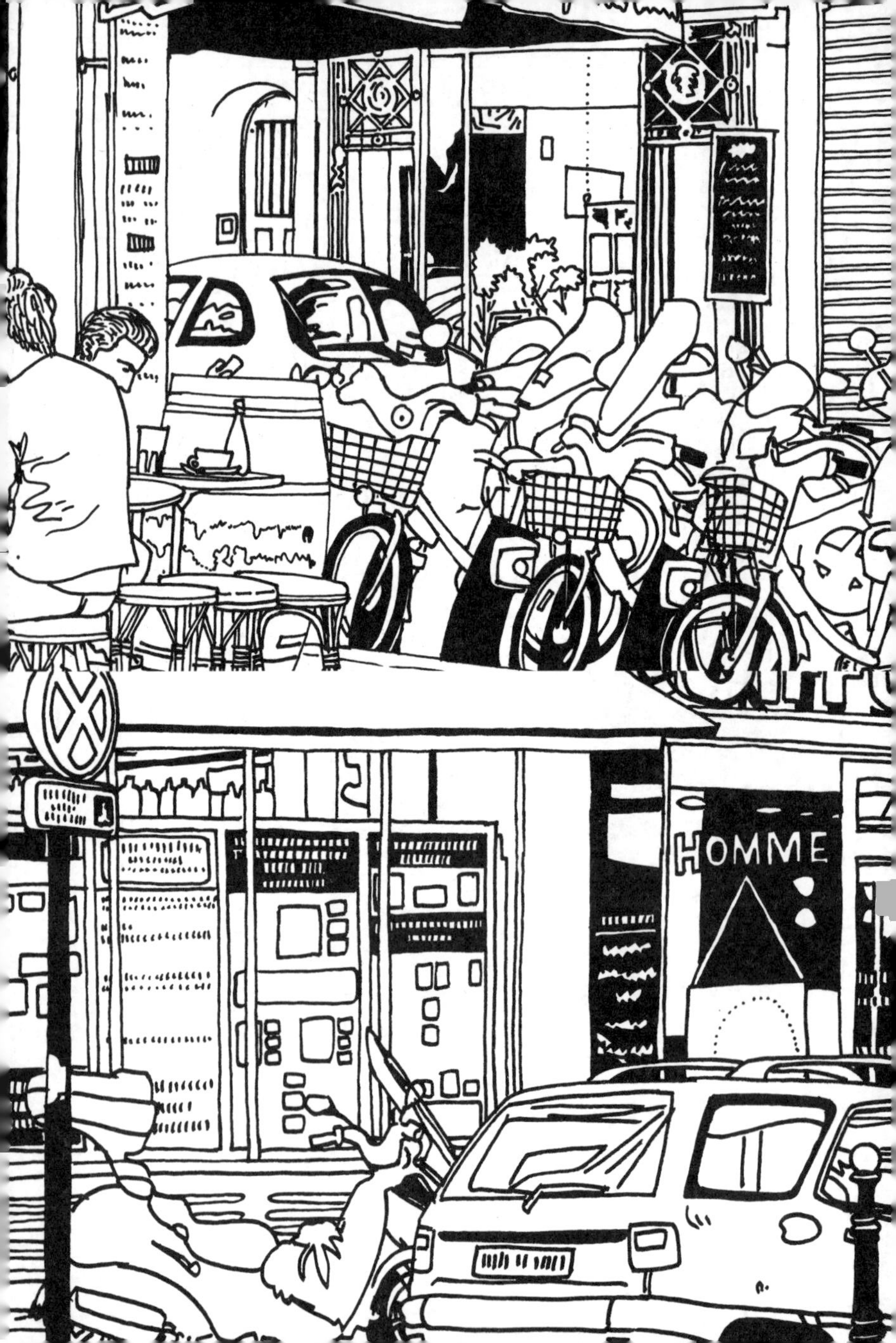
HOMME

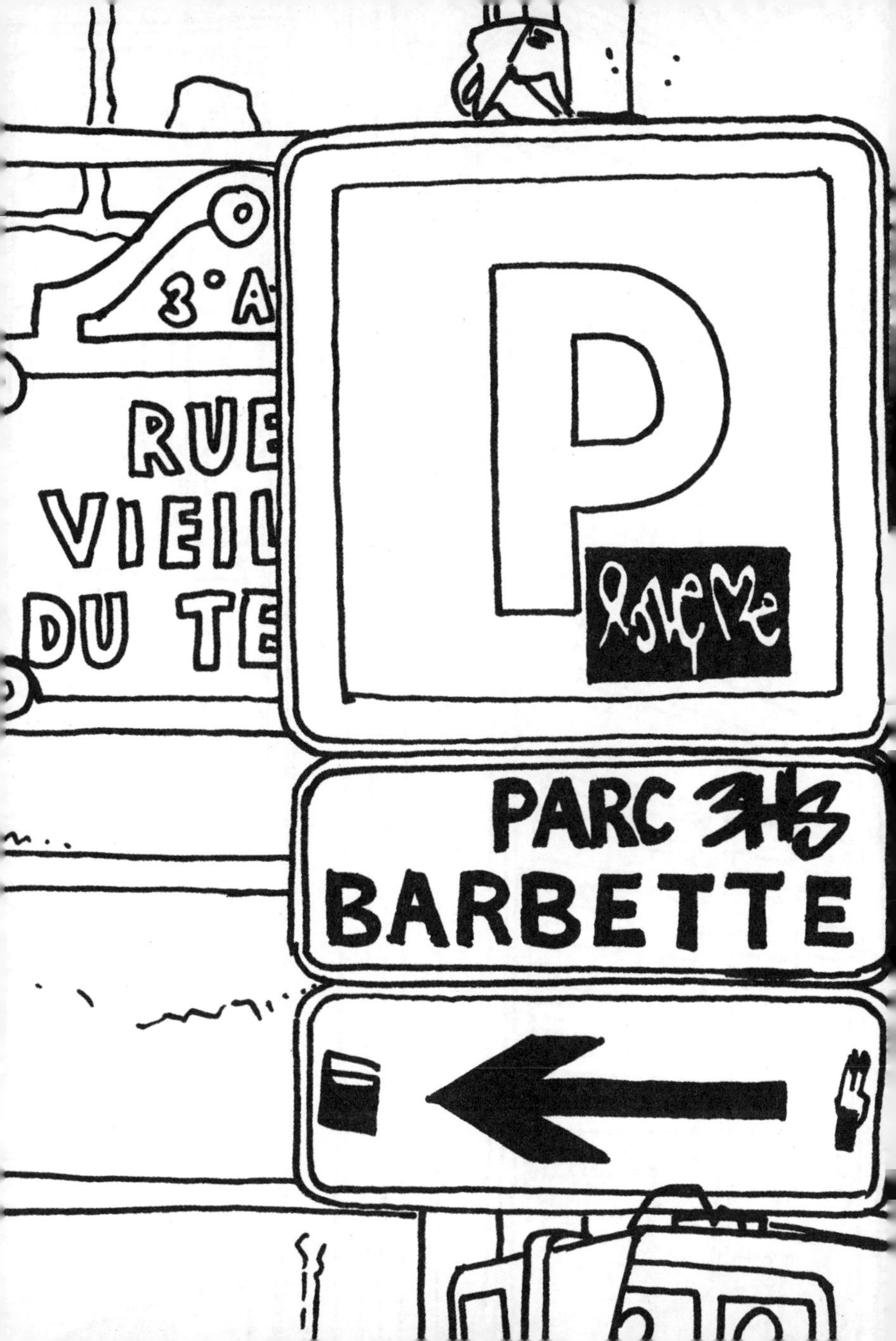
3°A
RUE
VIEIL
DU TE
P
PARC
BARBETTE

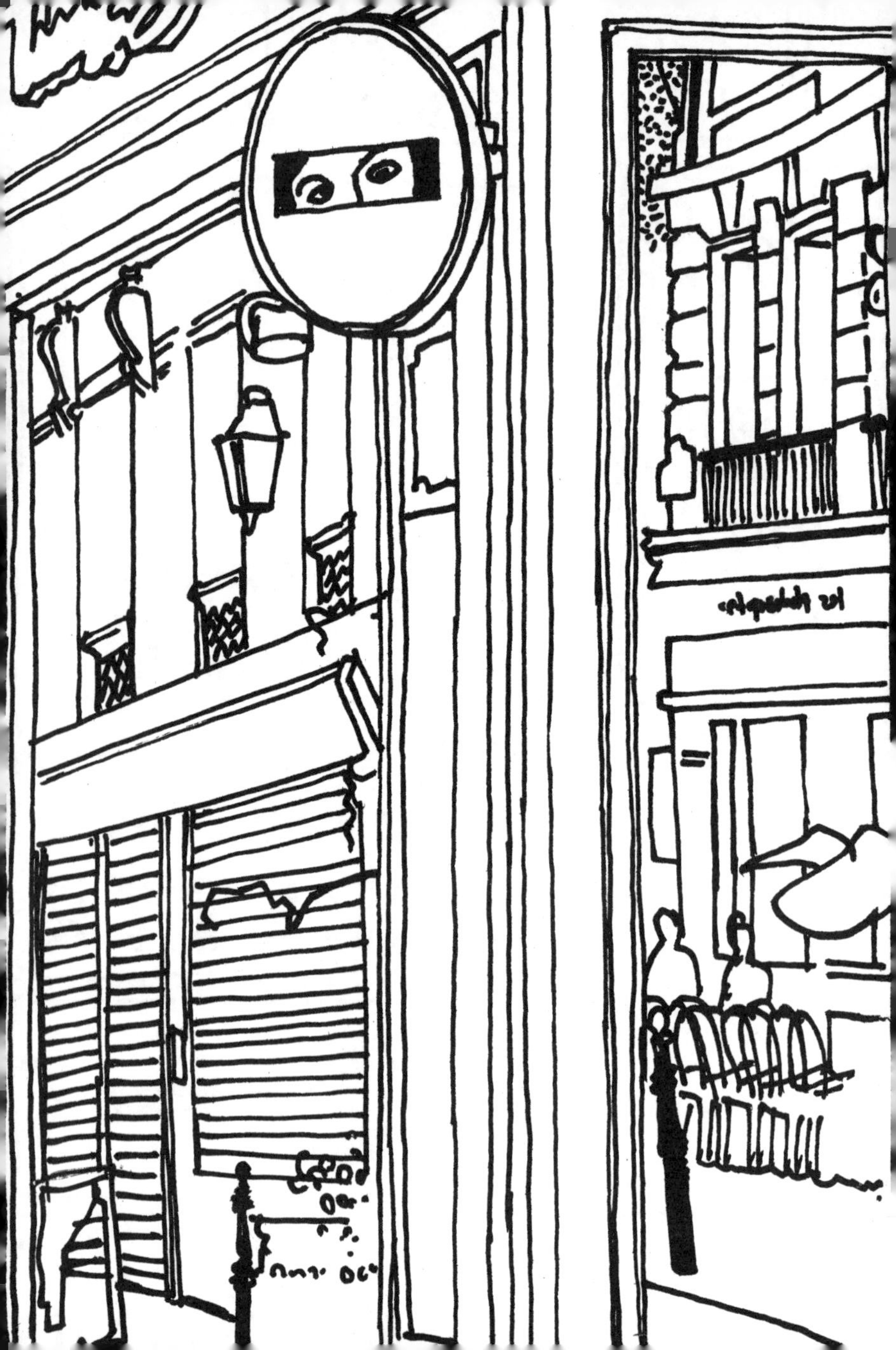

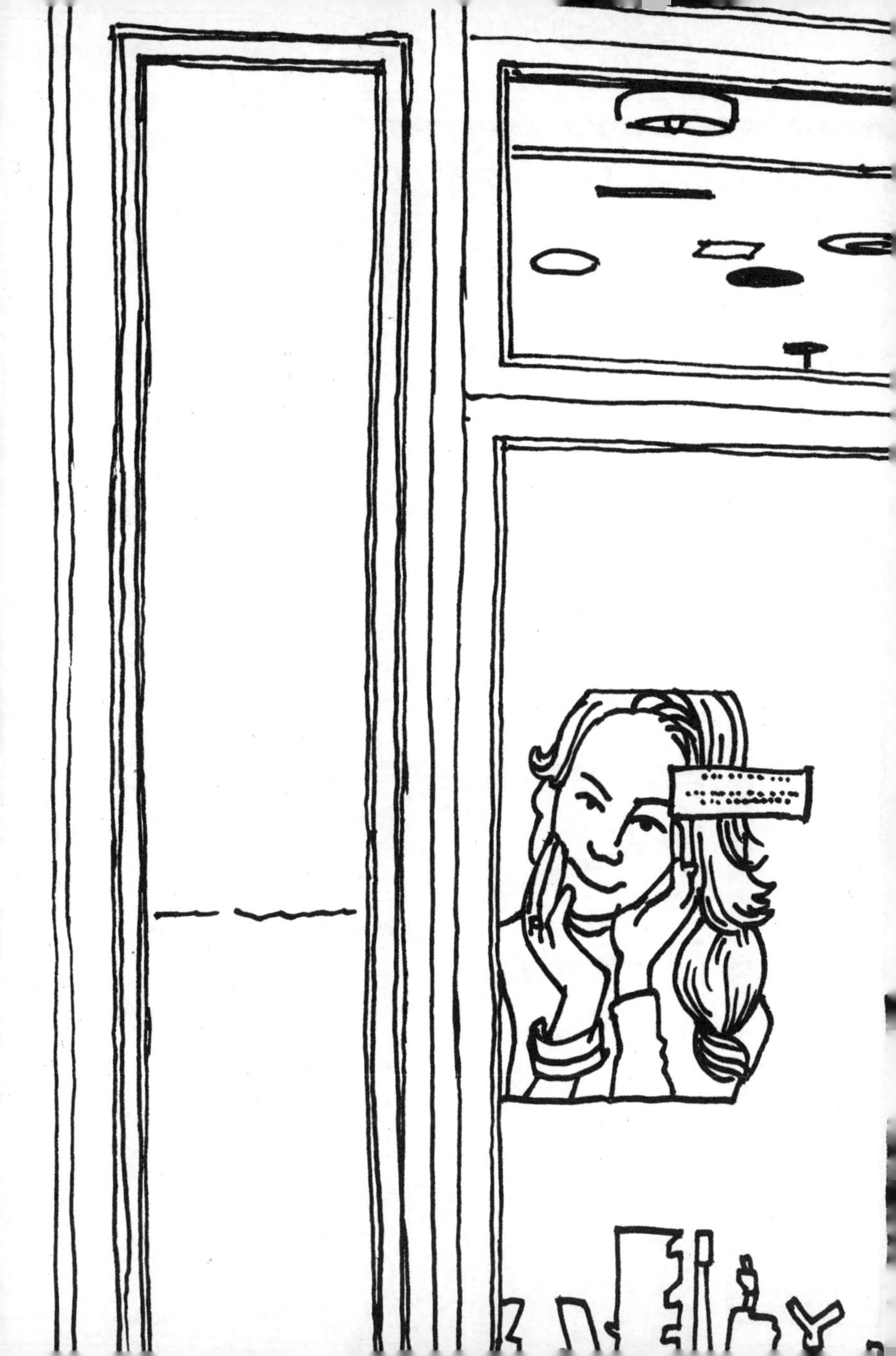

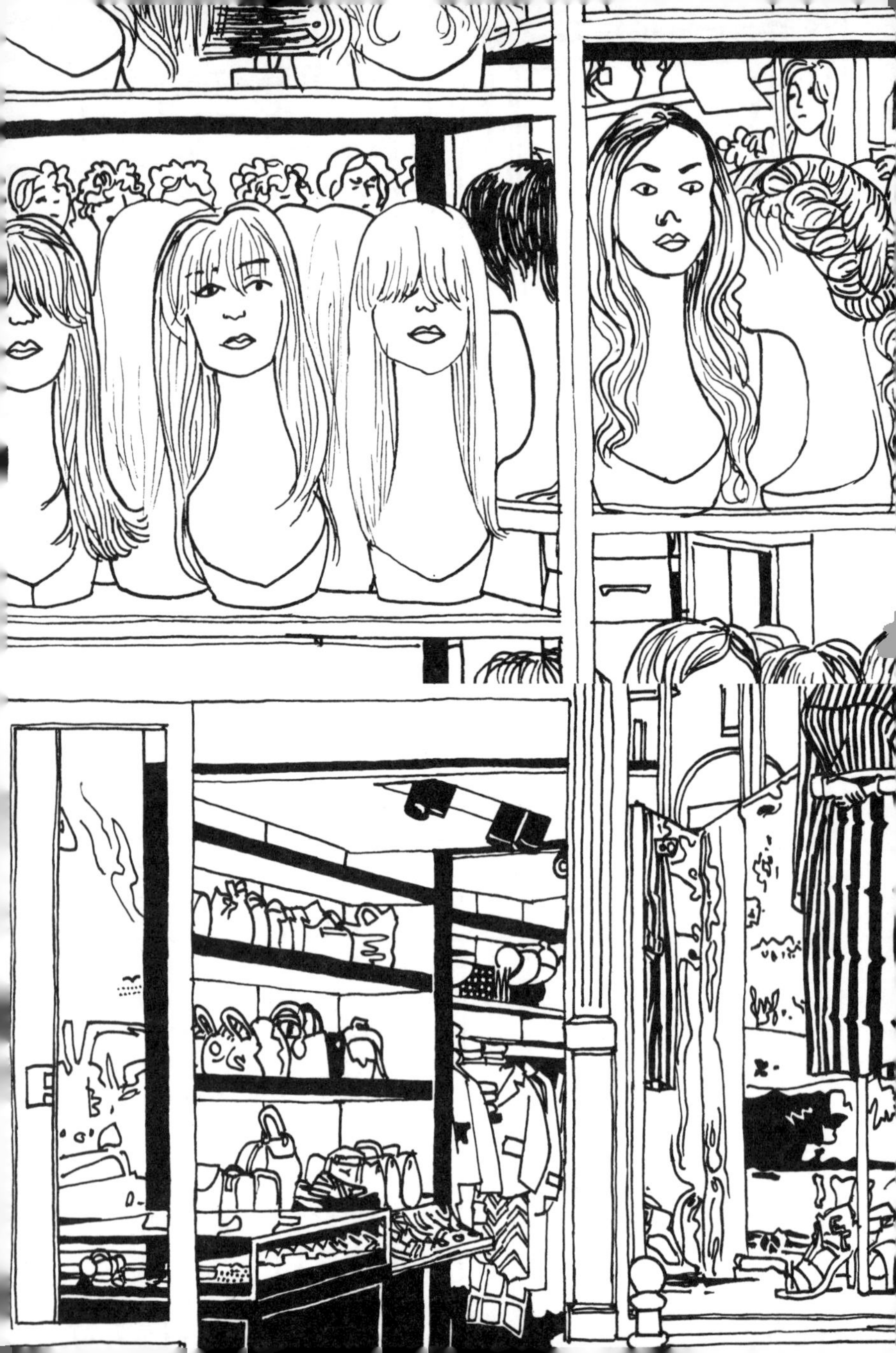

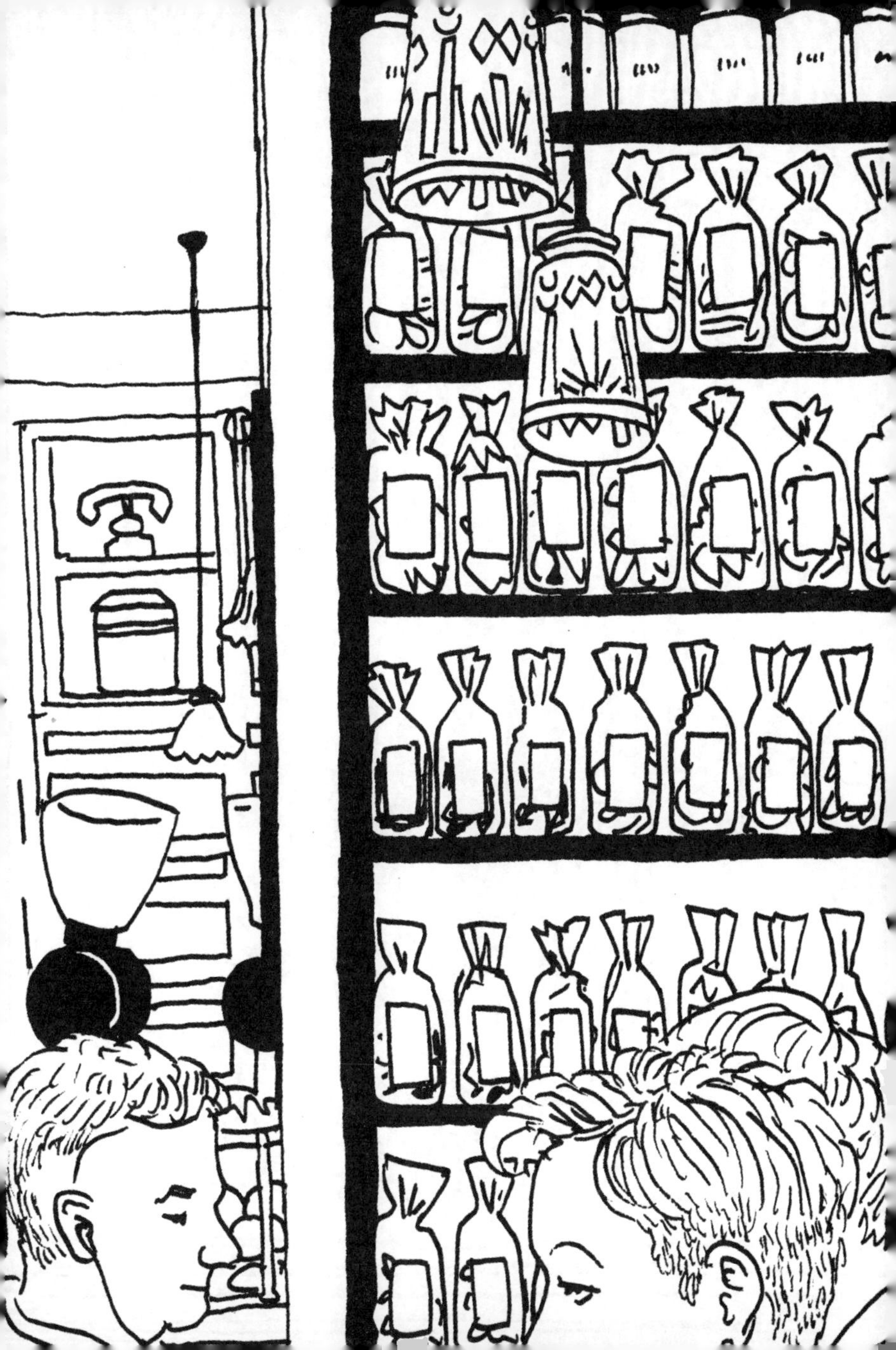

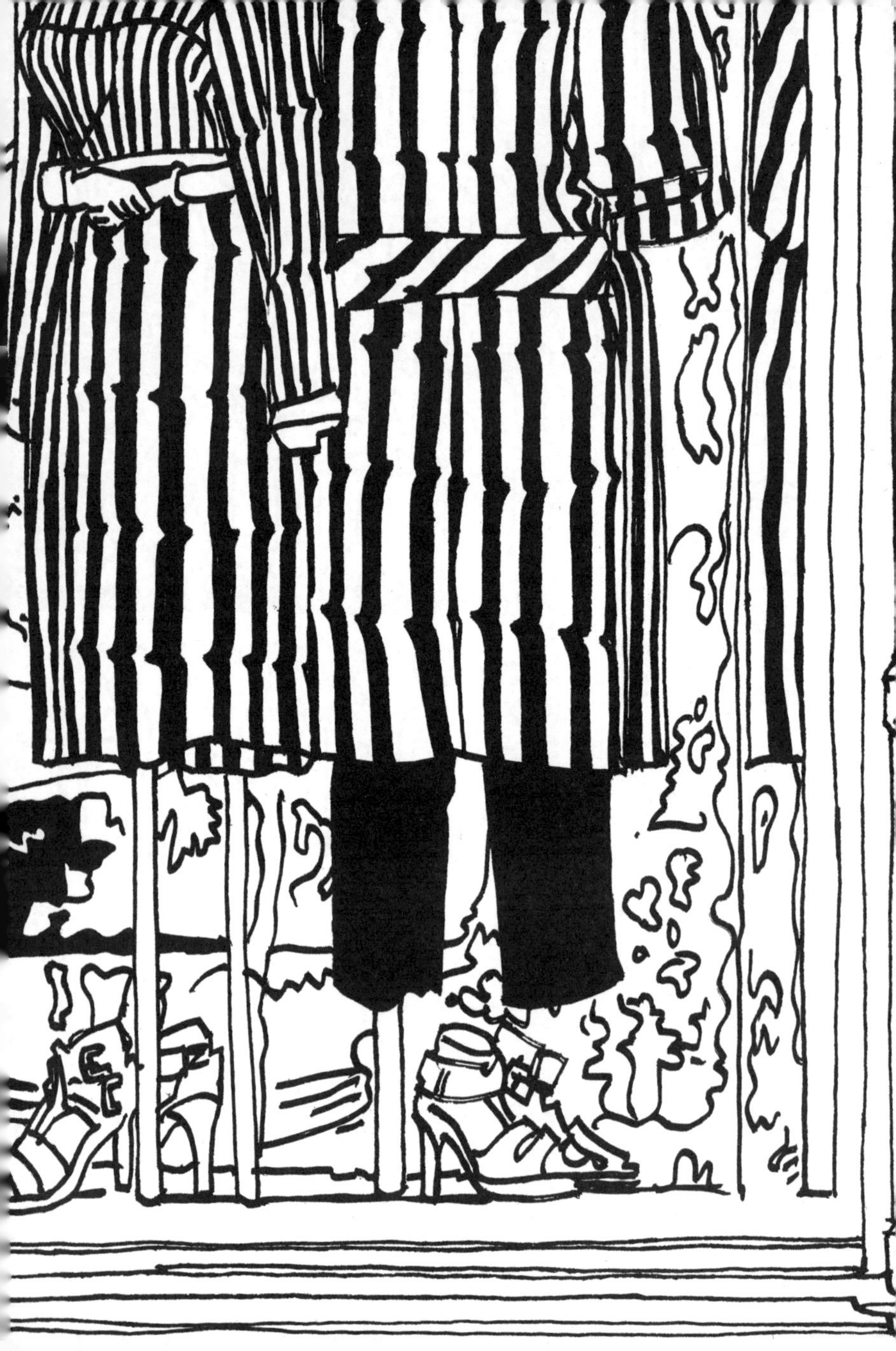

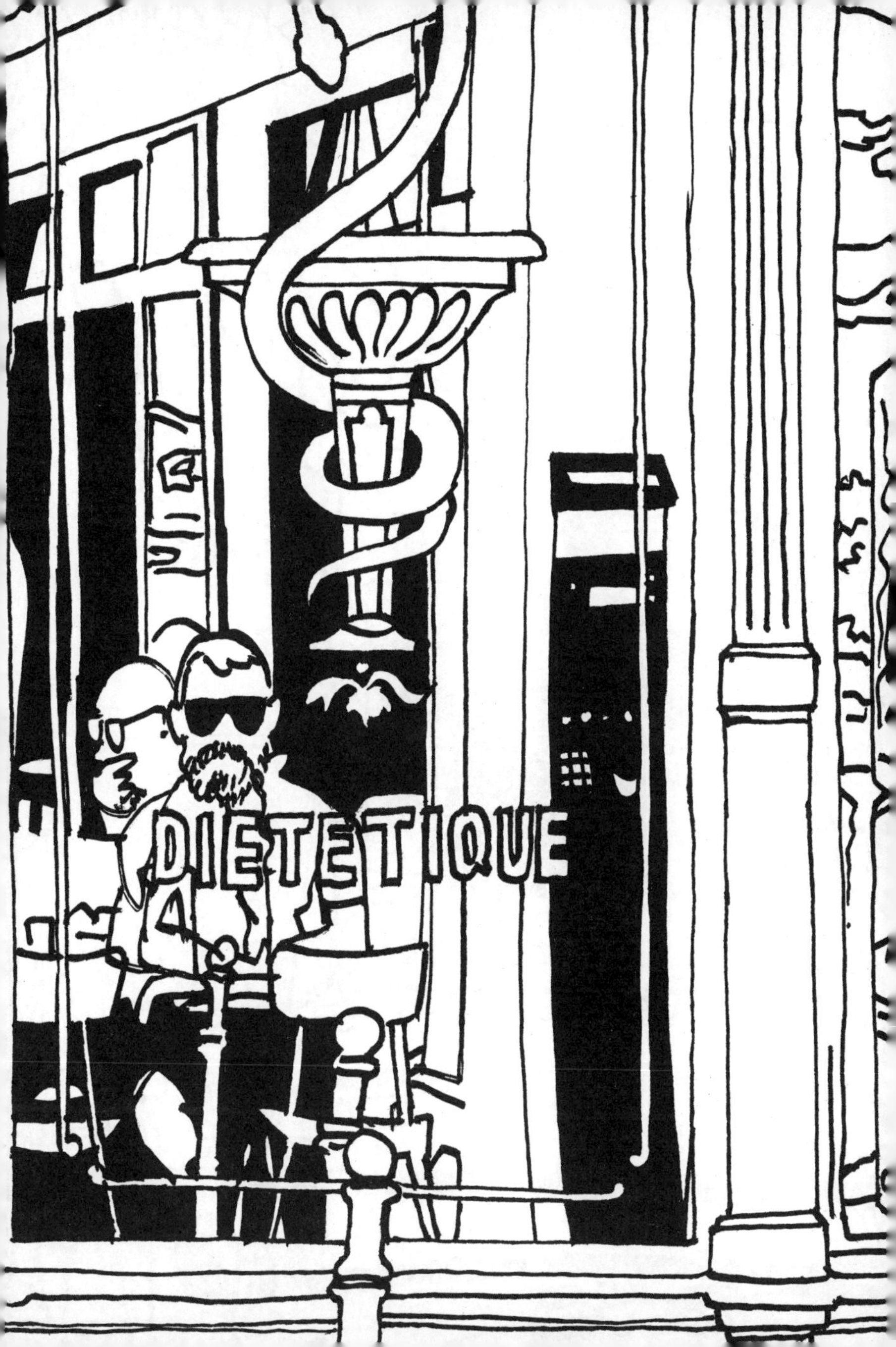
DIETETIQUE

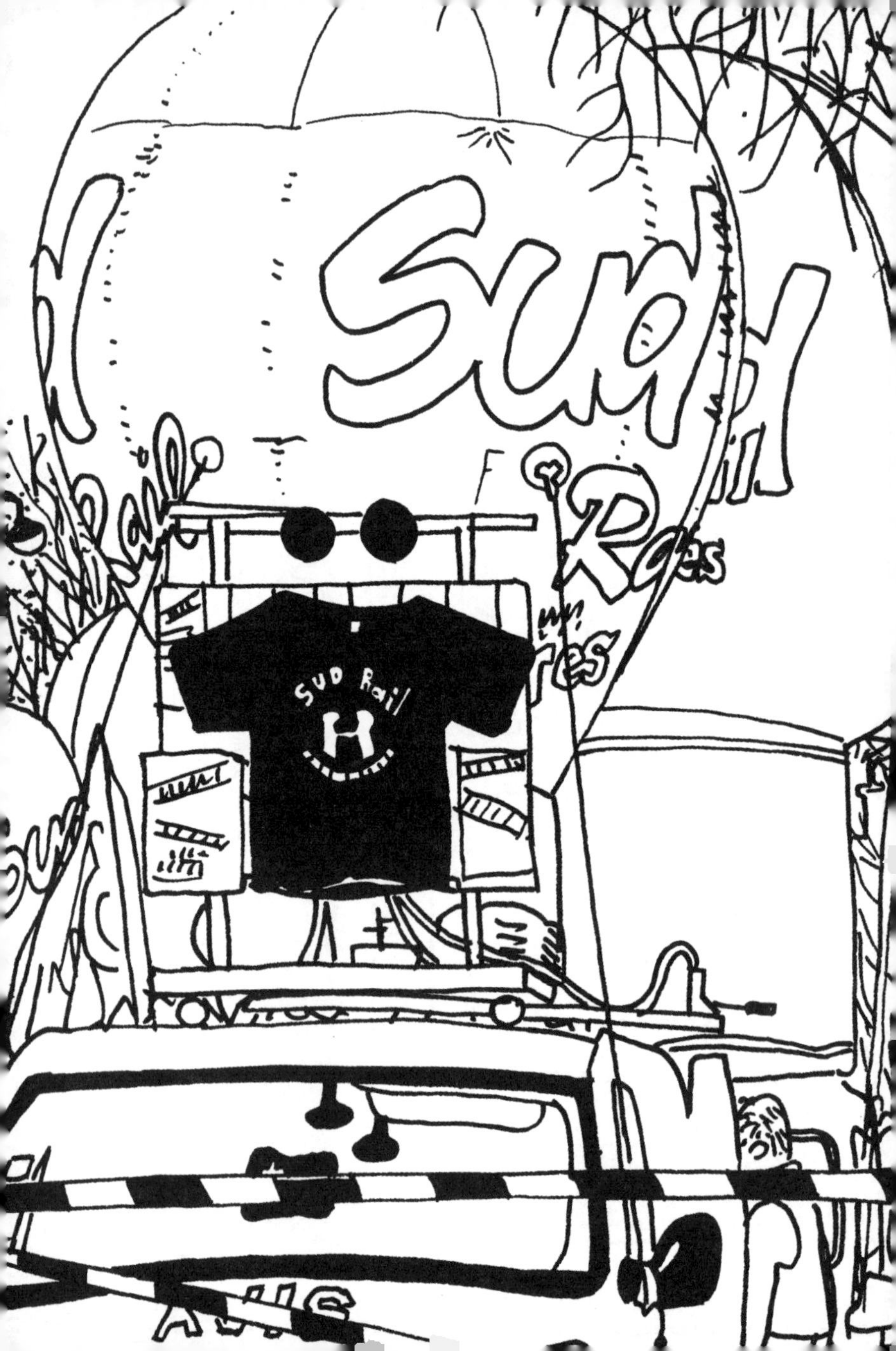
SUD Rail

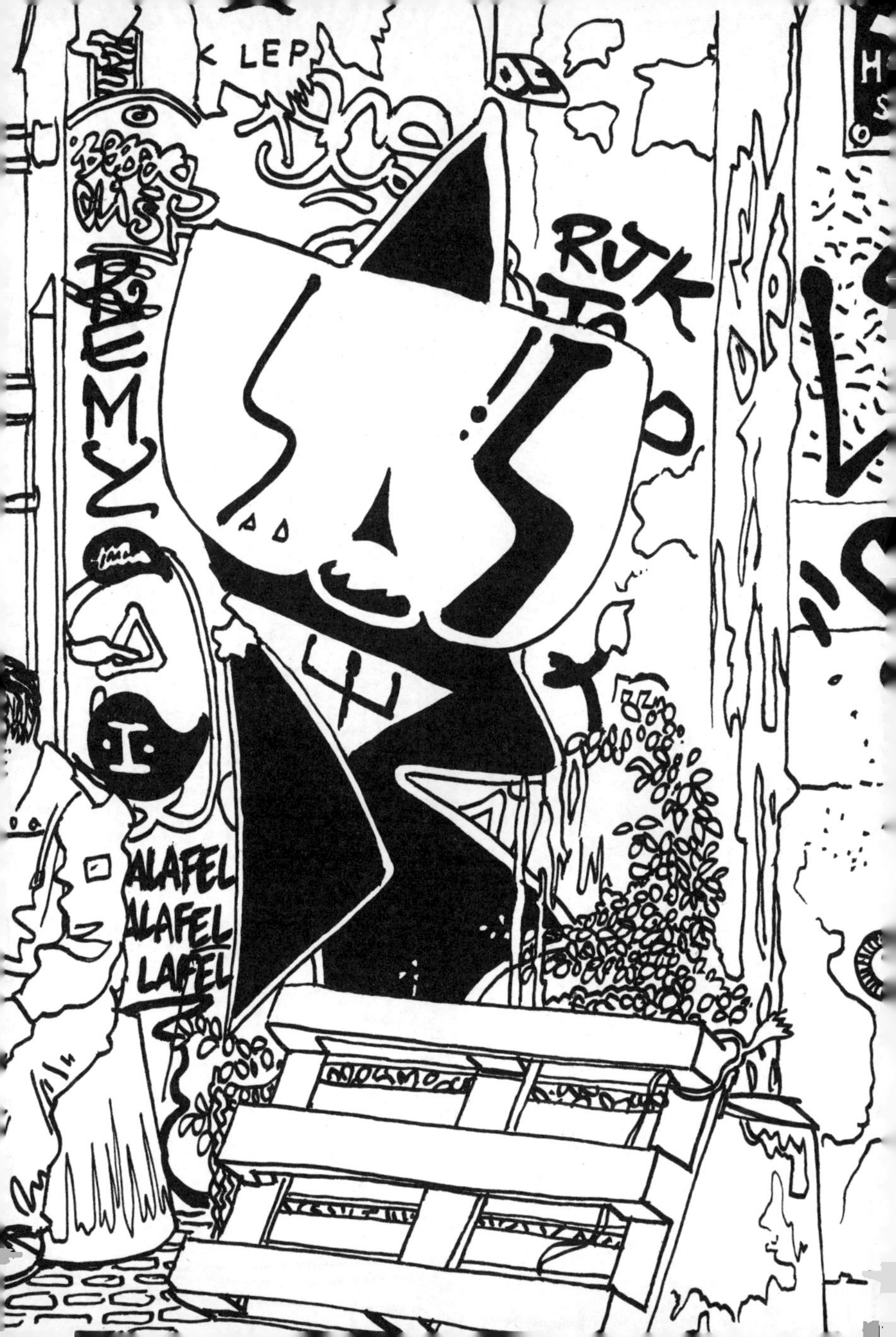
K LEP
RJK
ALAFEL
ALAFEL
LAFEL

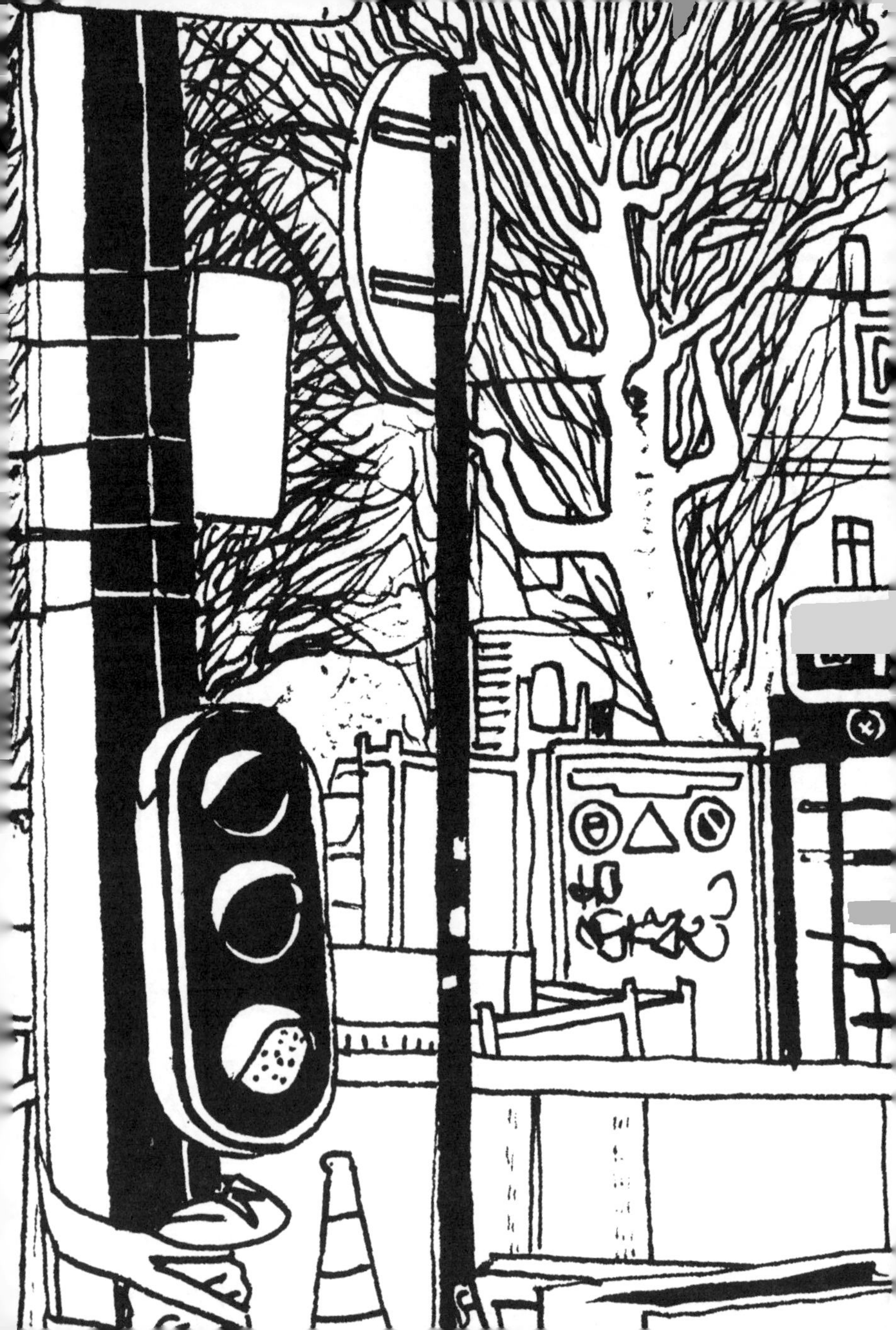

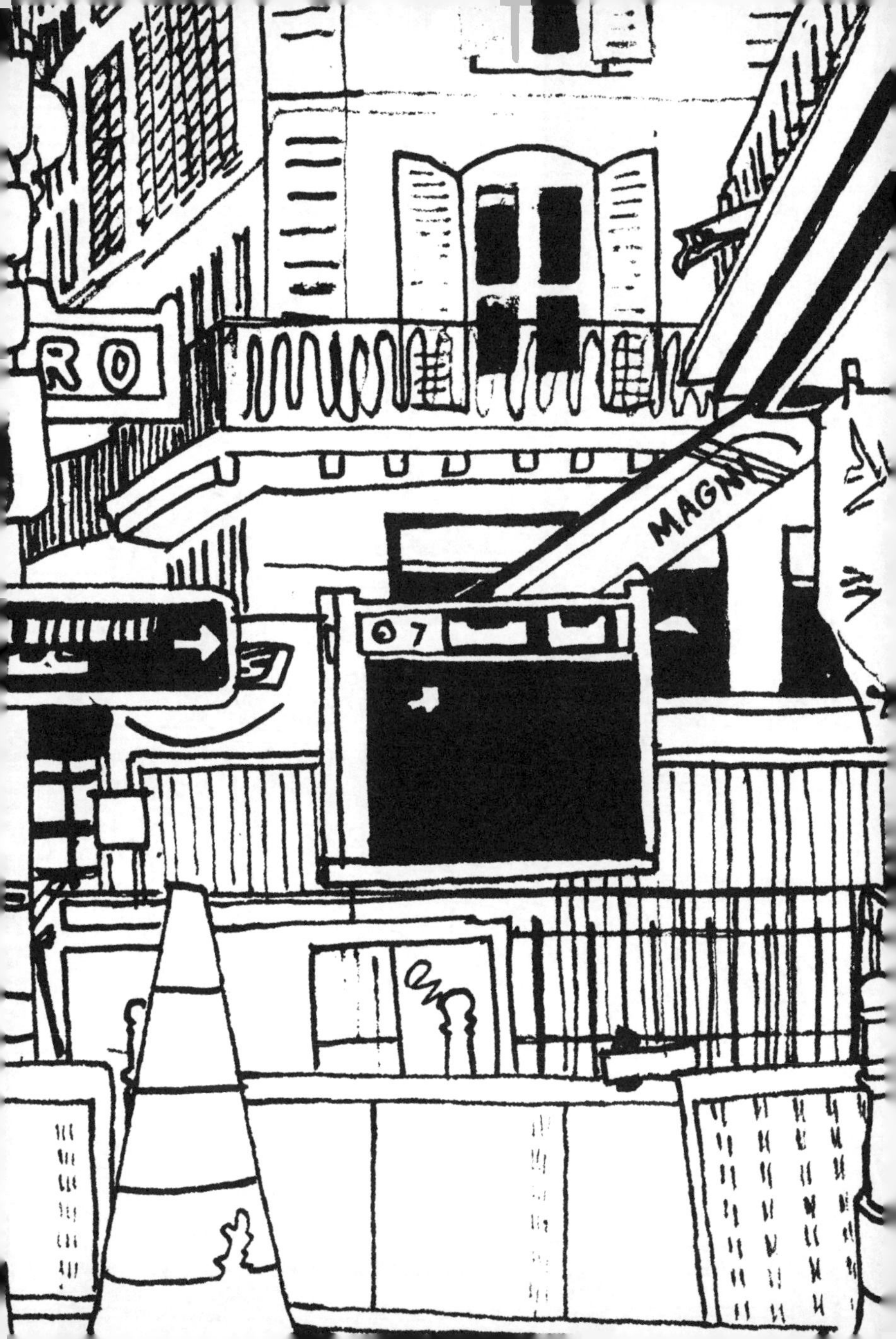
R O
MAGN

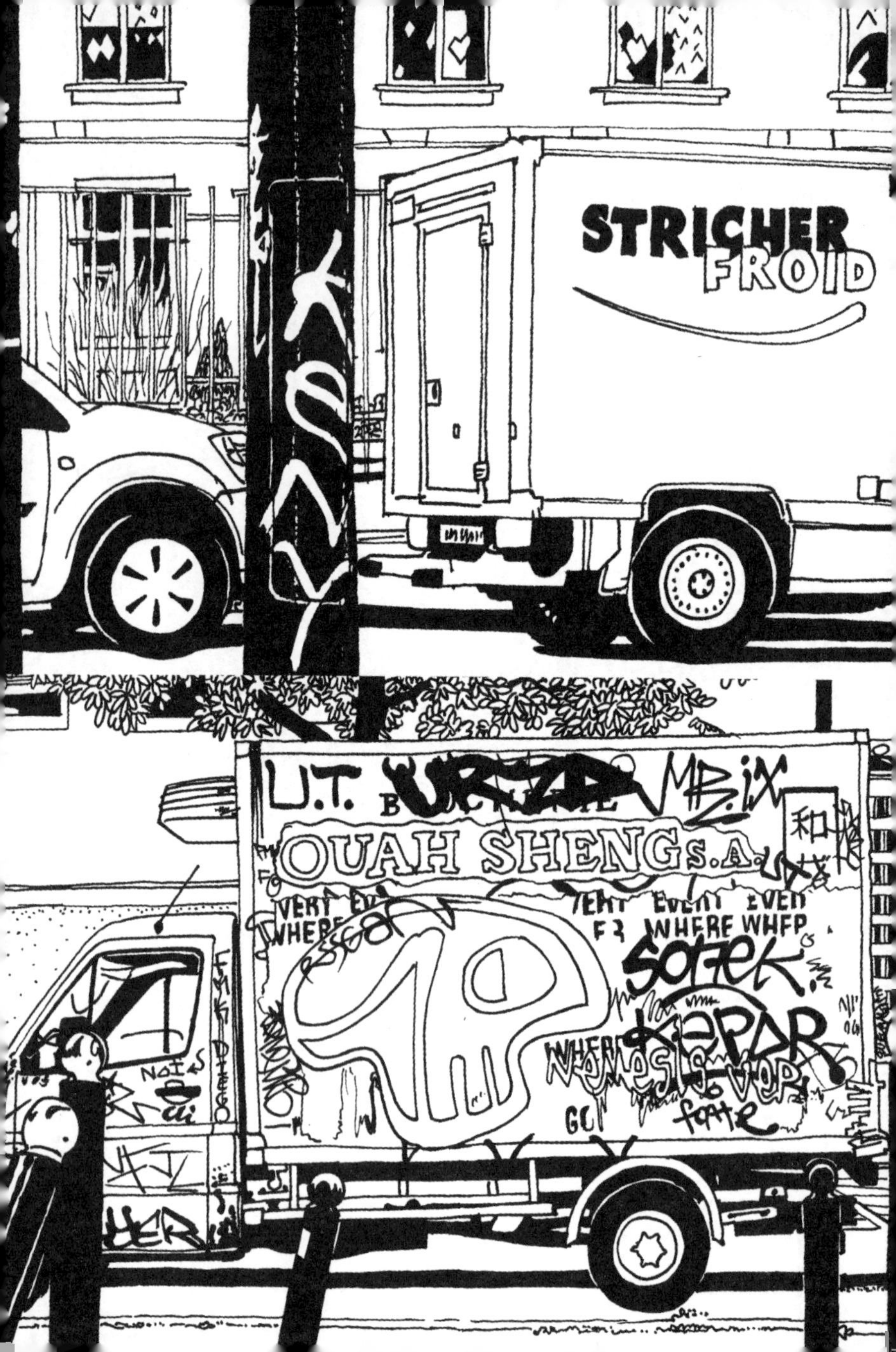

STRICHER
FROID
U.T.
OUAH SHENG S.A.

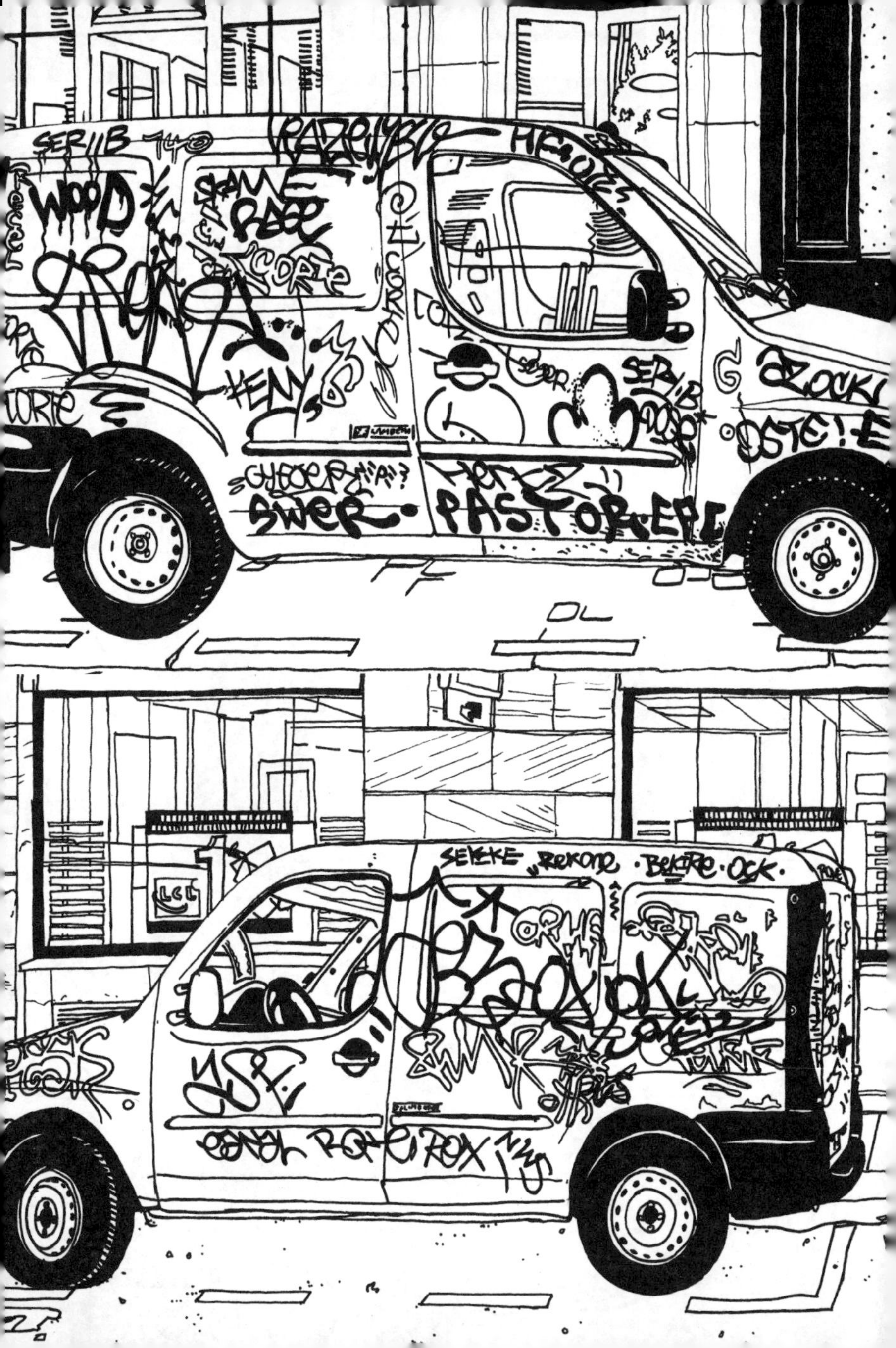

WOOD
SWER
PASTOR

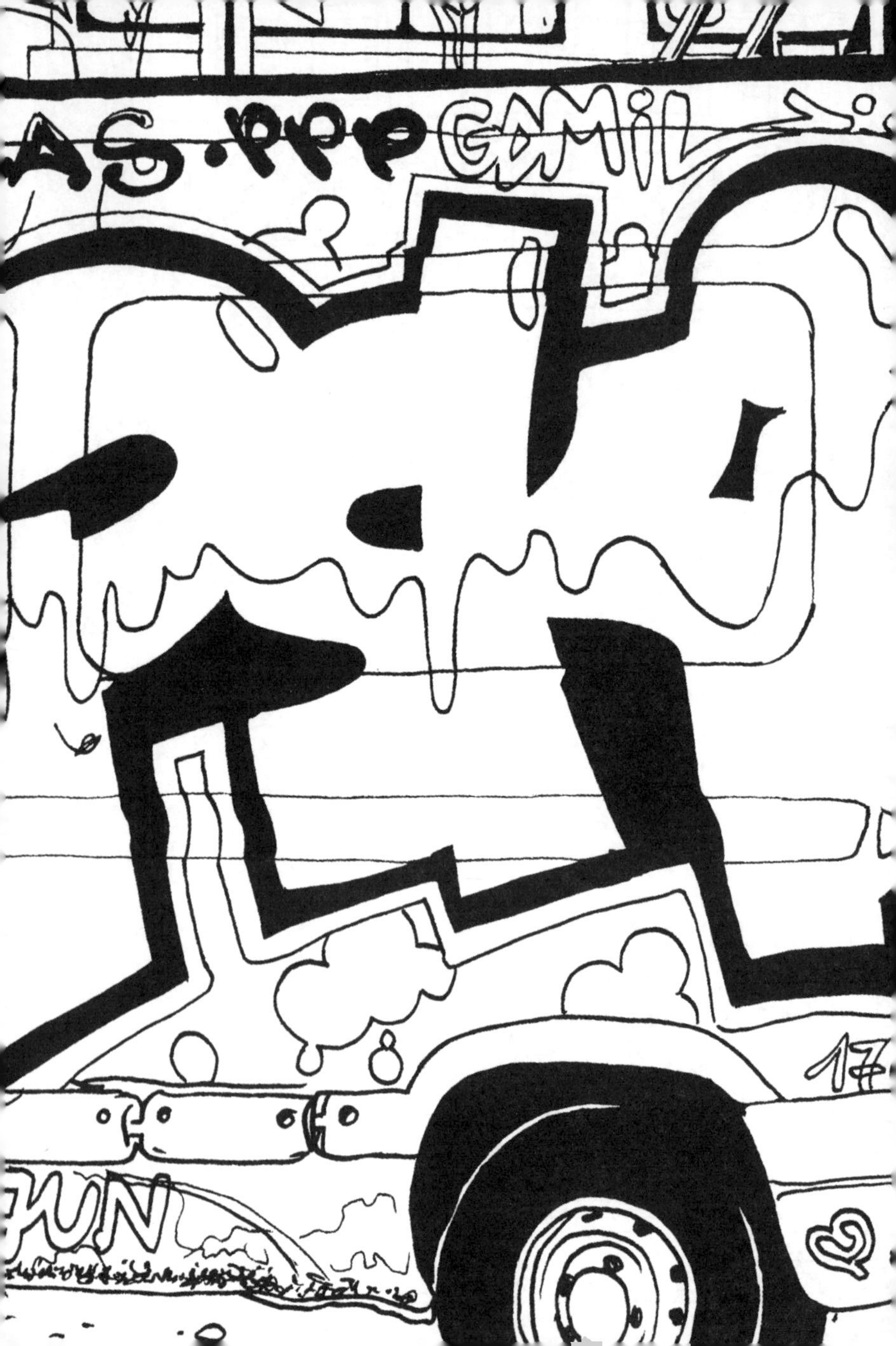

76
CAMIL
MESK
SANCHO
AZ592GV
RENAULT
OREY.OREY.

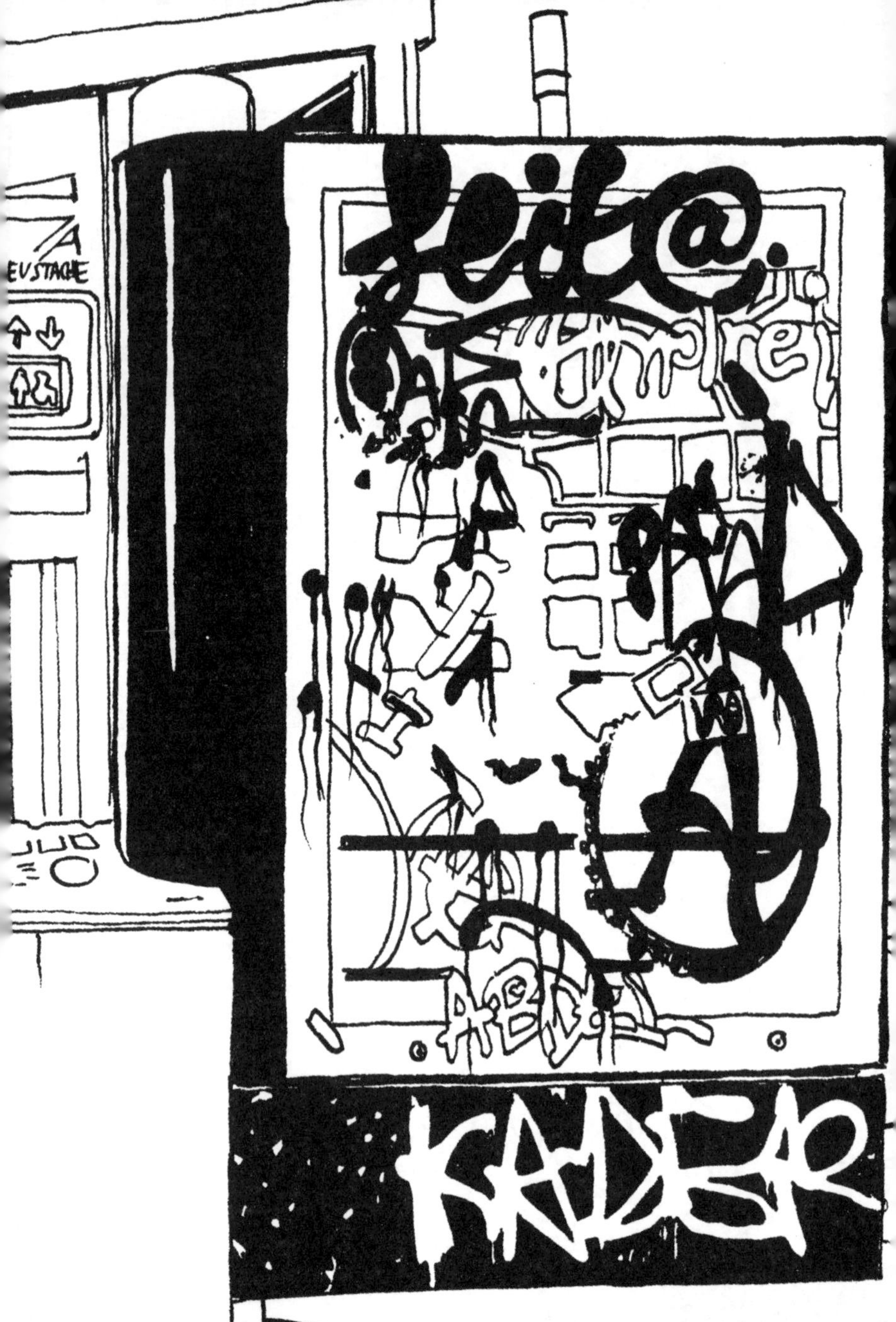
EUSTACHE

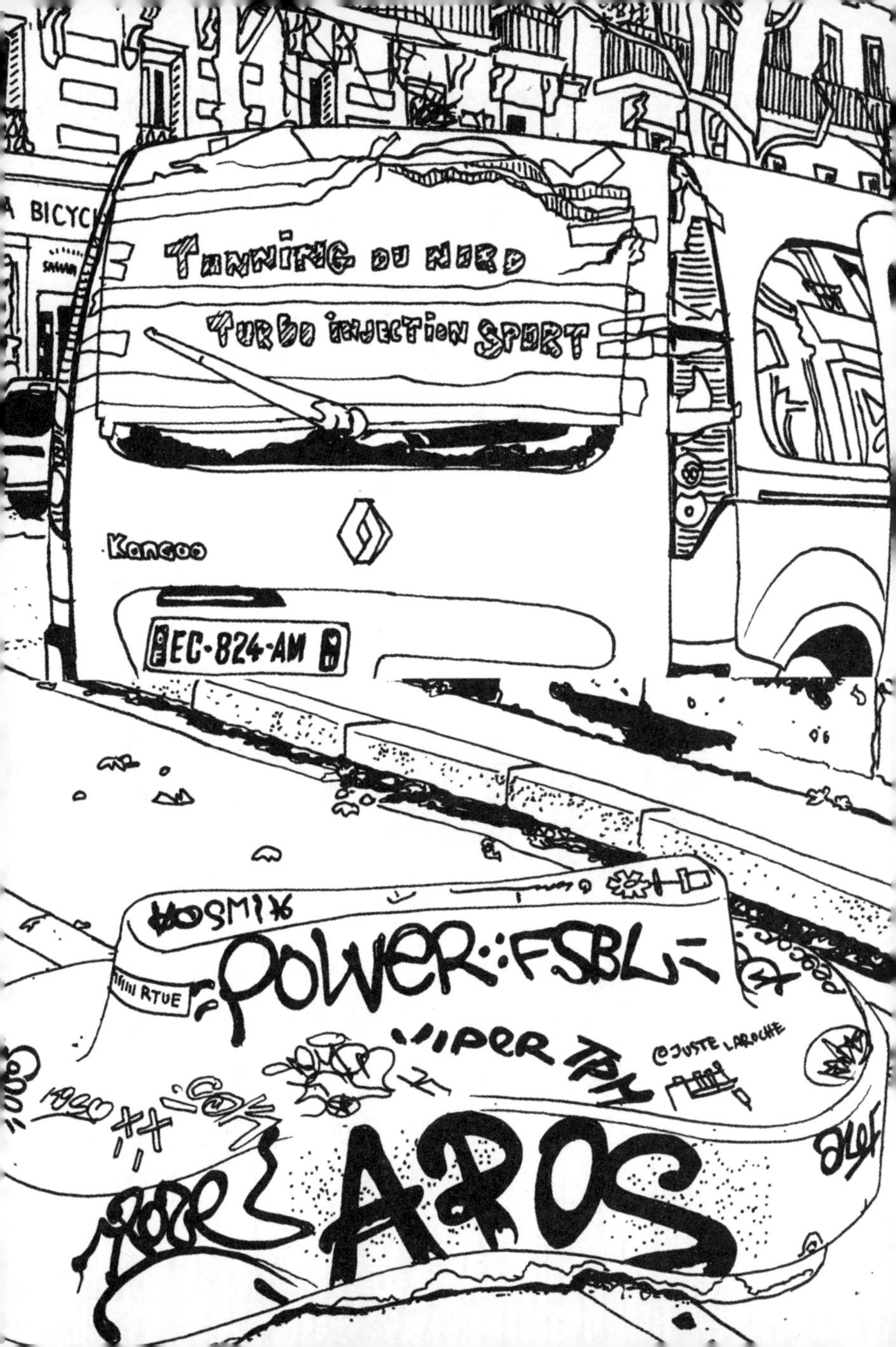

A BICYC
TUNNING DU NORD
Turbo injection SPORT
Kangoo
EC-824-AM
POWER:FSBL
@JUSTE LAROCHE

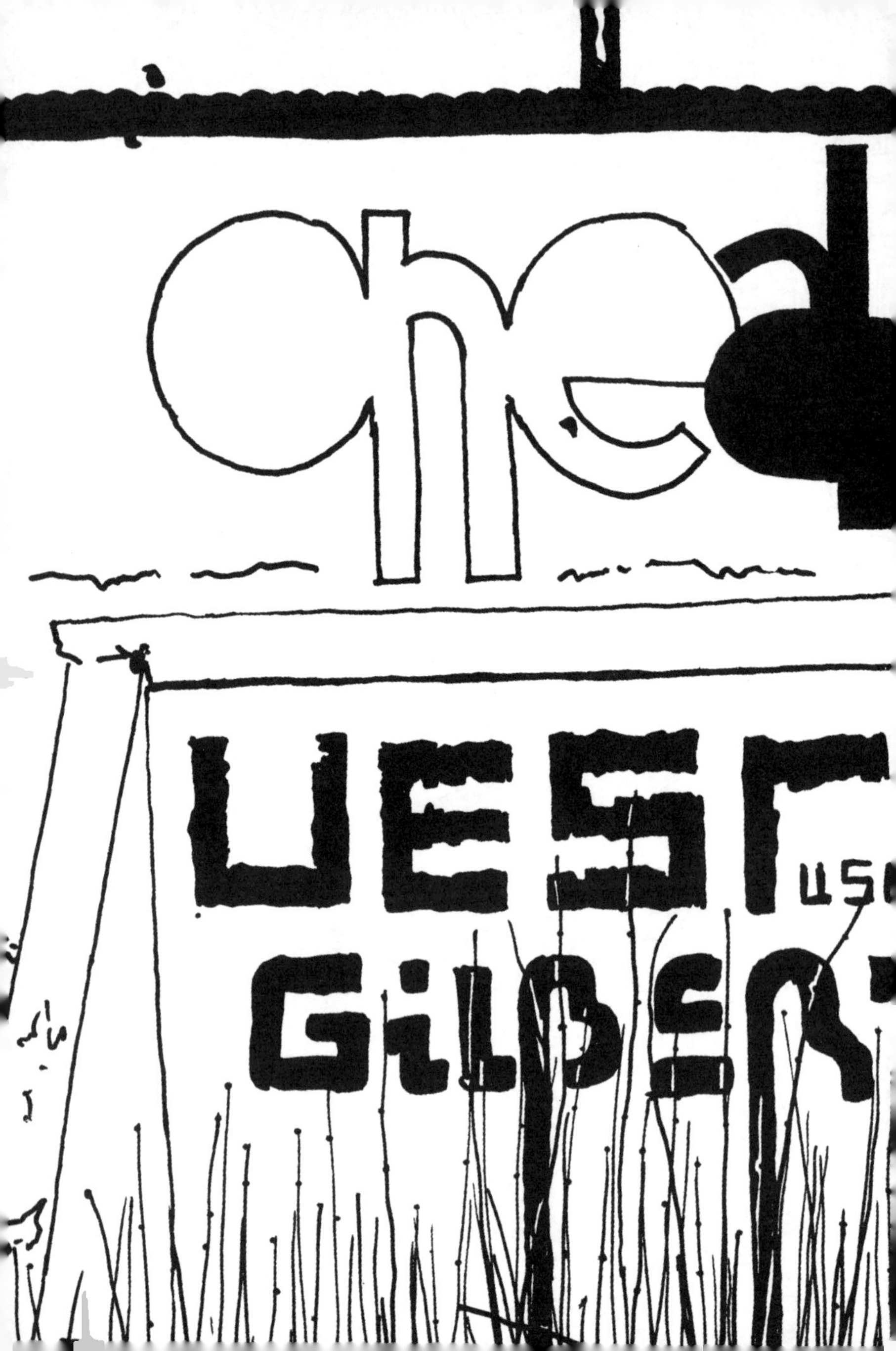

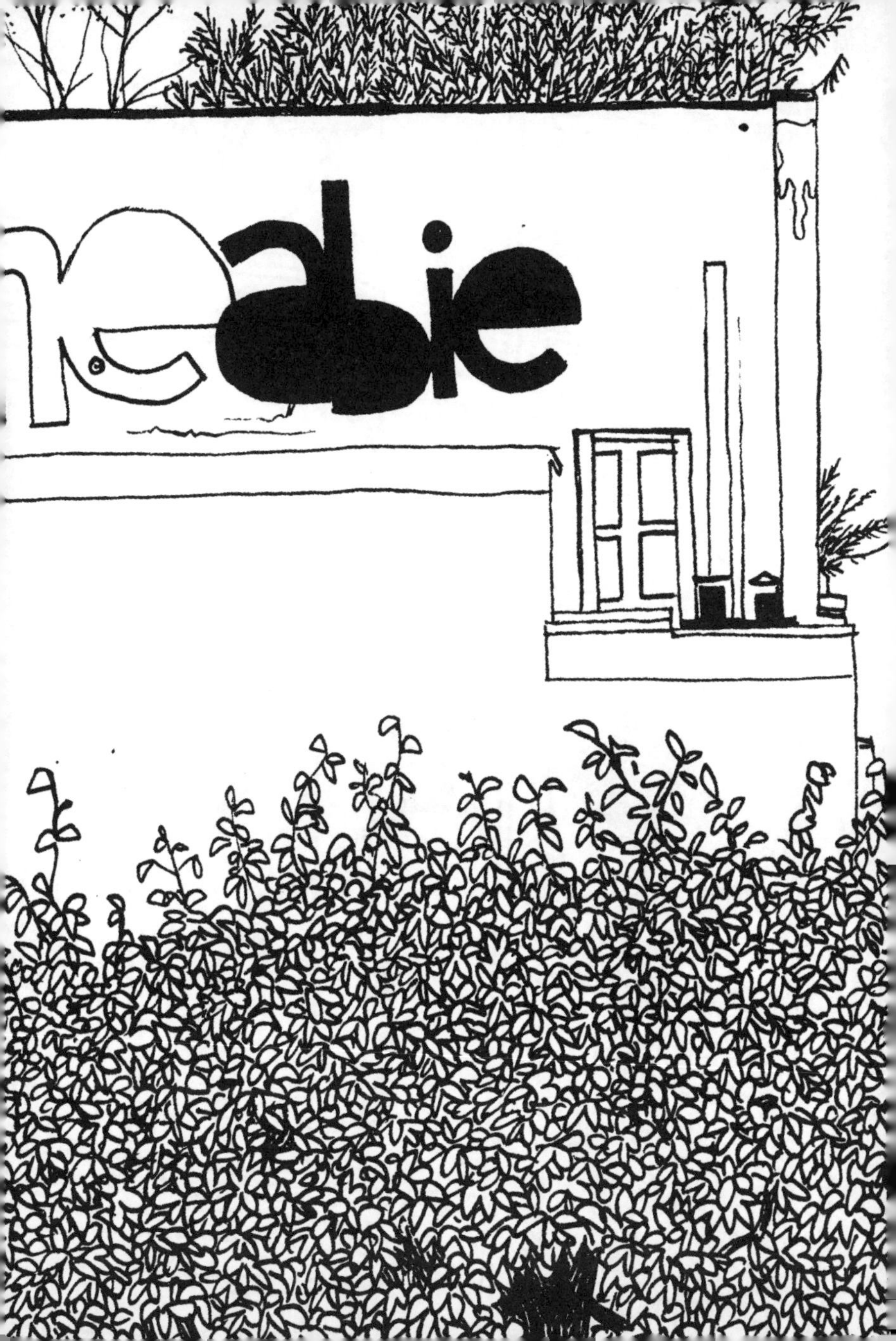

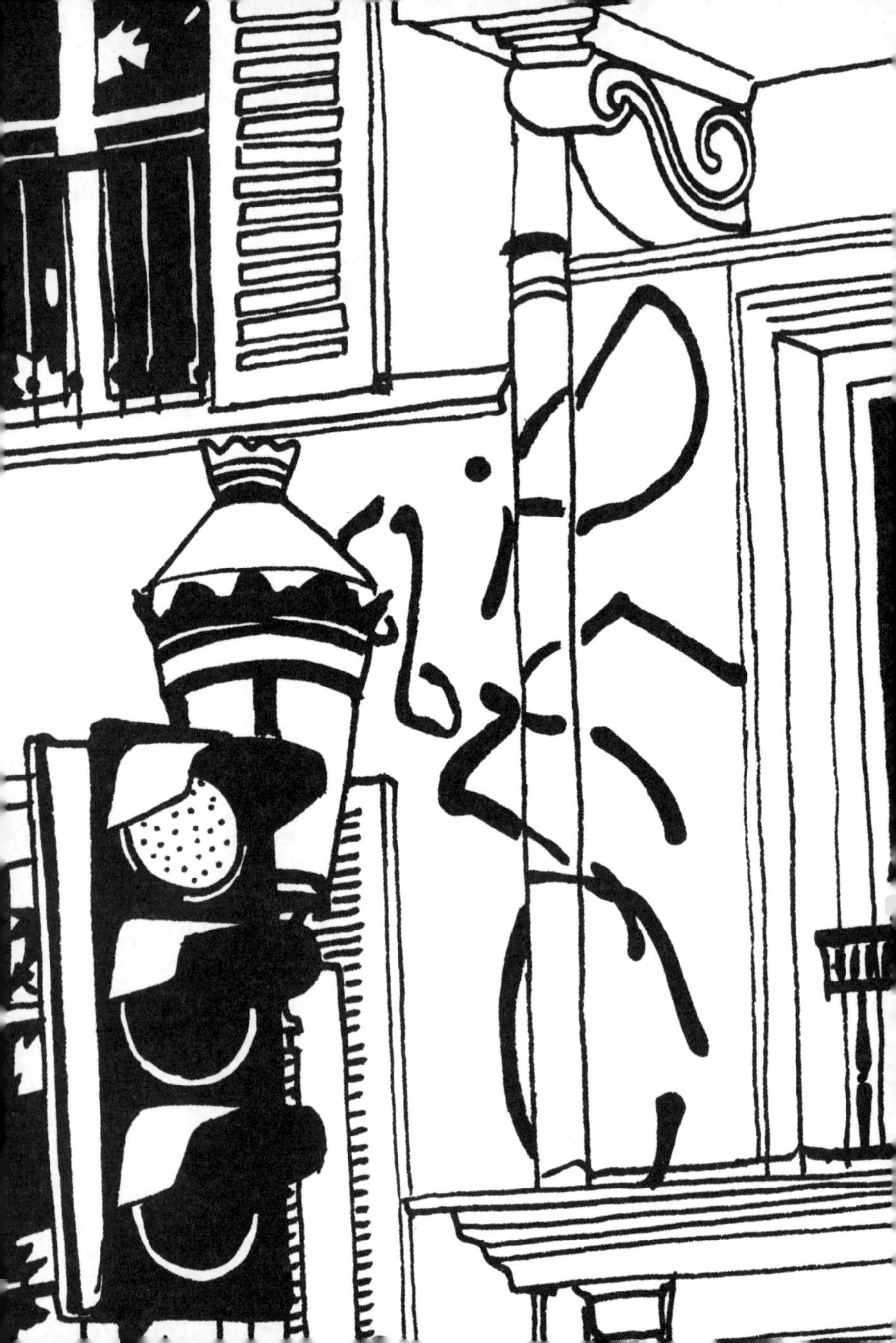

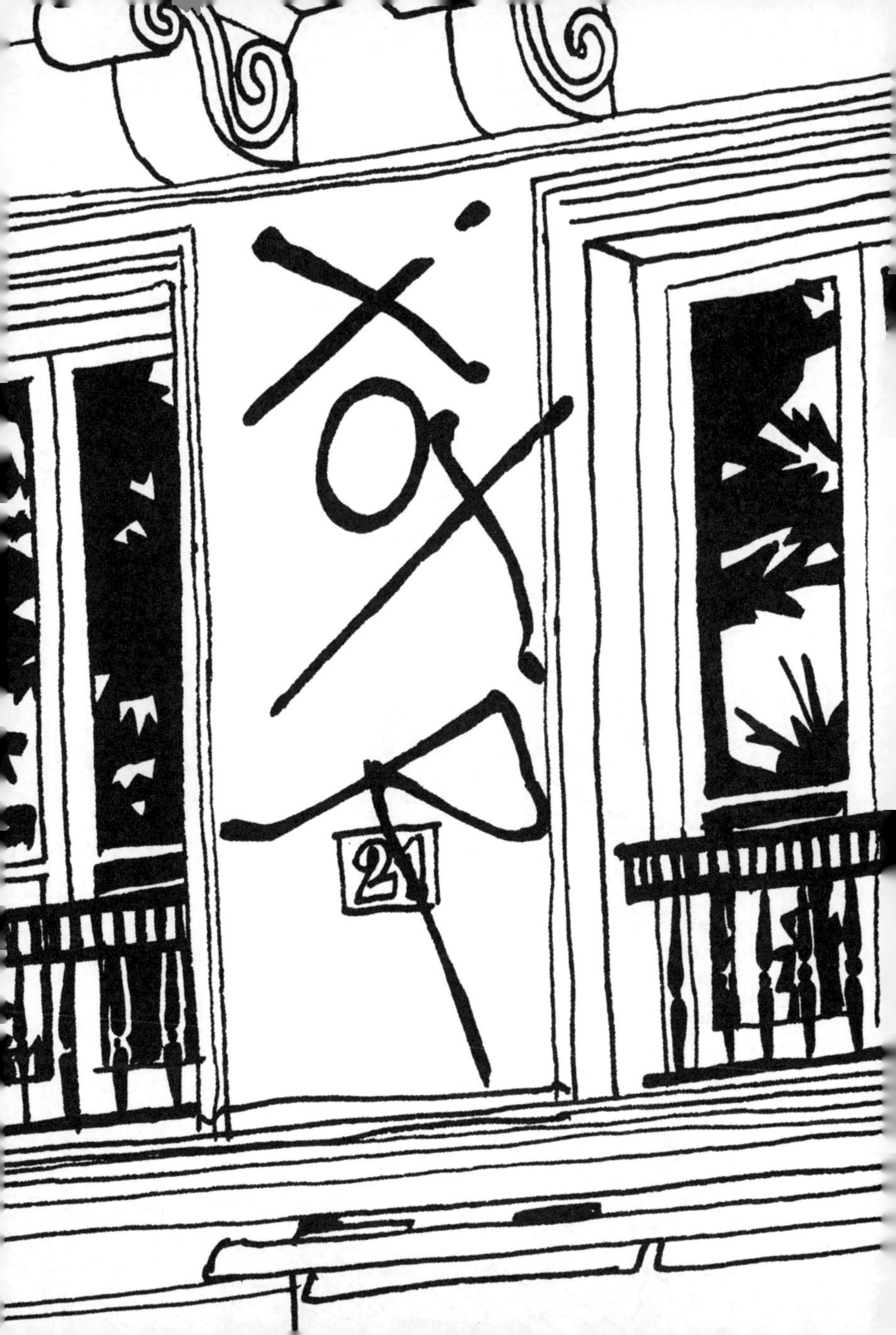
21

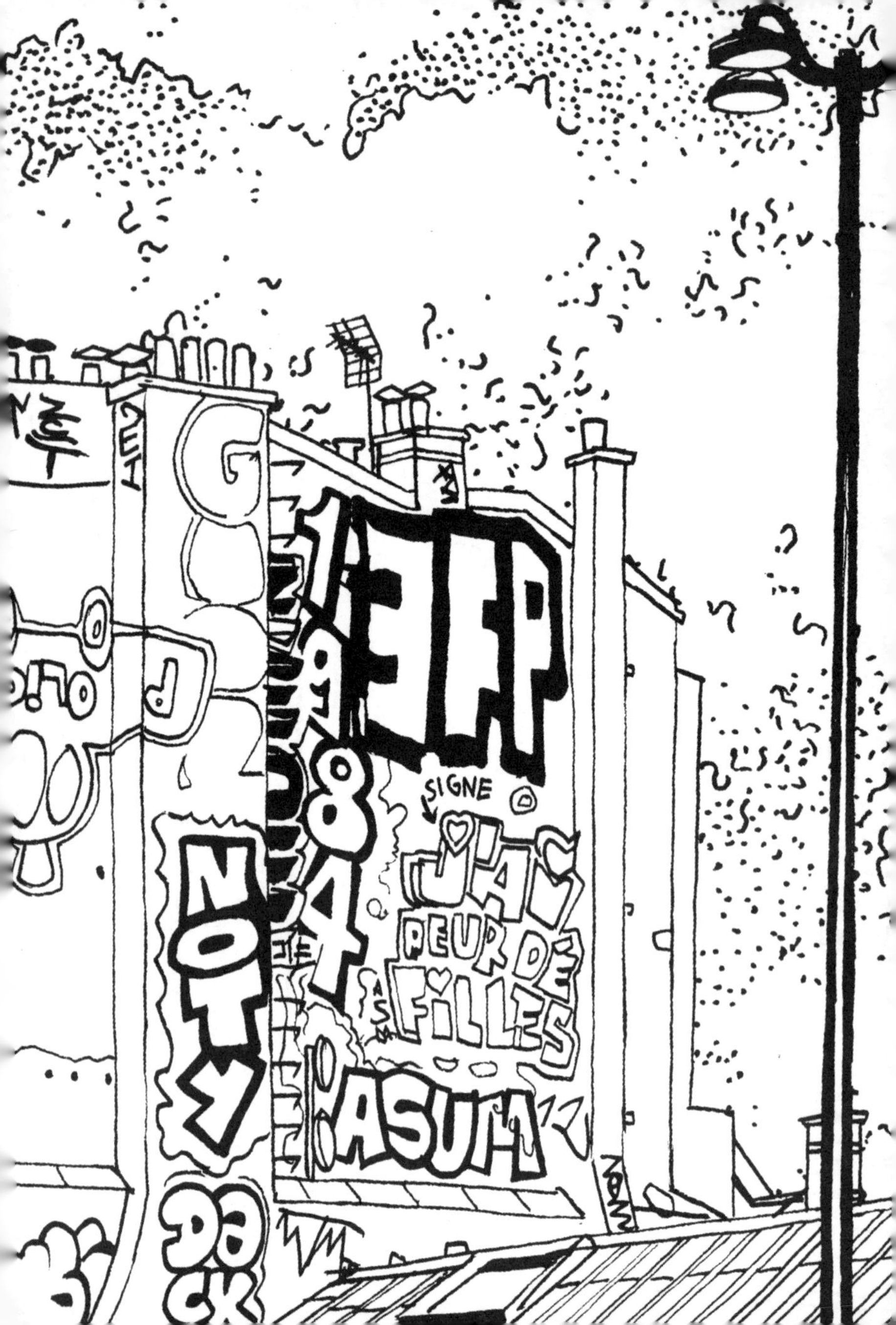
SIGNE
J'AI
PEUR DE
FILLES
NOTY
ASUM

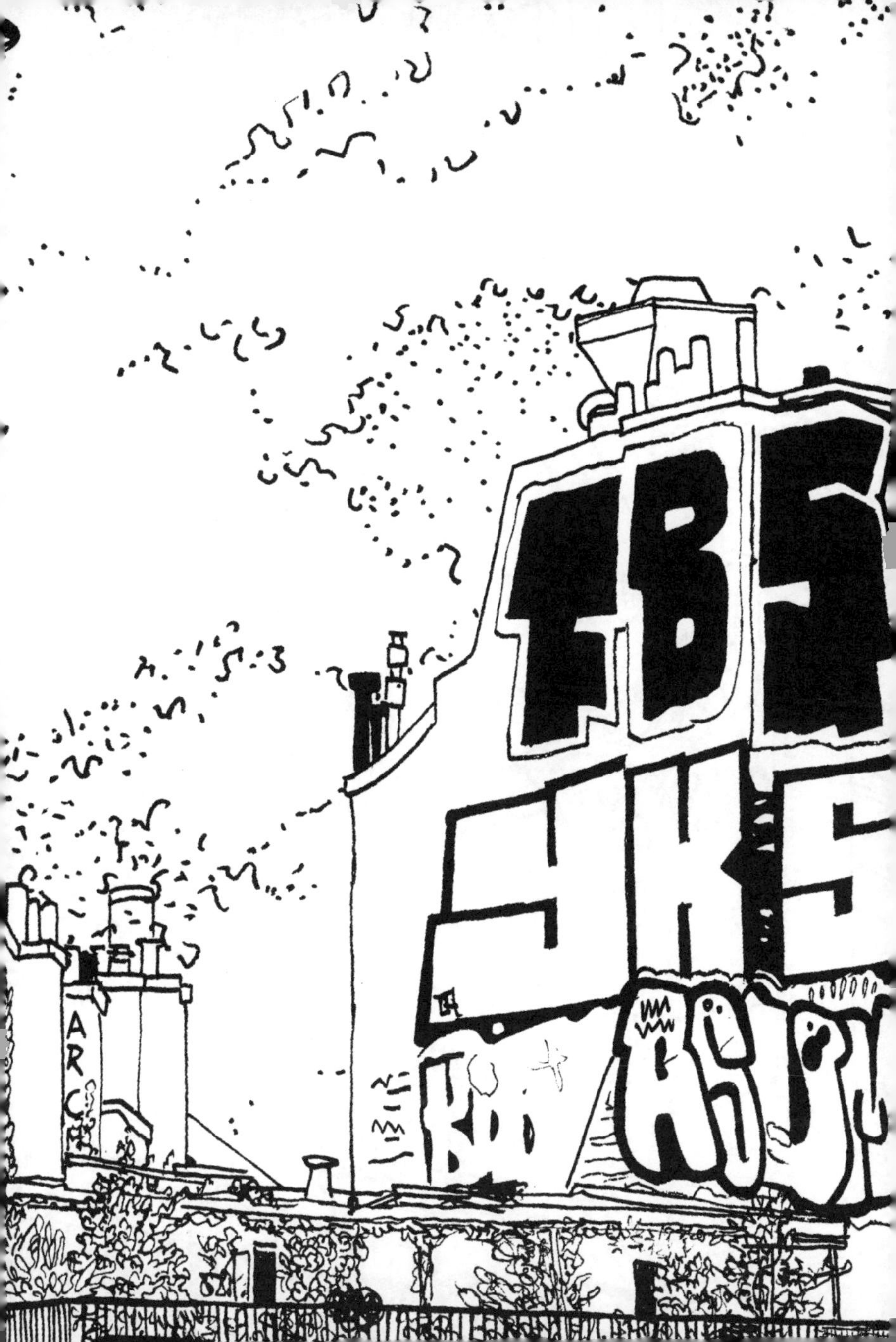

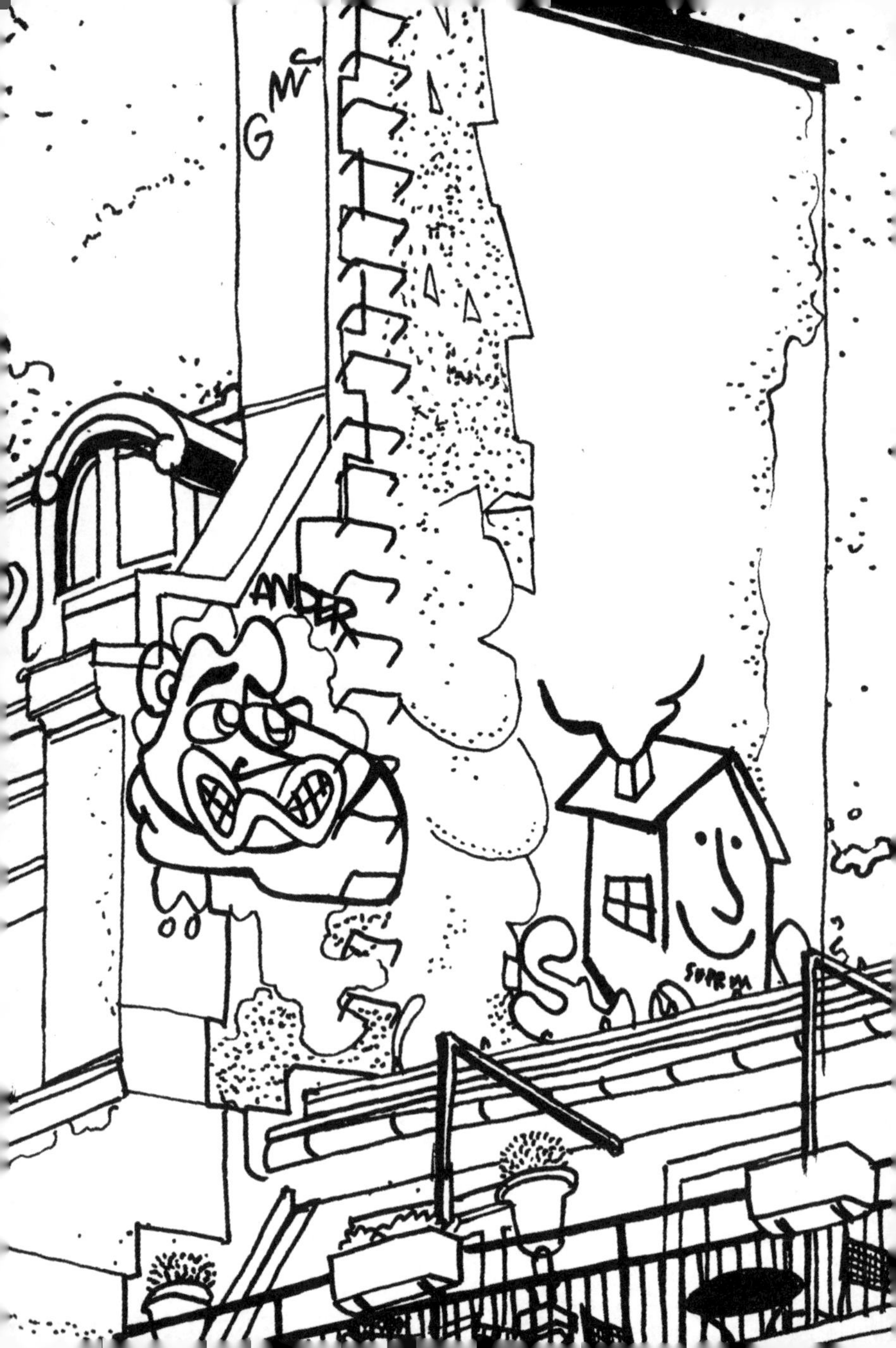
ANDER

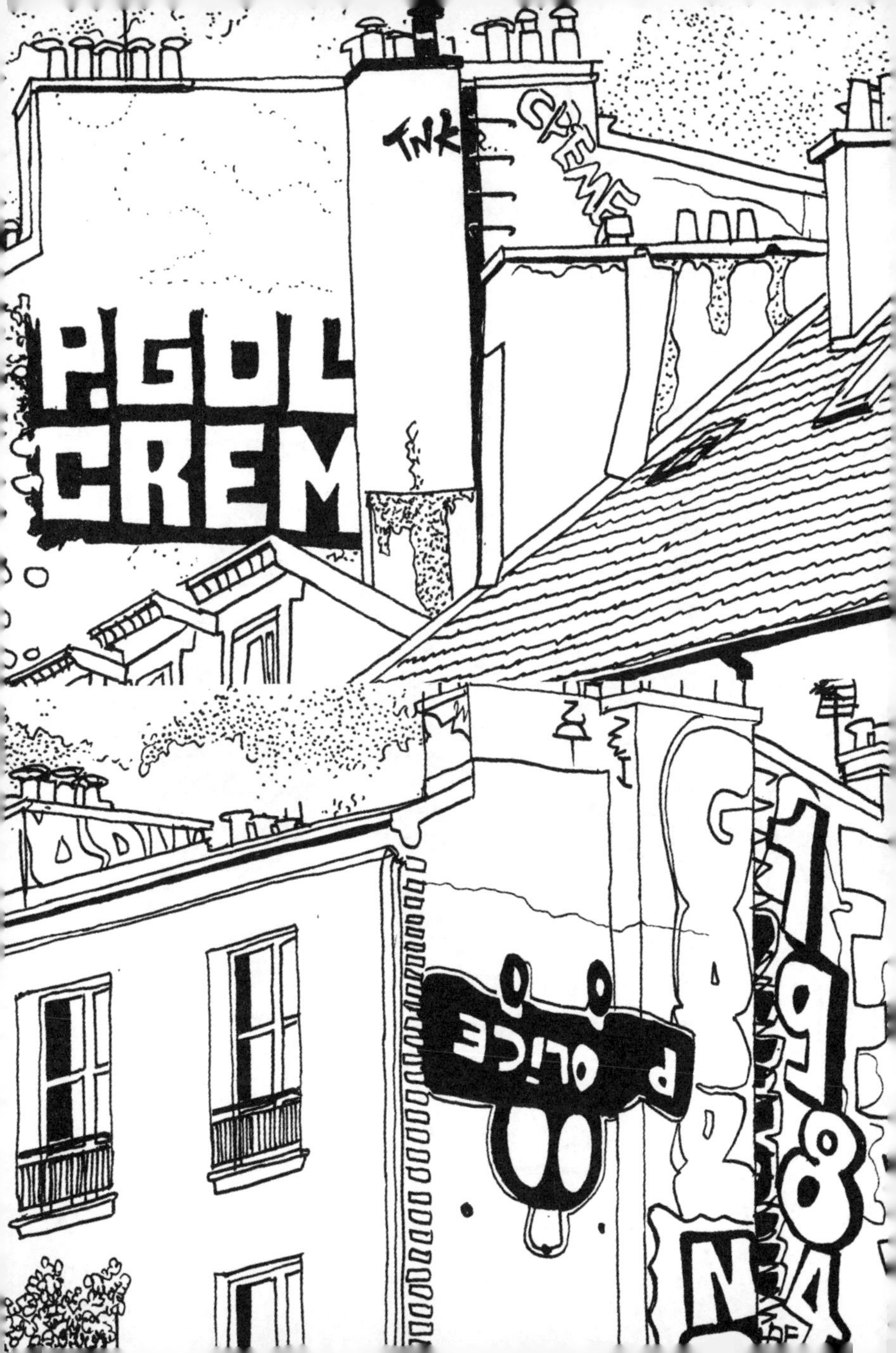
P.GOL
CREM
TNK
CREME

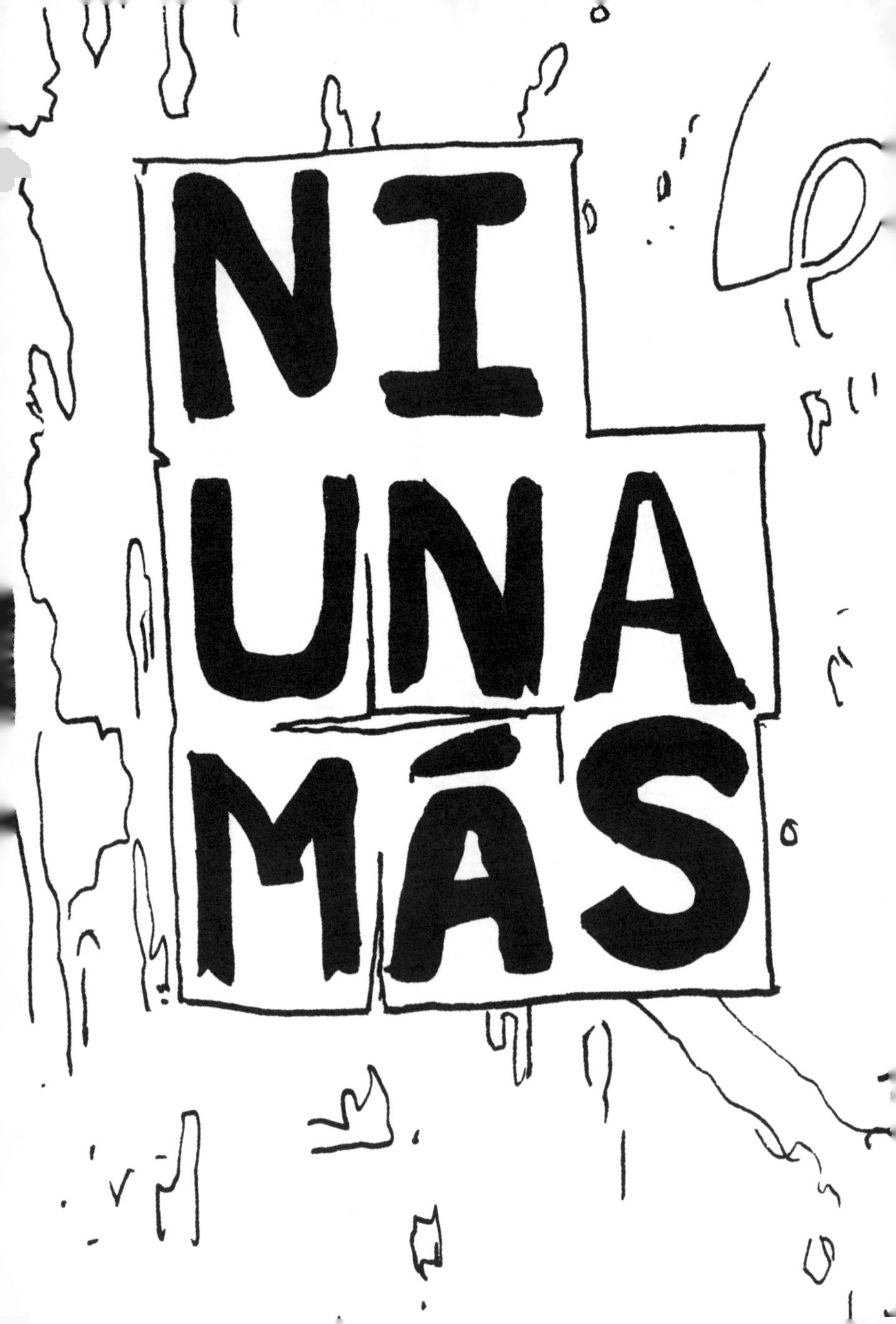
NI
UNA
MÁS

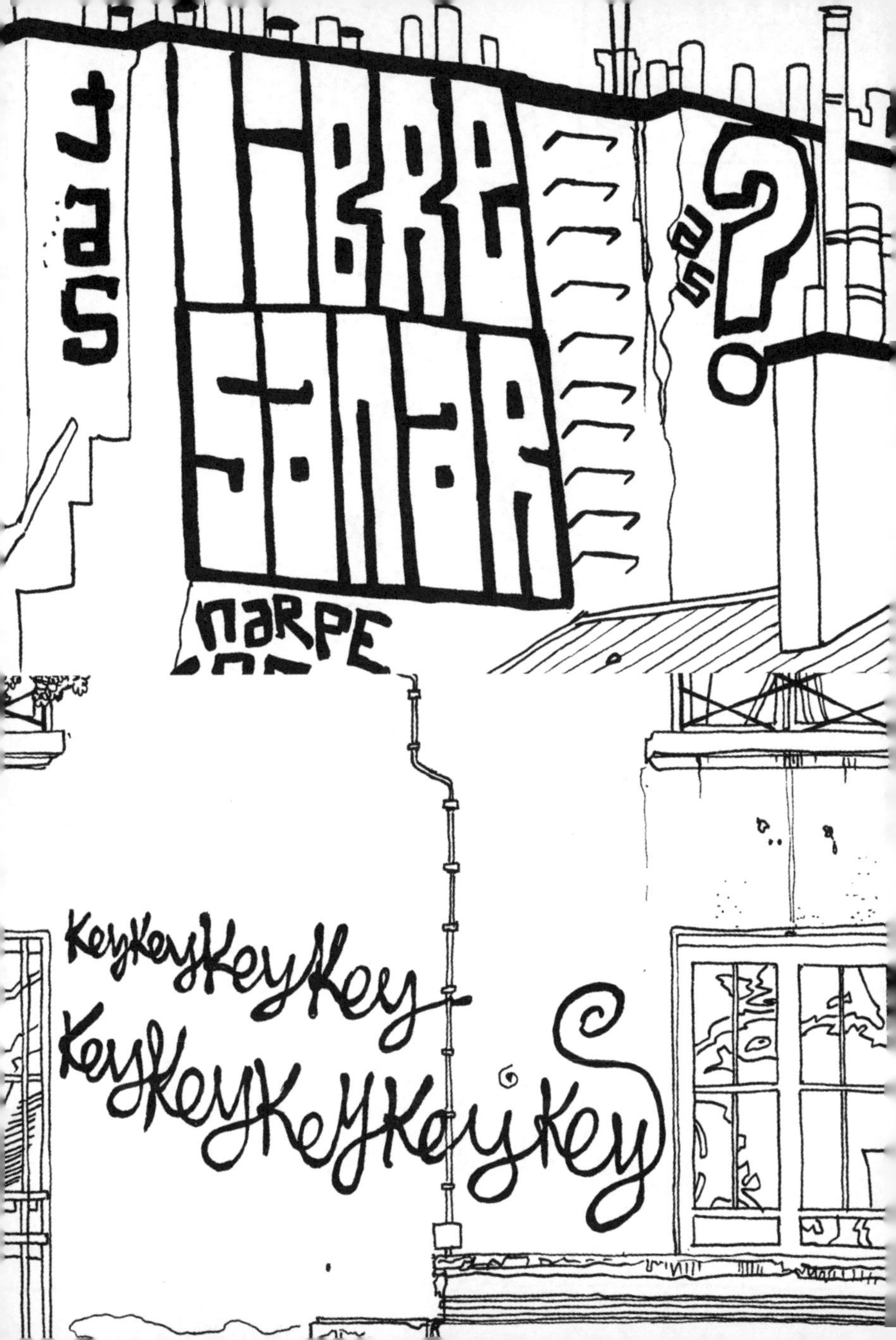
KeyKeyKeyKey
KeyKeyKeyKeyKey

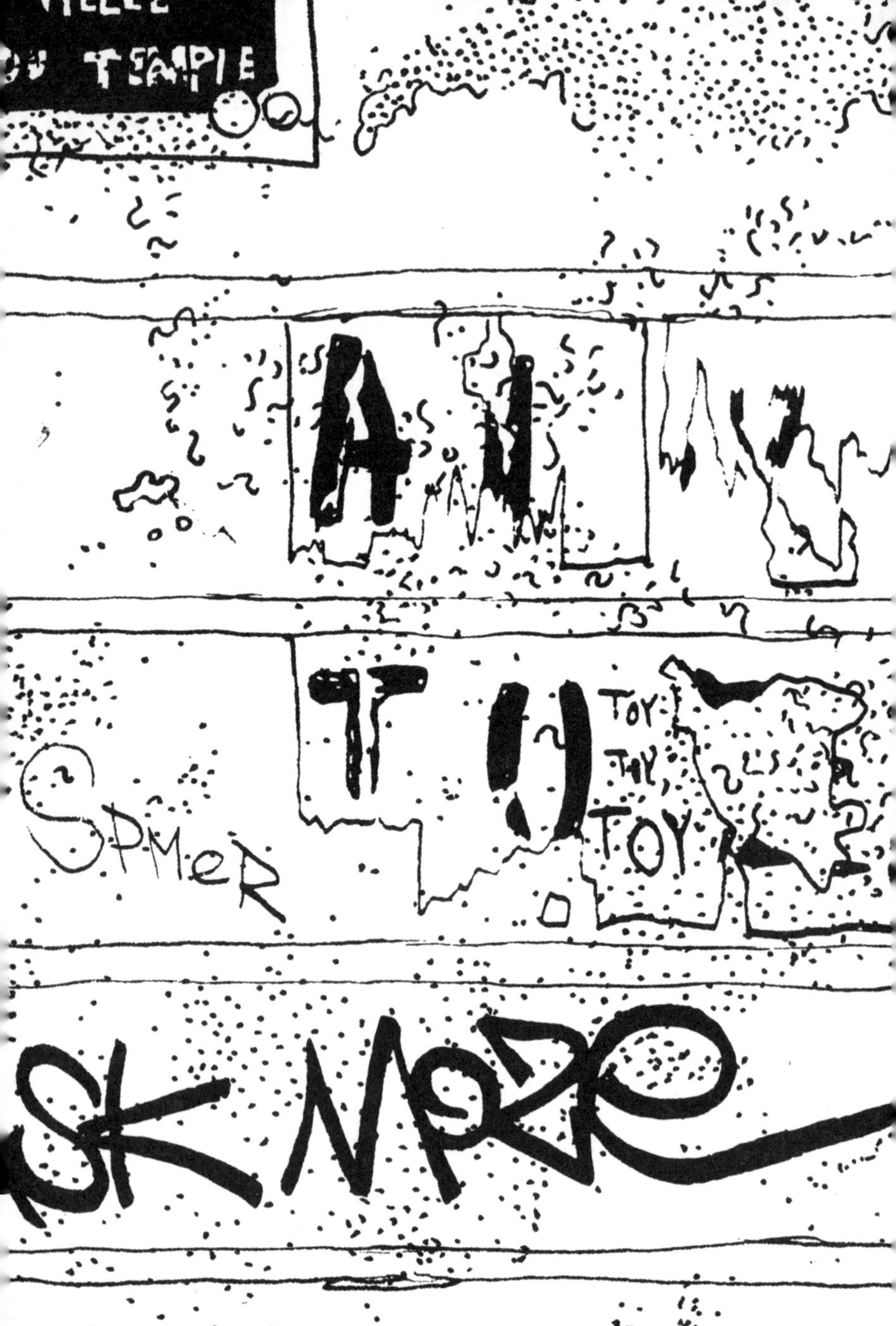
TOY
TOY

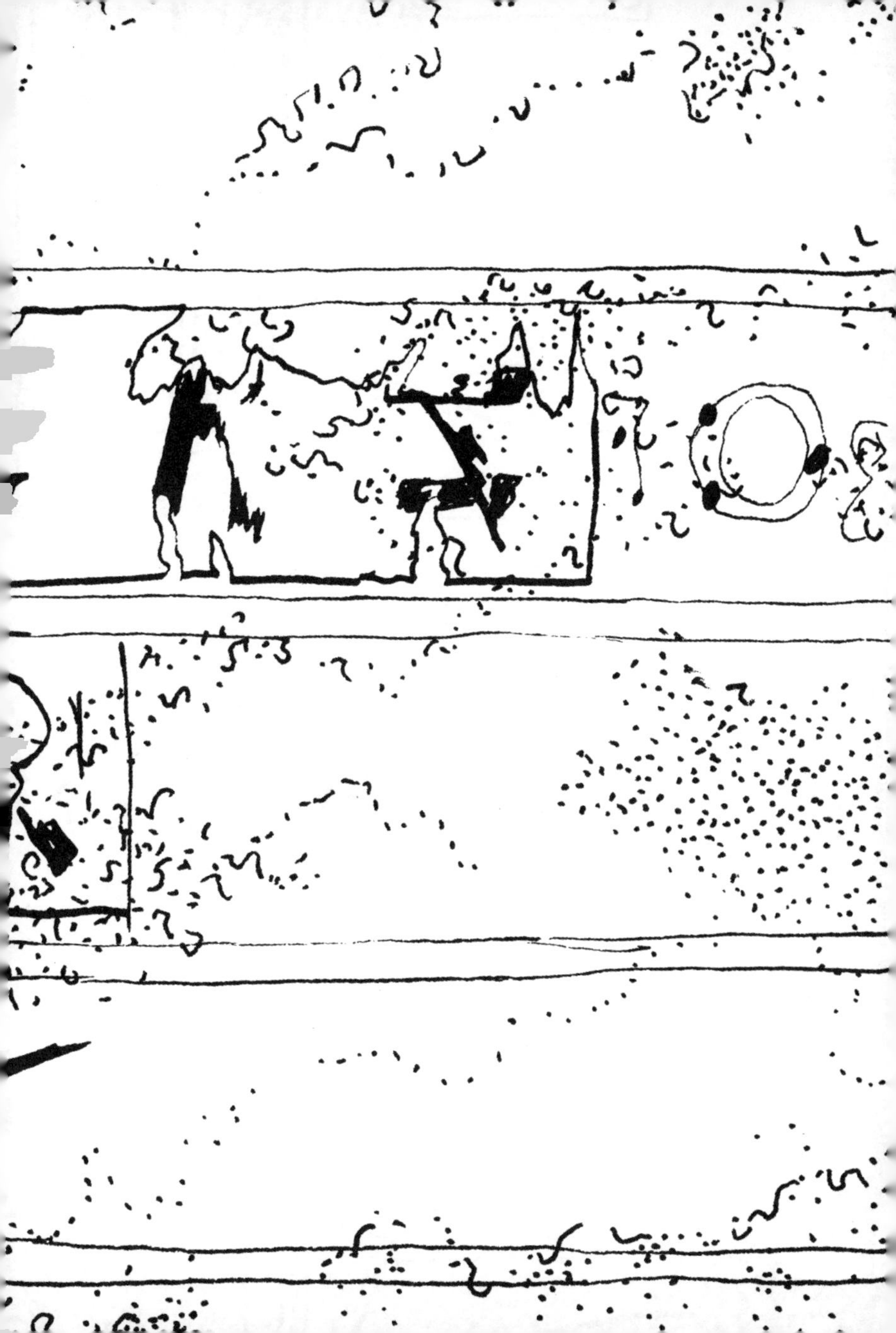

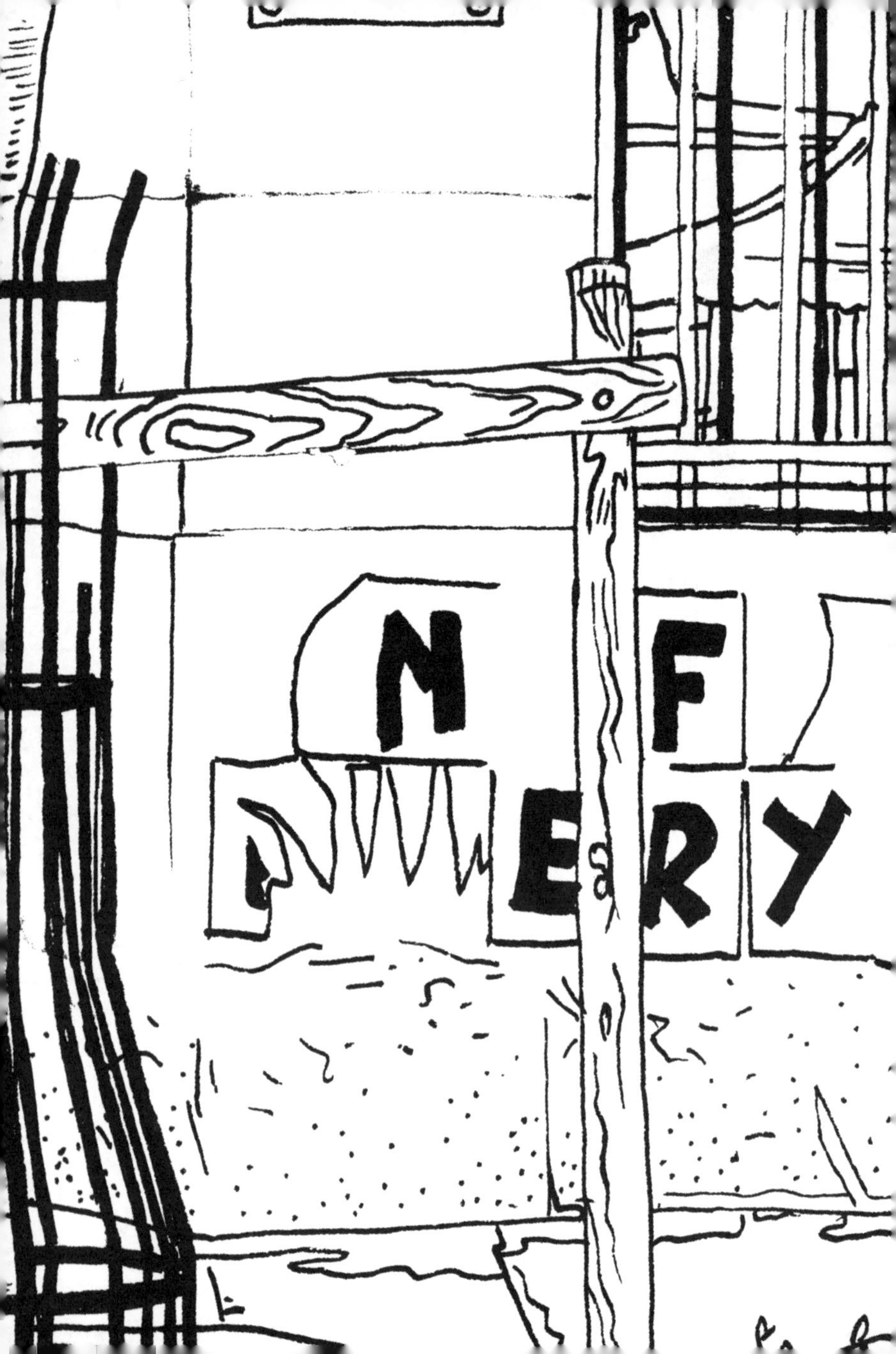
N F
ERY

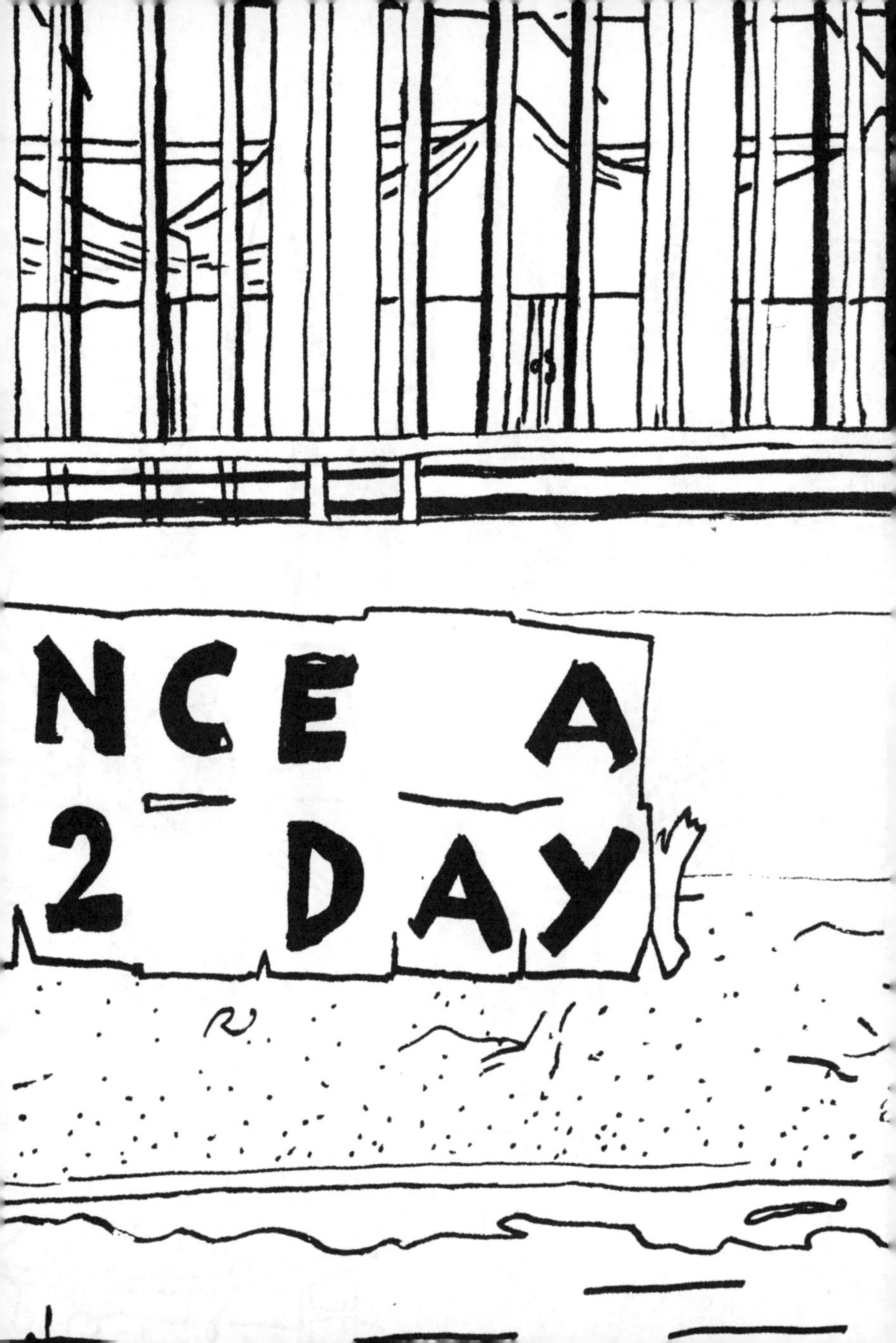
NCE A
2 DAY

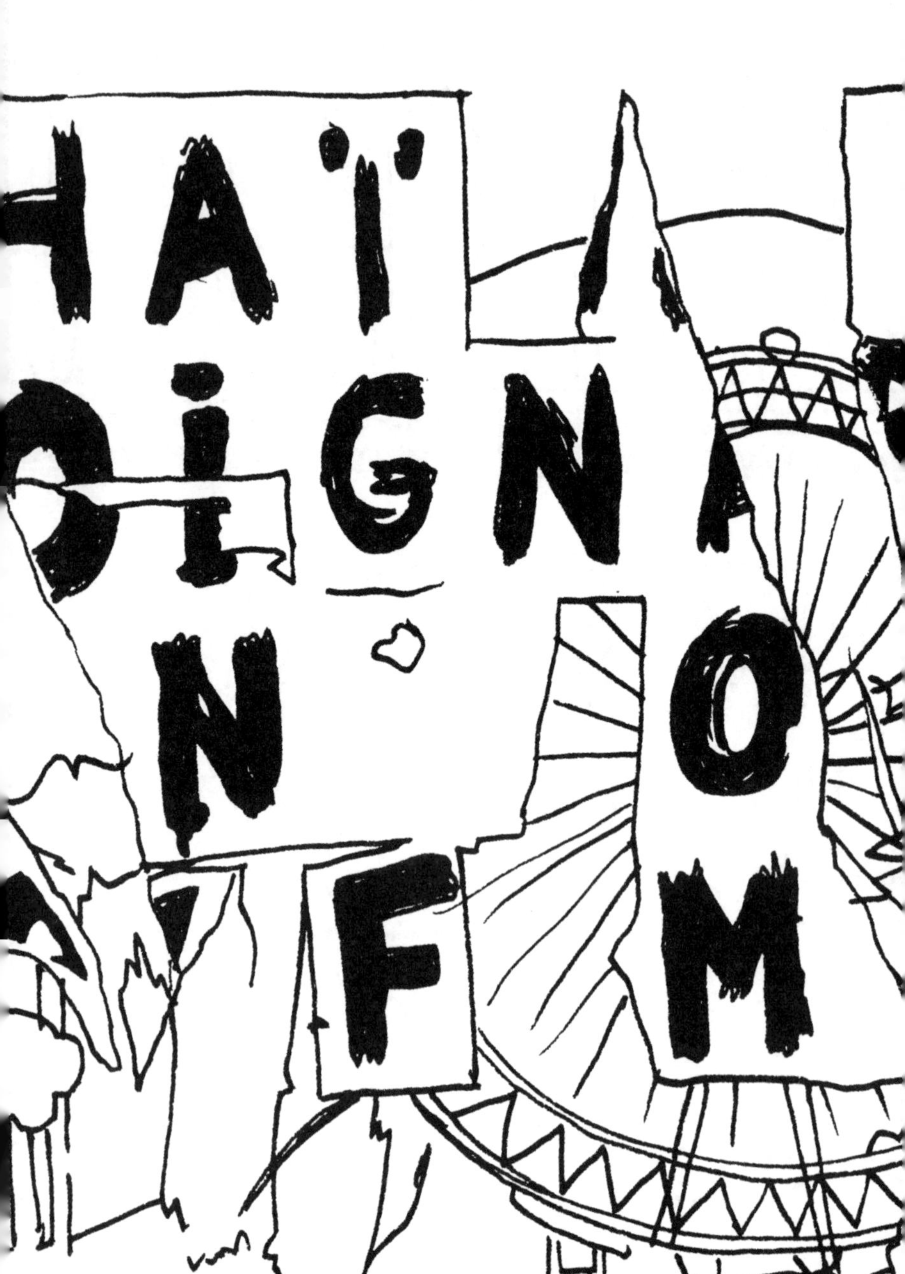
HAÏ
GN
N
O
F
M

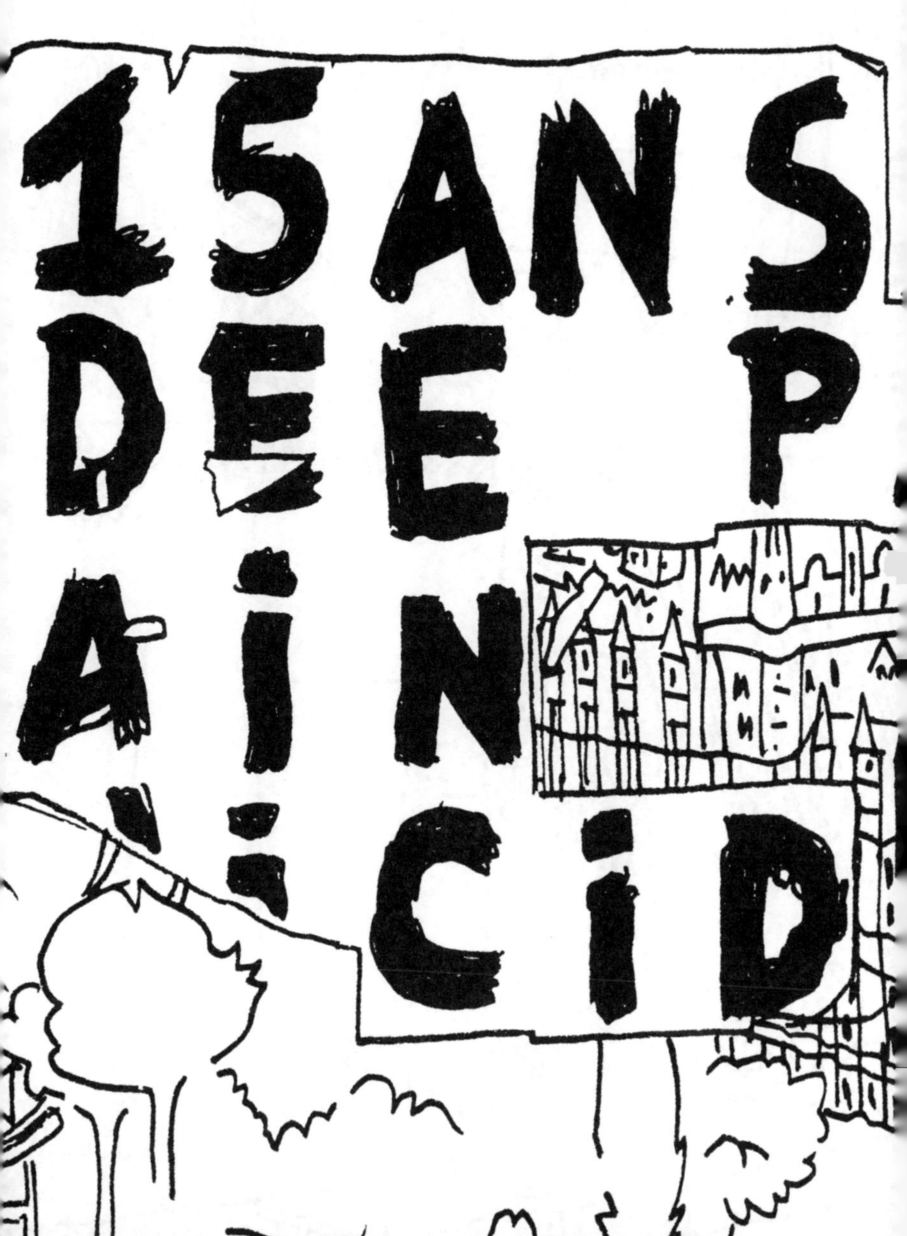
15ANS
DEE P
AiN
ÀiCiD

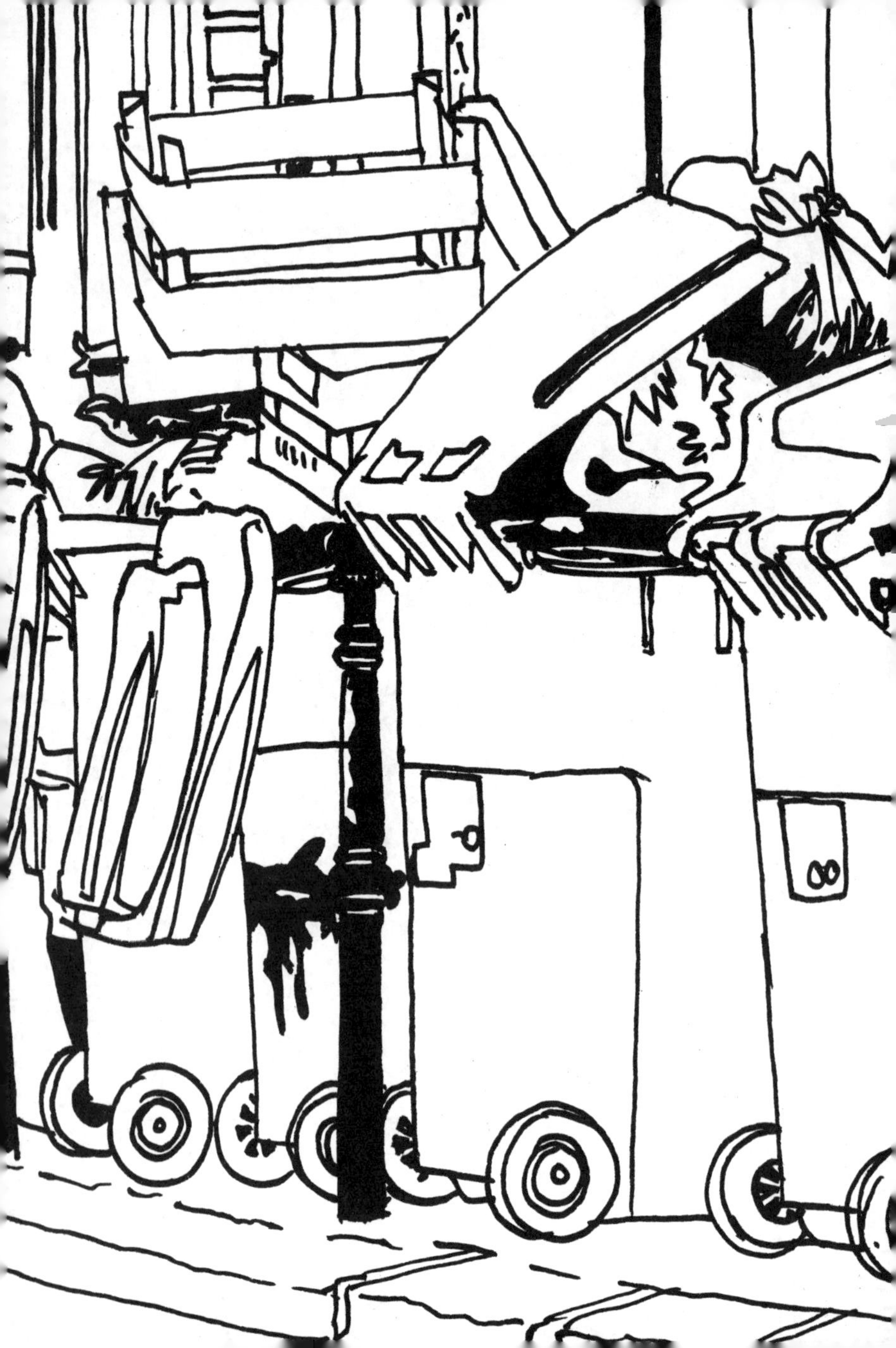

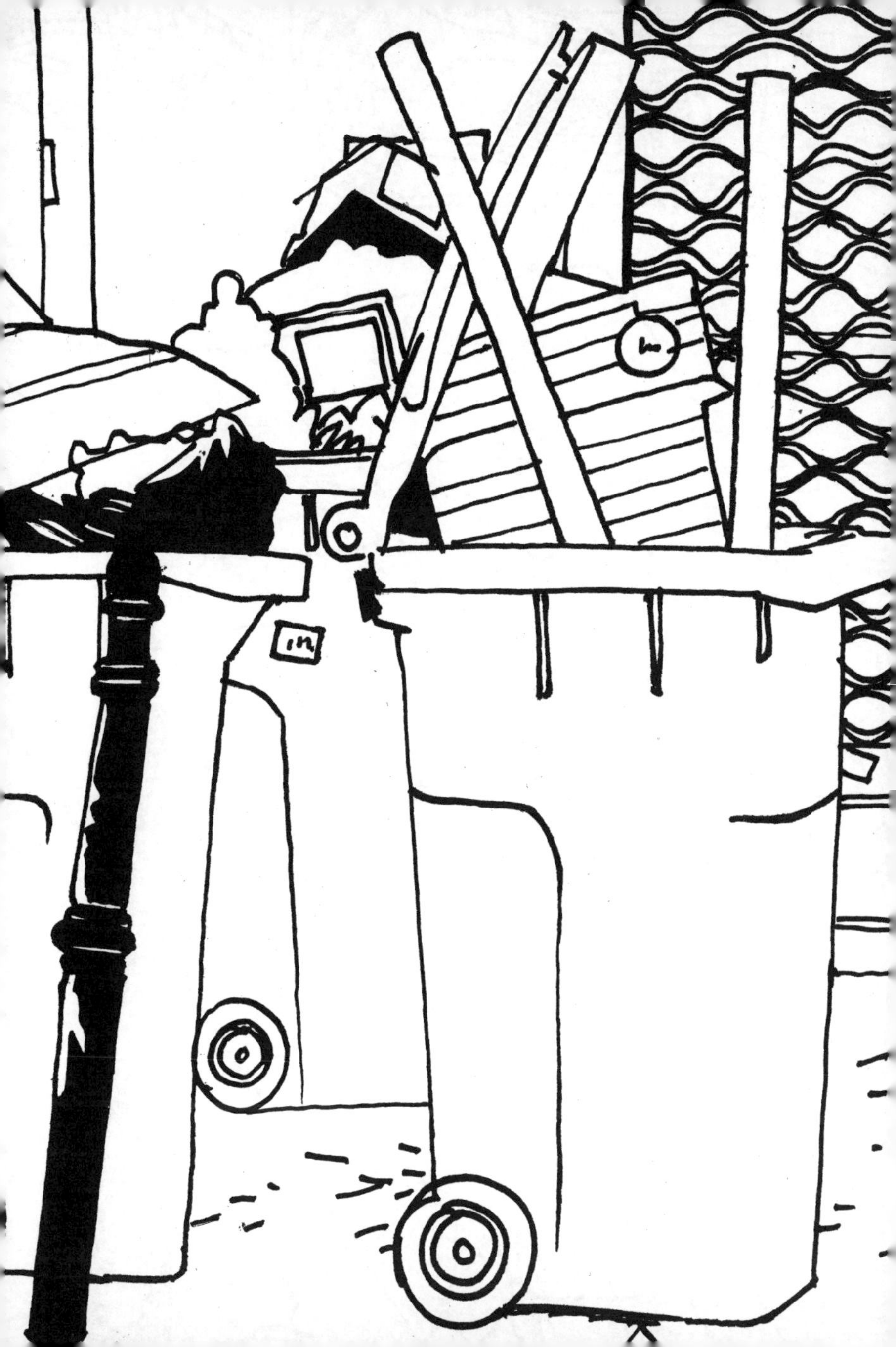

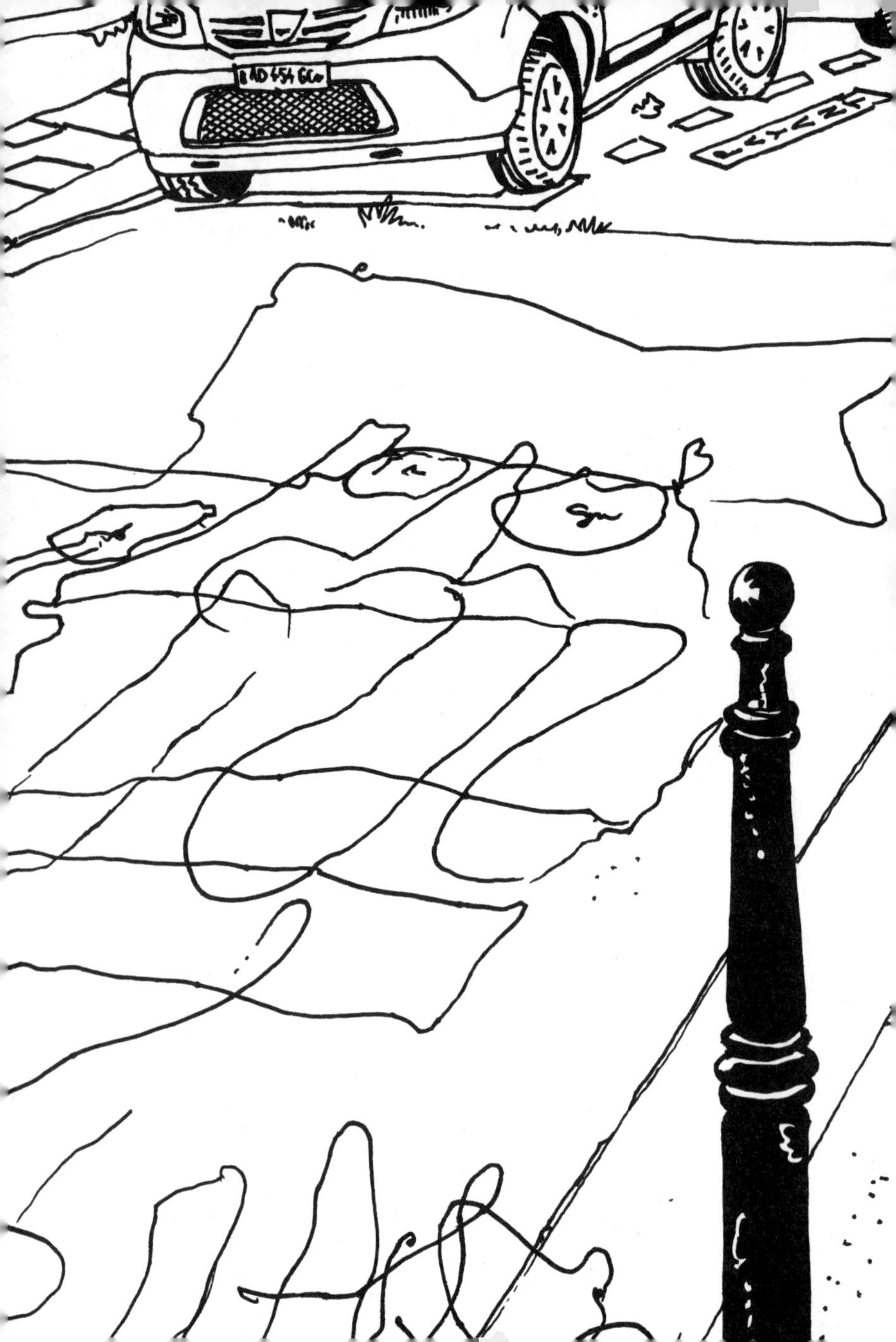

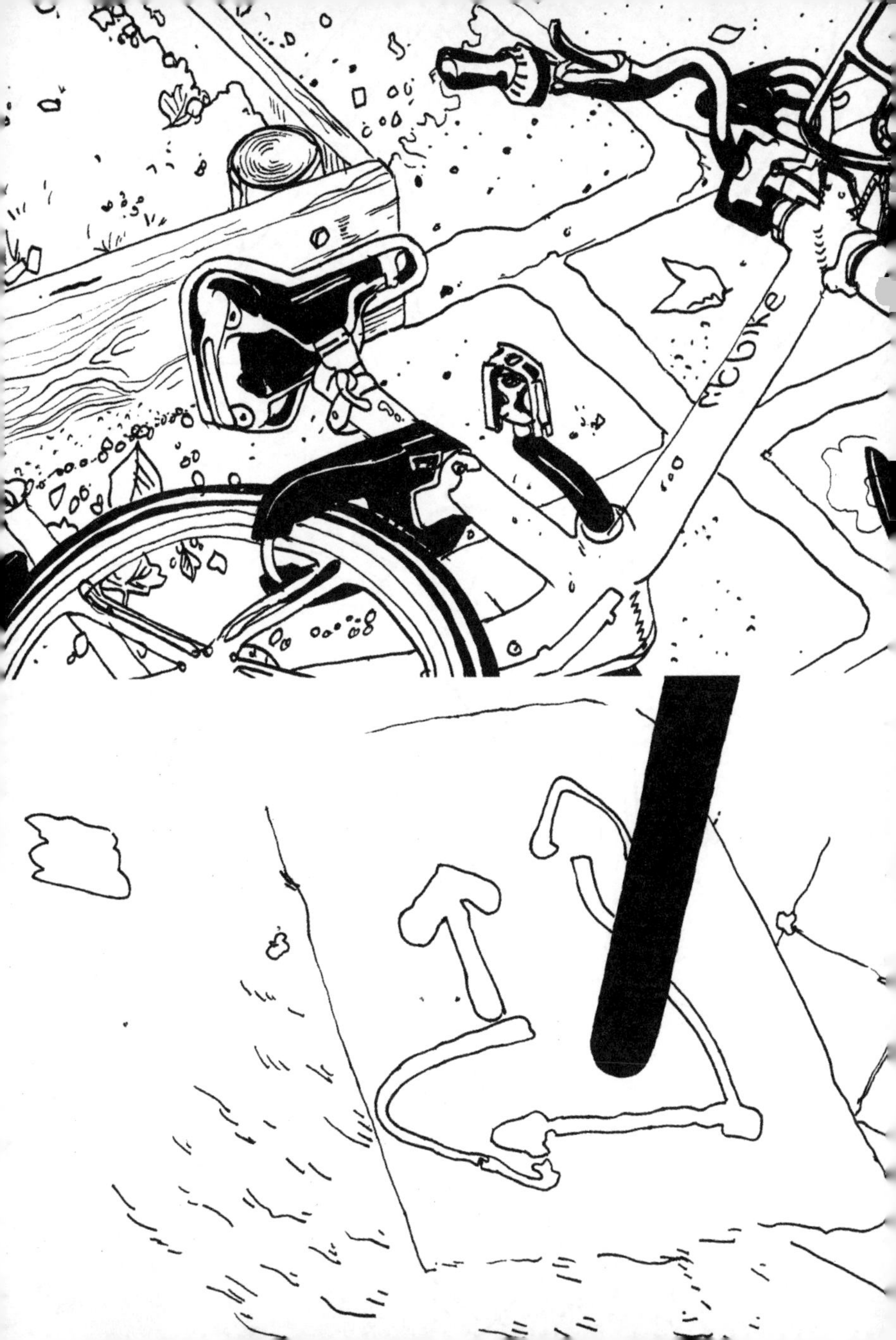

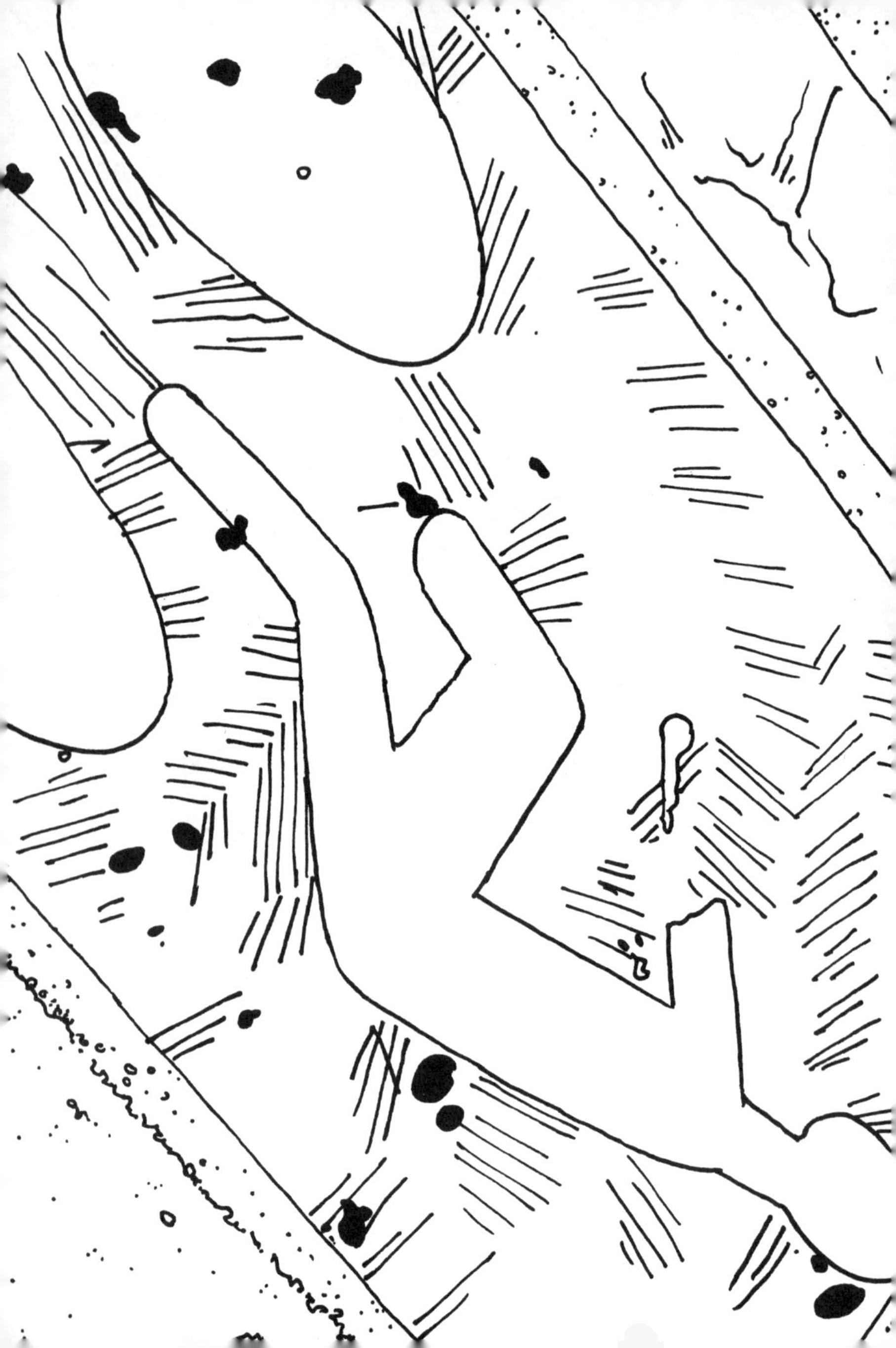

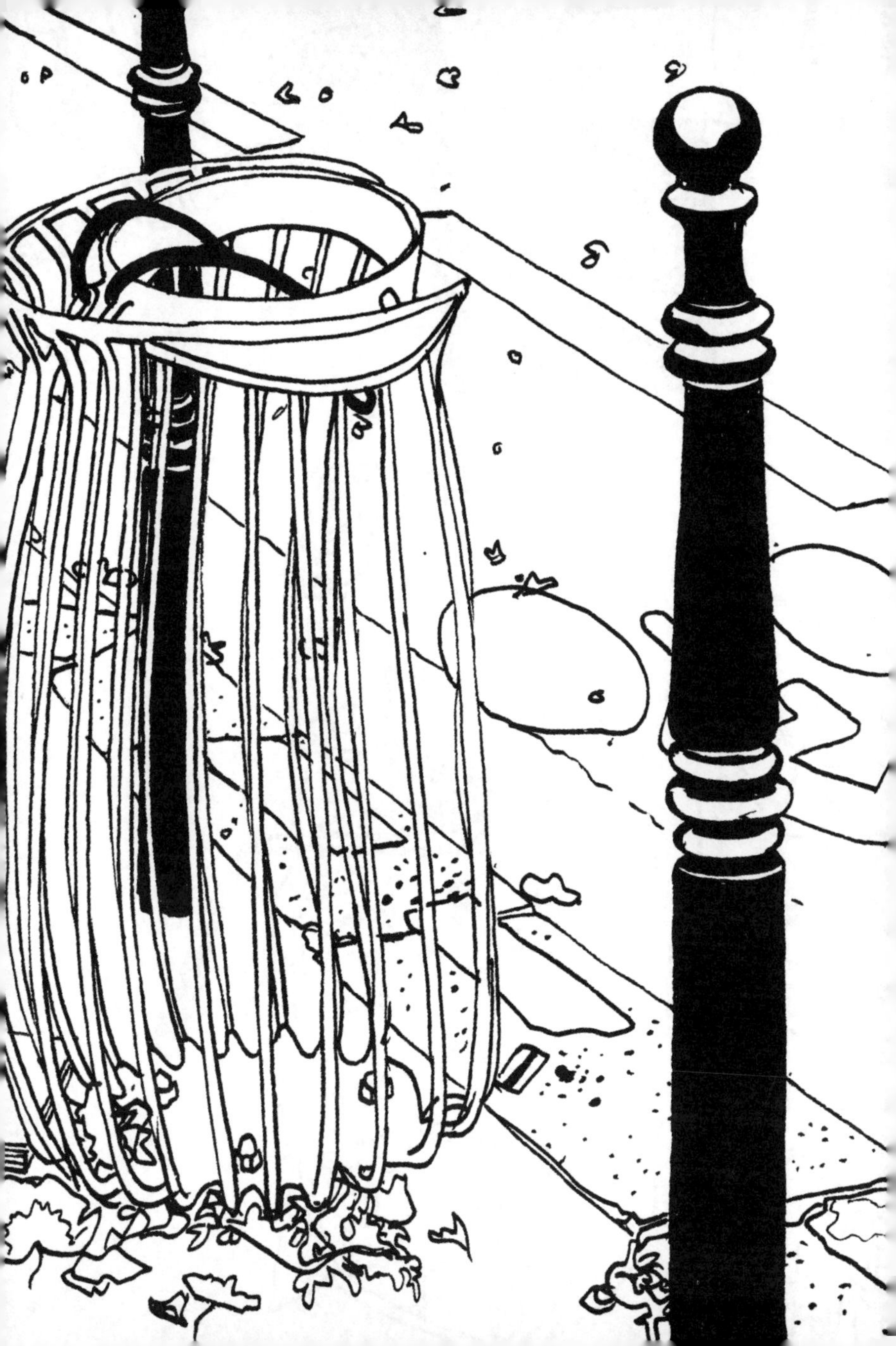

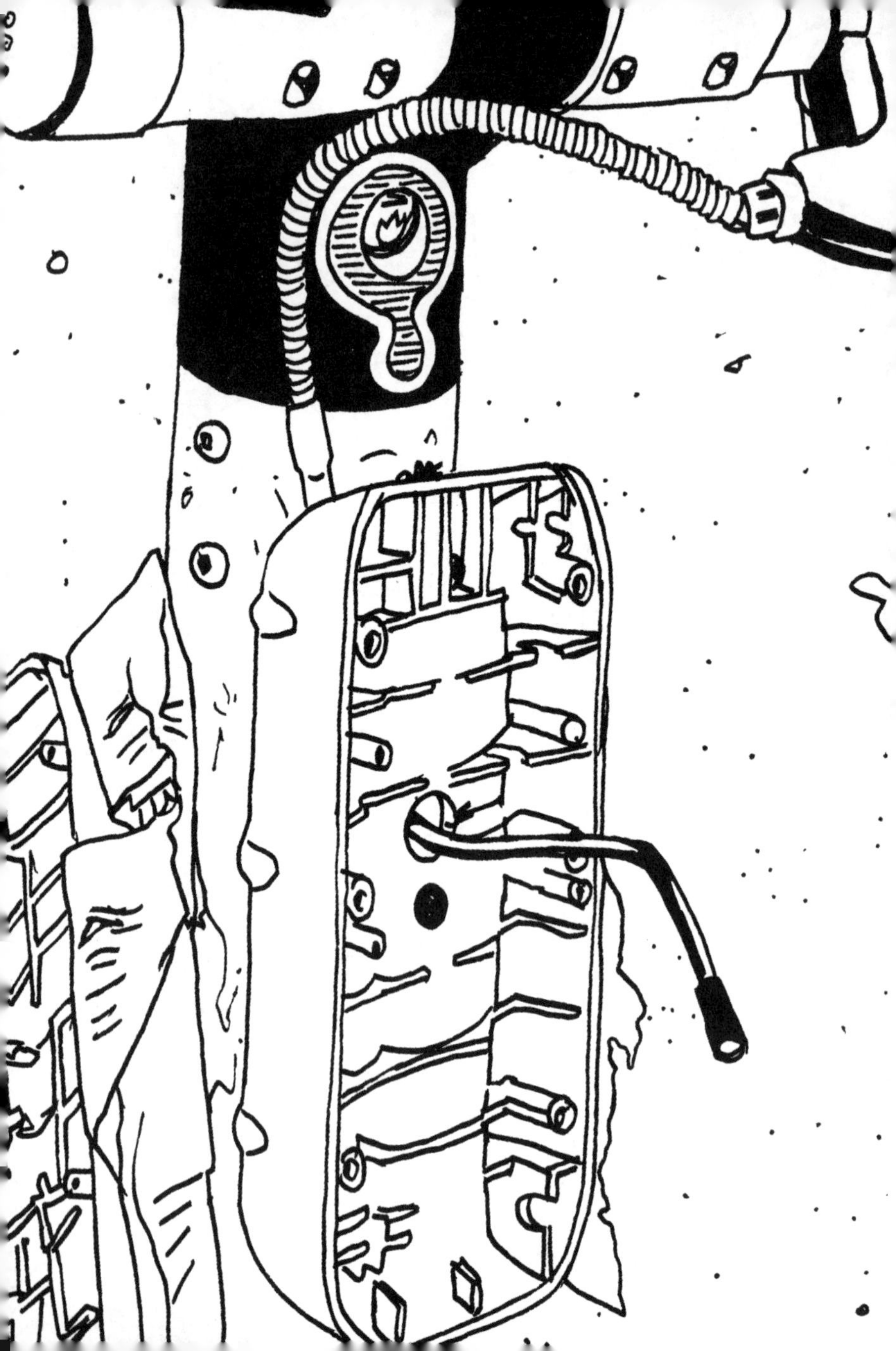

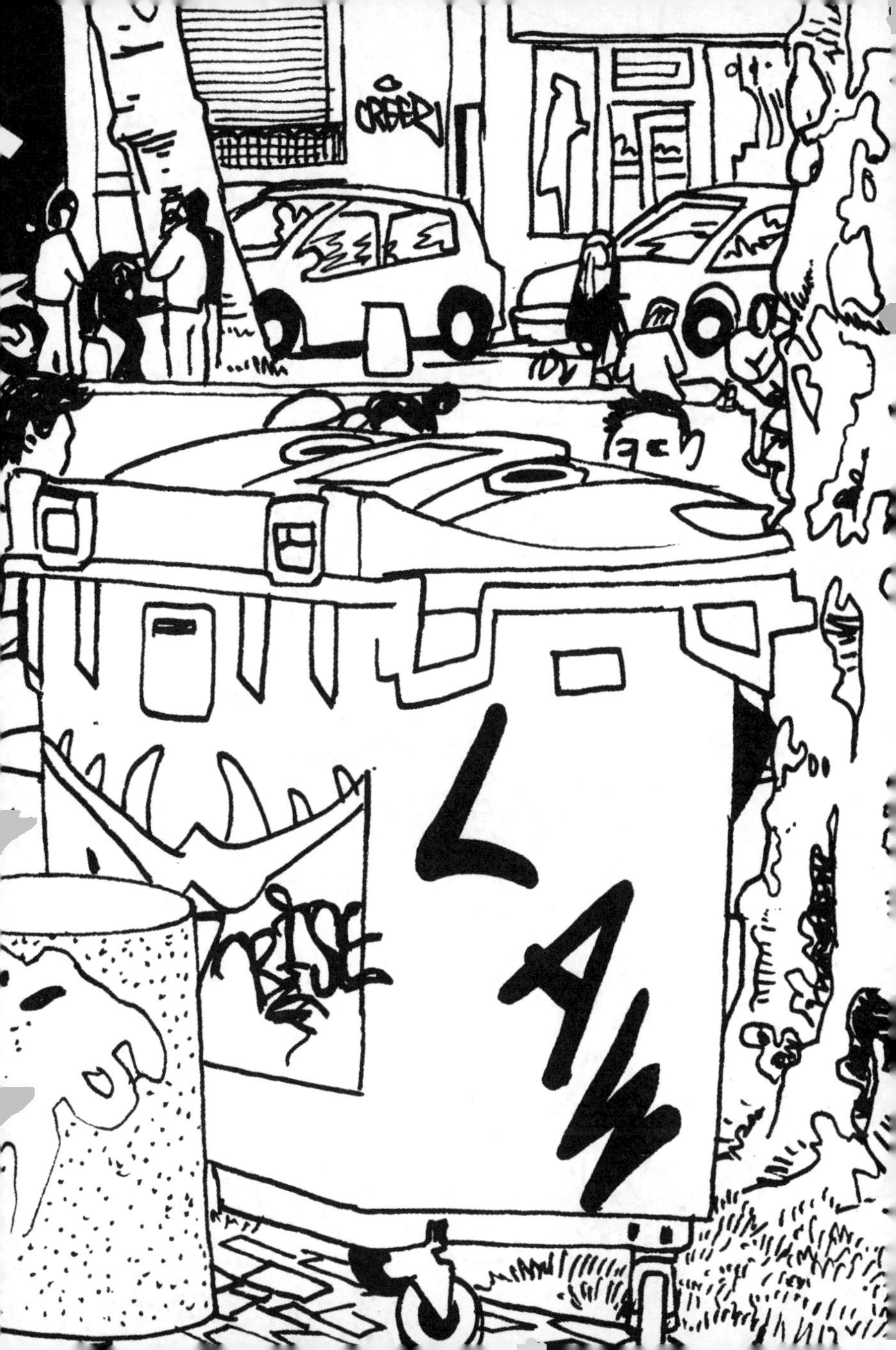
LAW

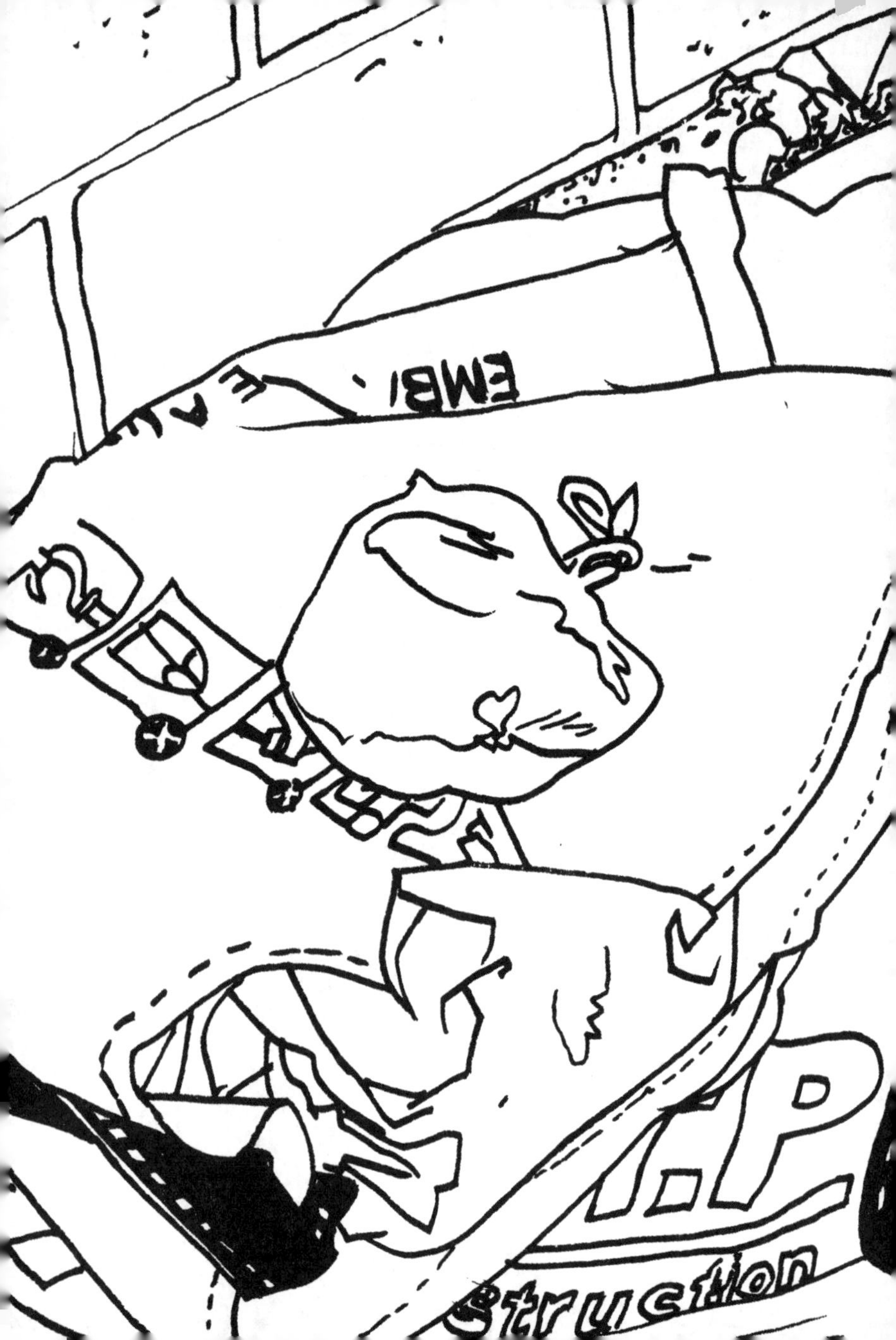
struction

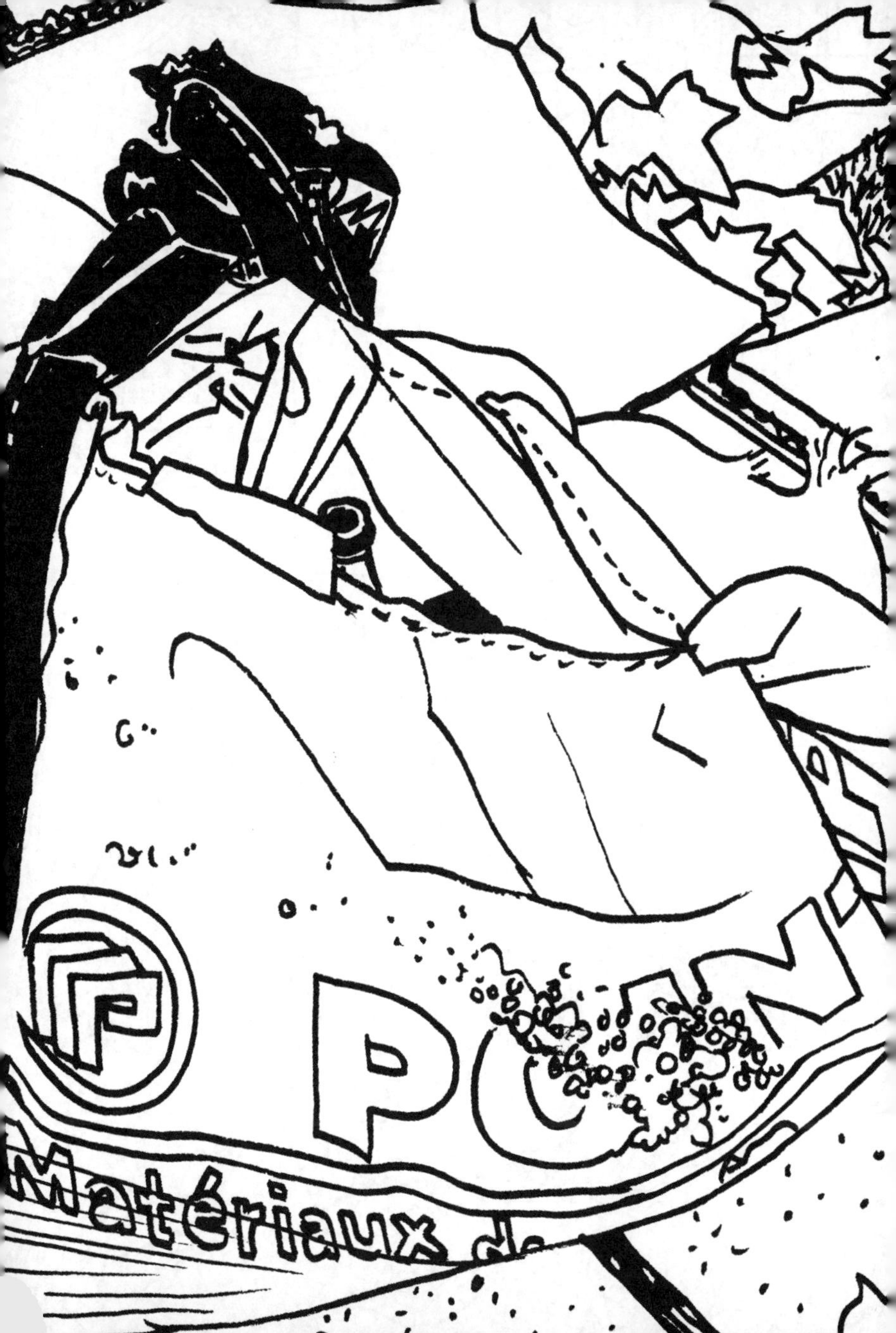
Matériaux

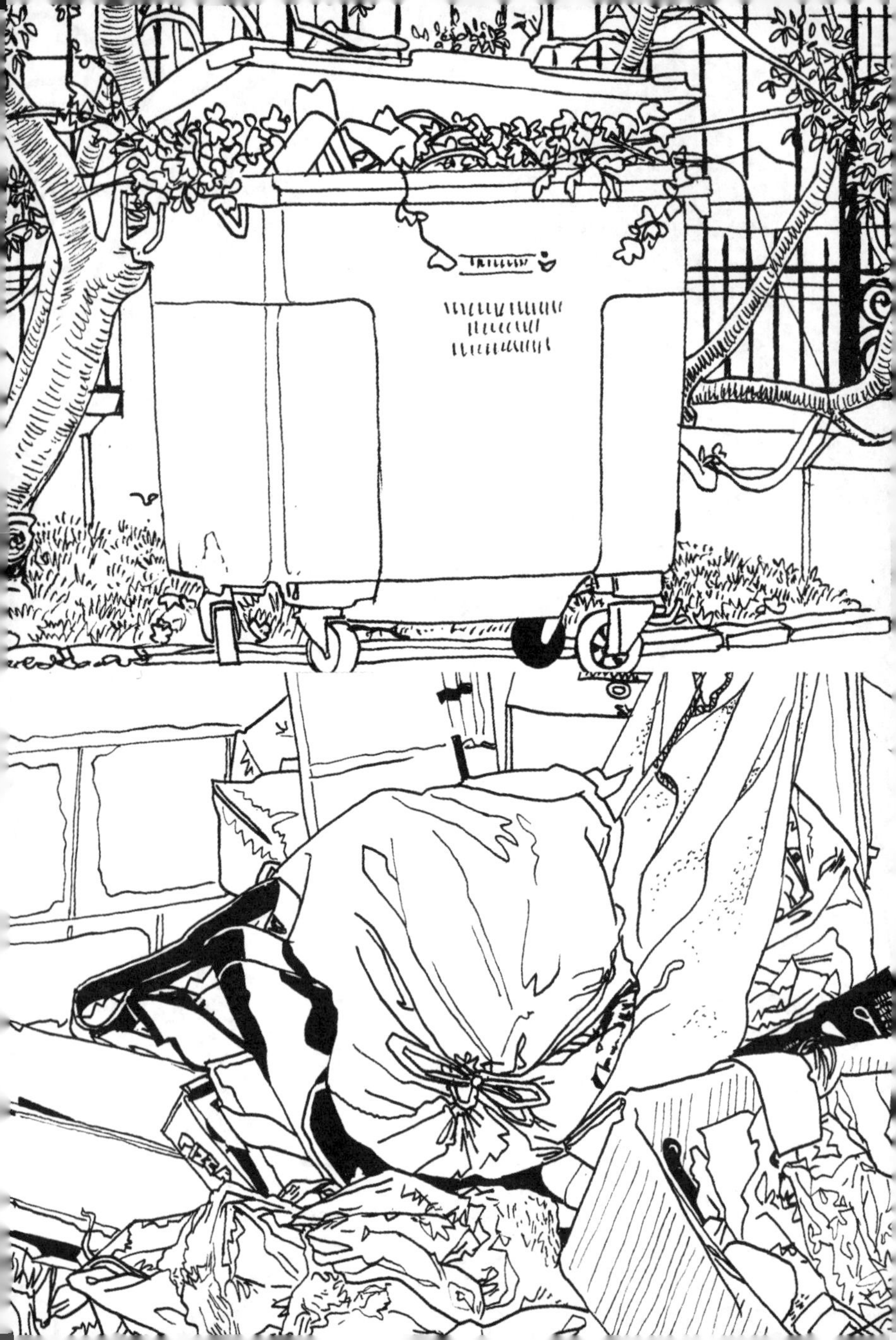

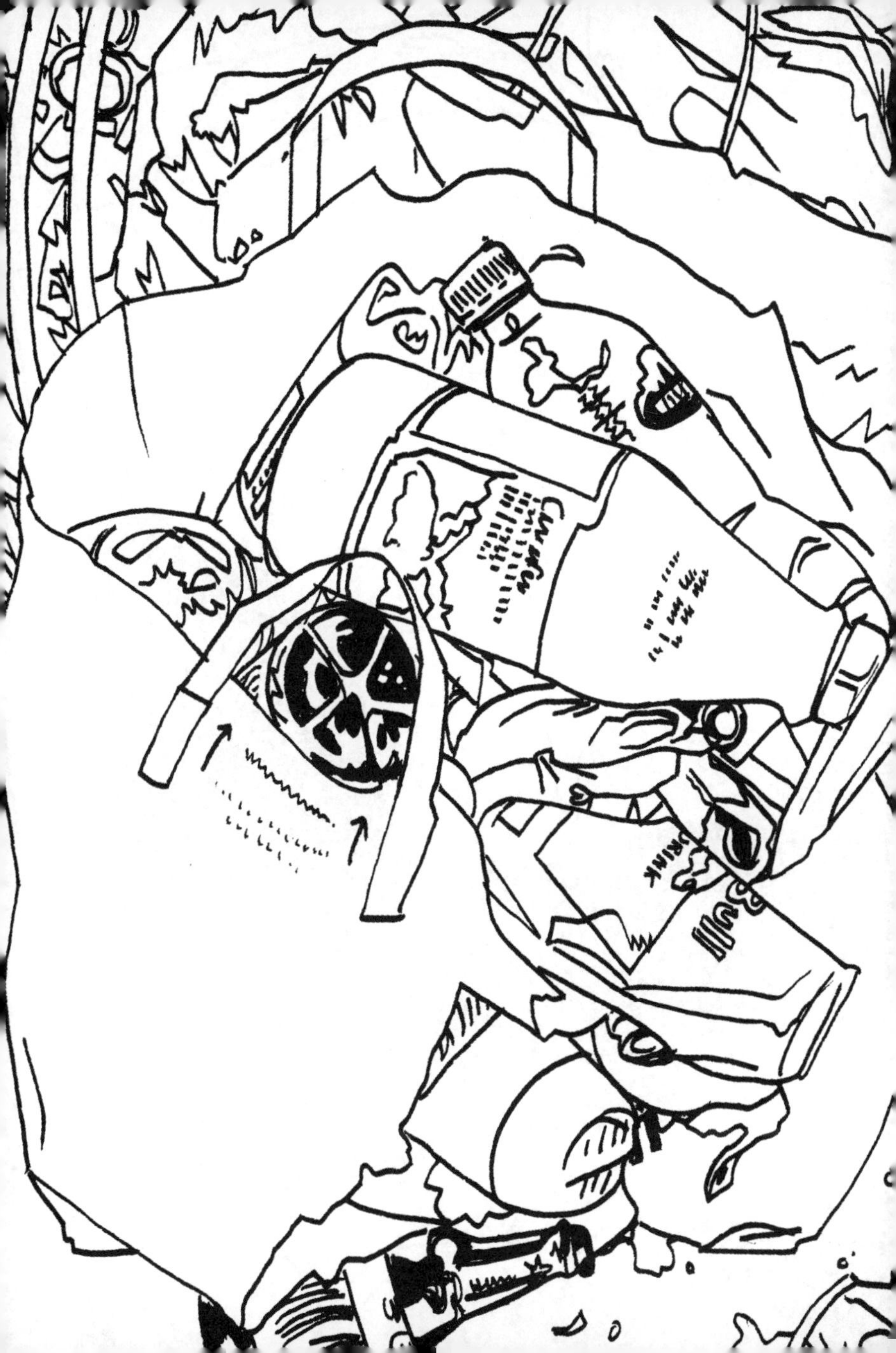
DRINK
Bull

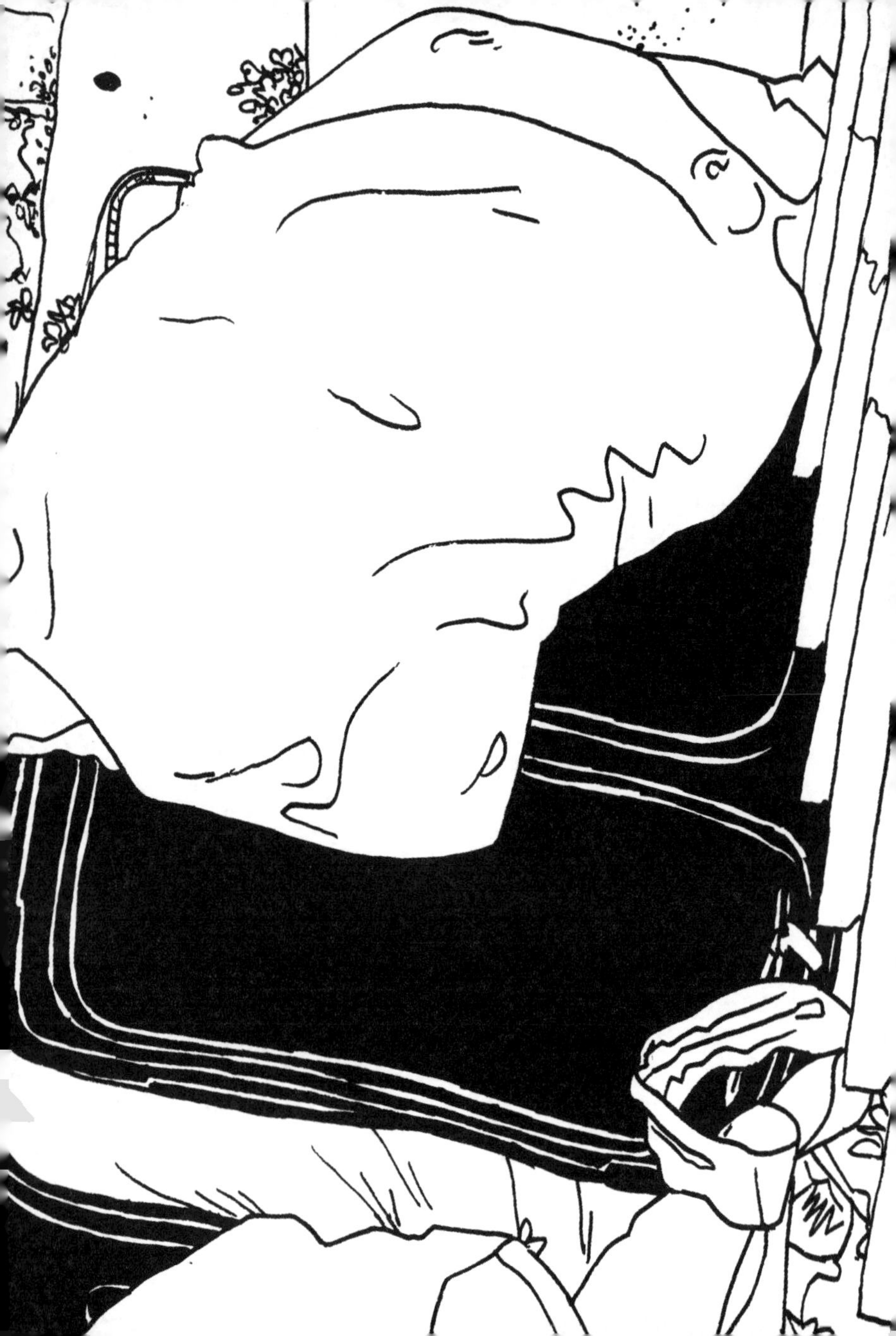

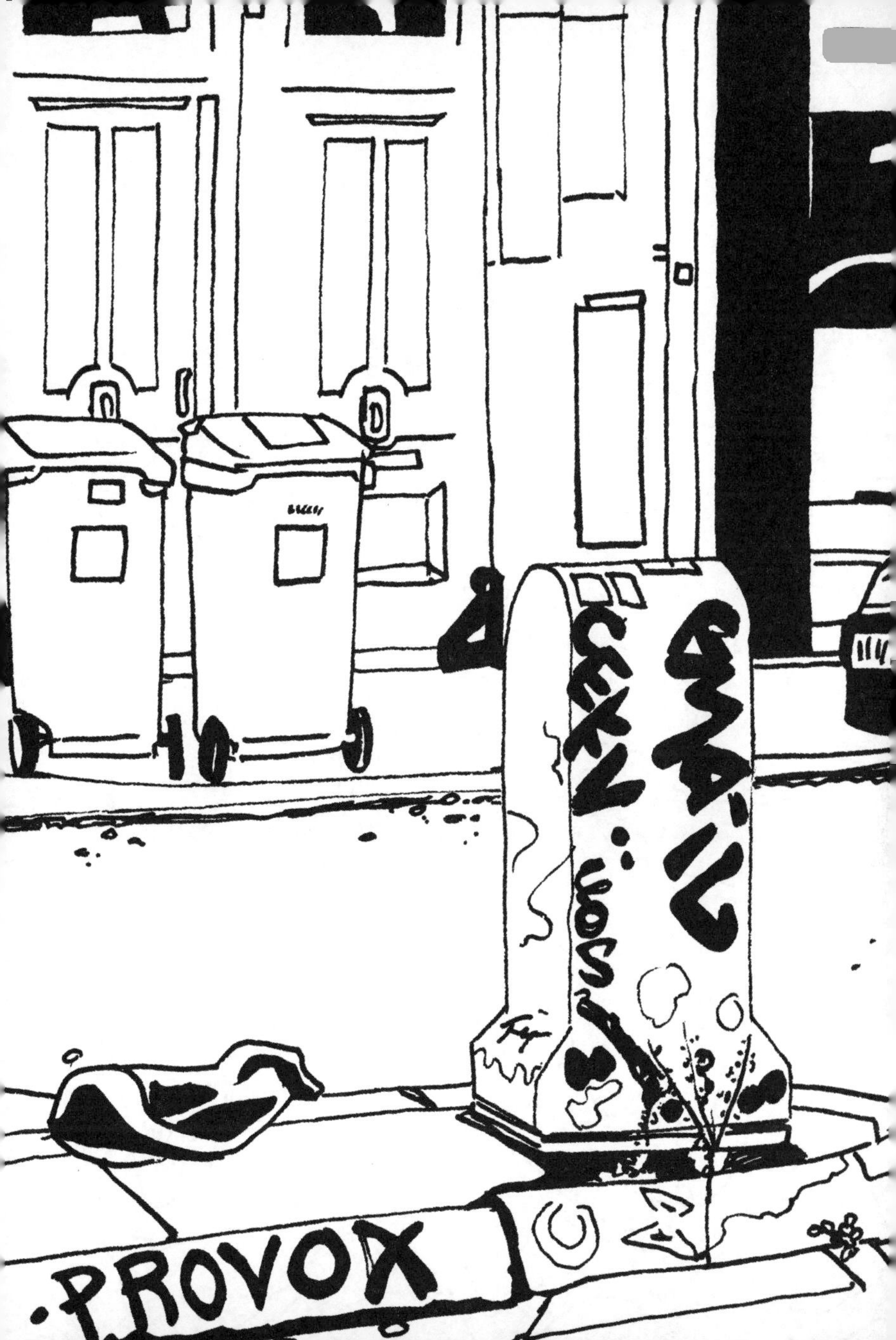
PROVOX

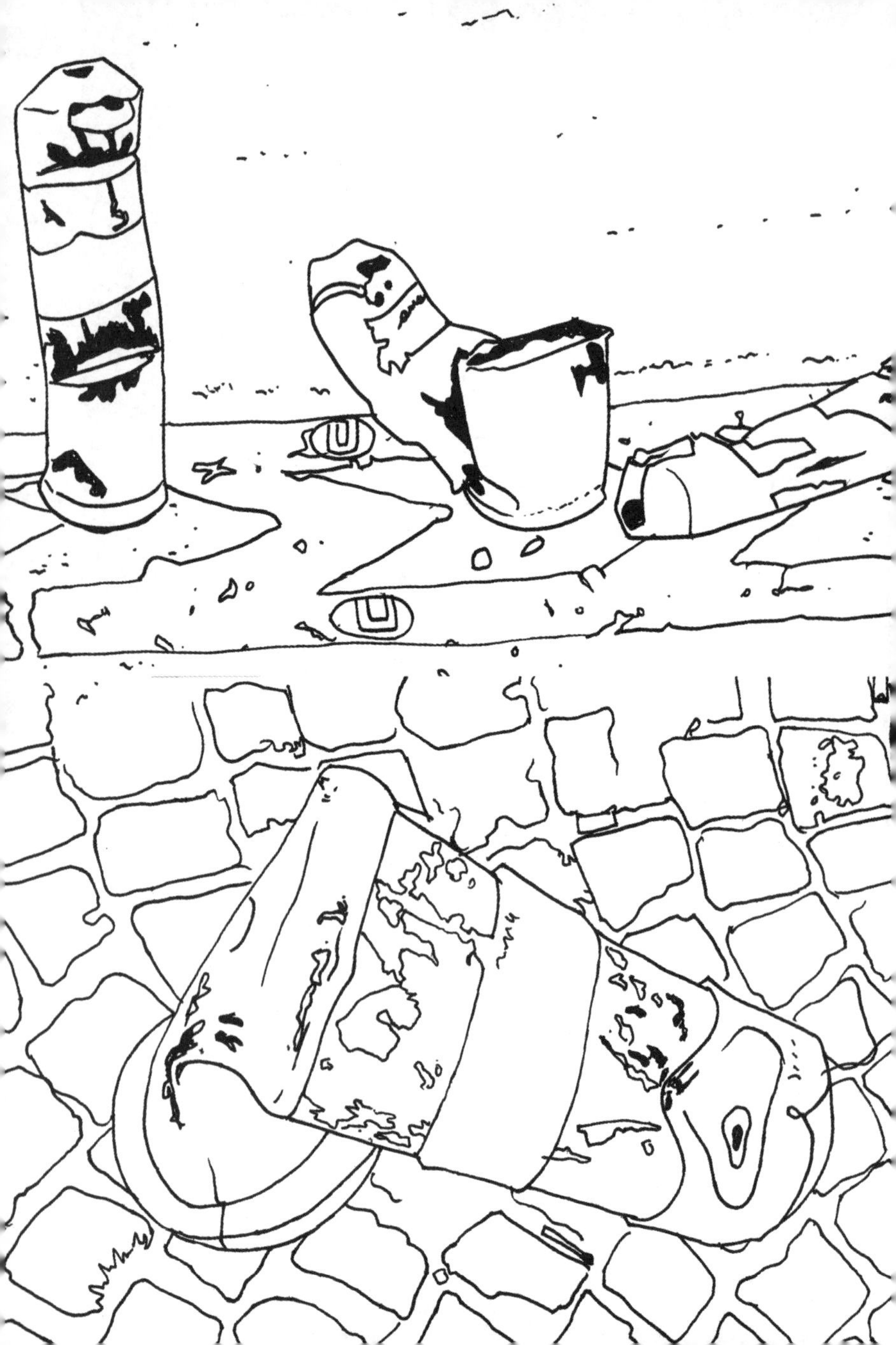

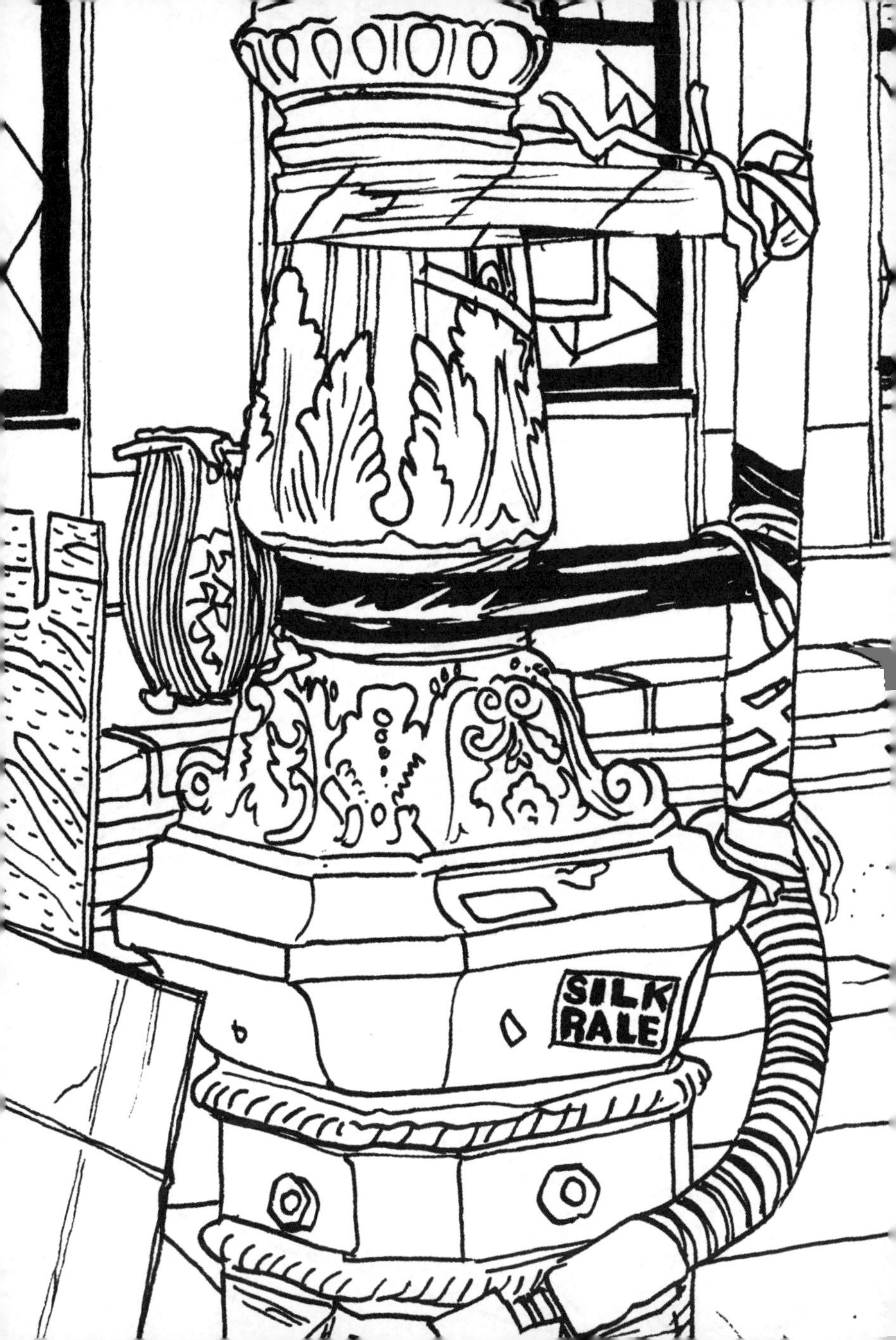
SILK
RALE

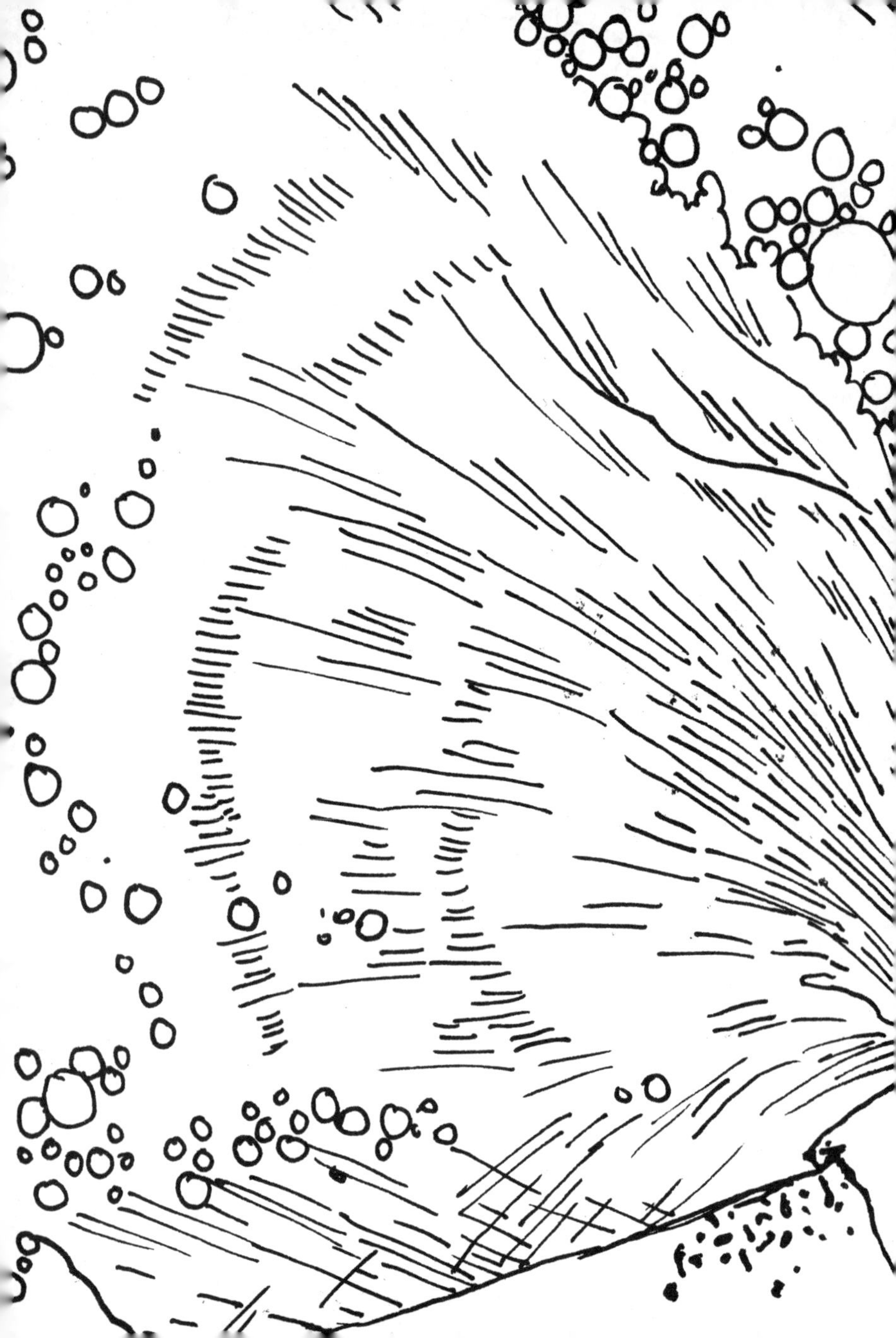

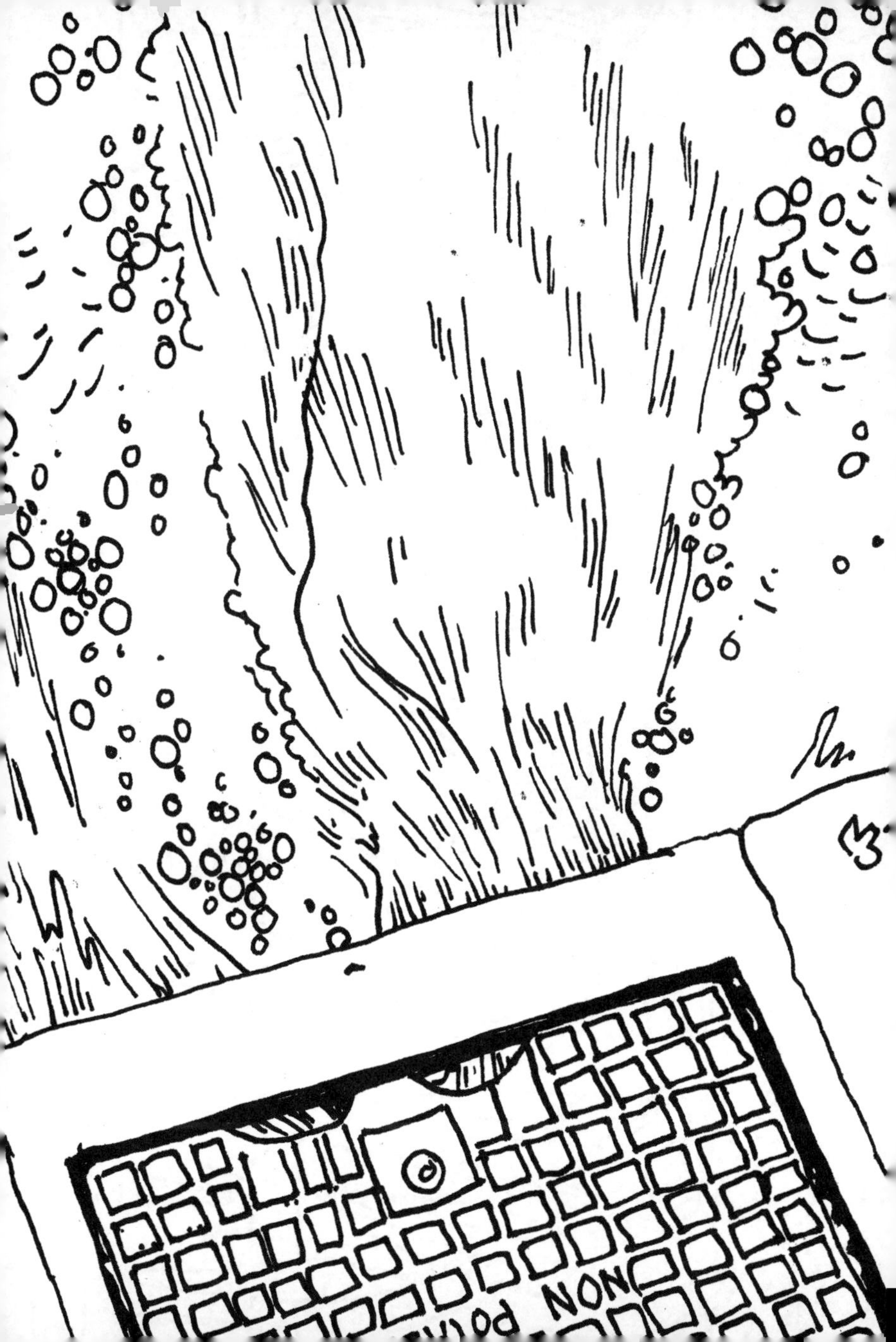
NON

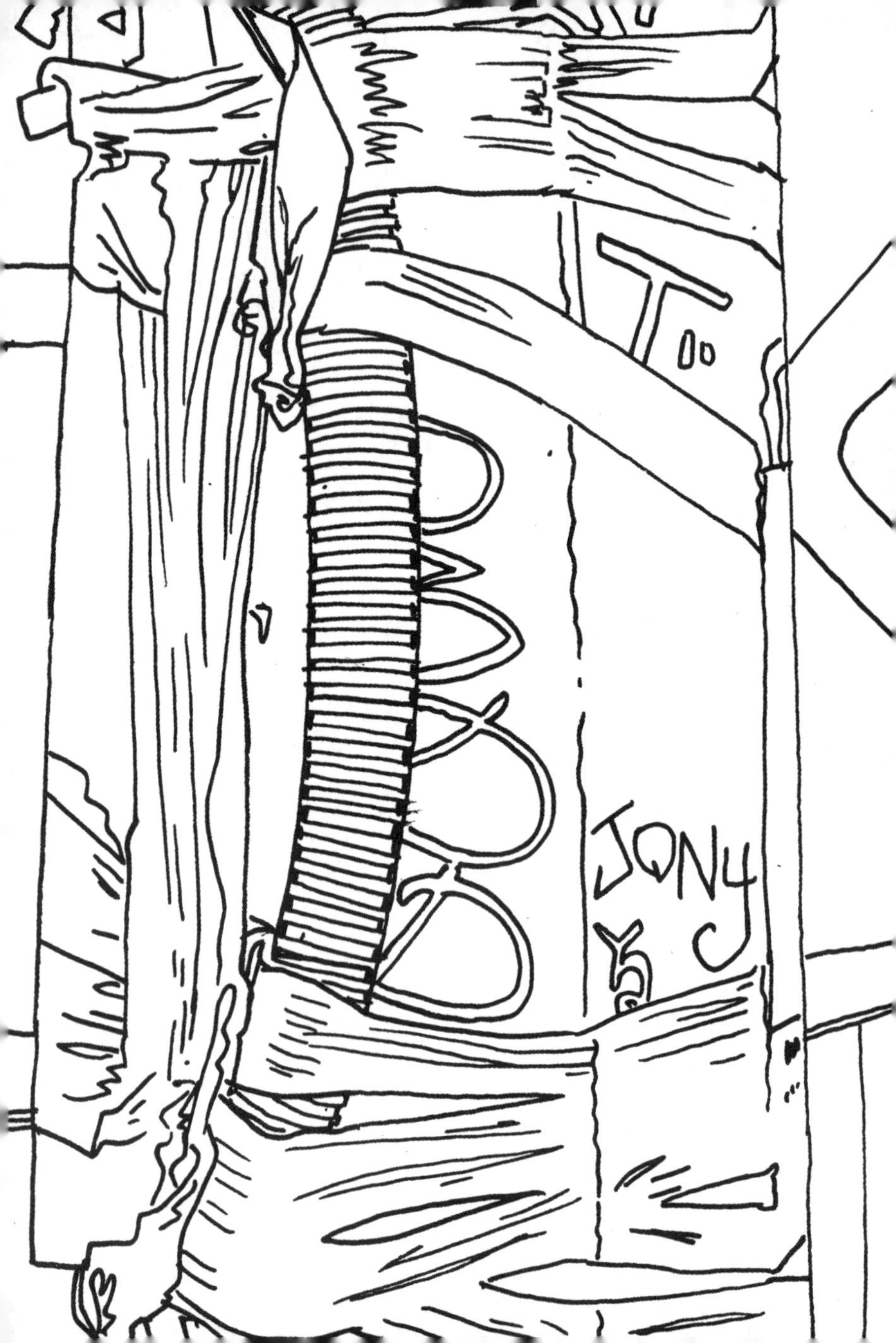

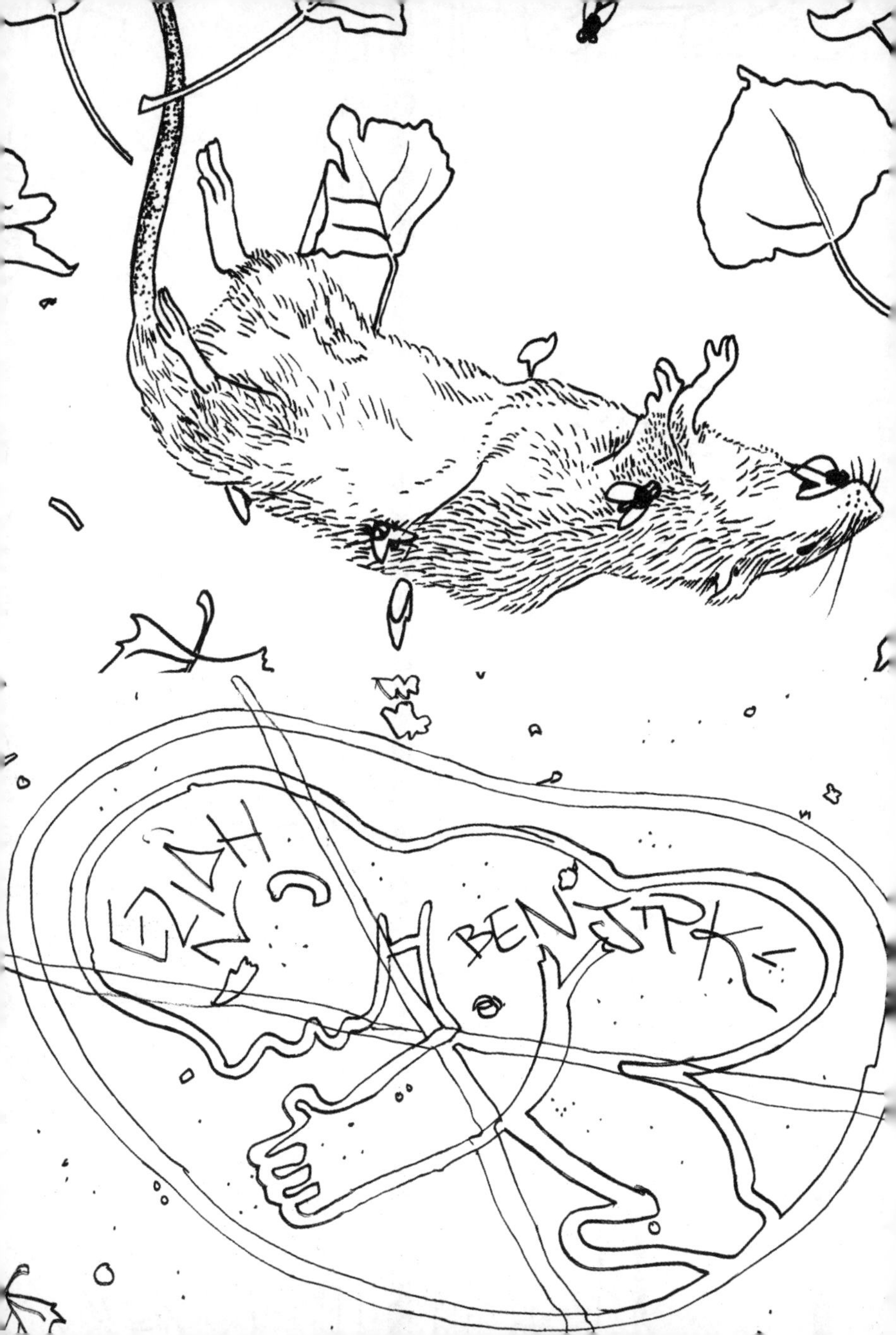

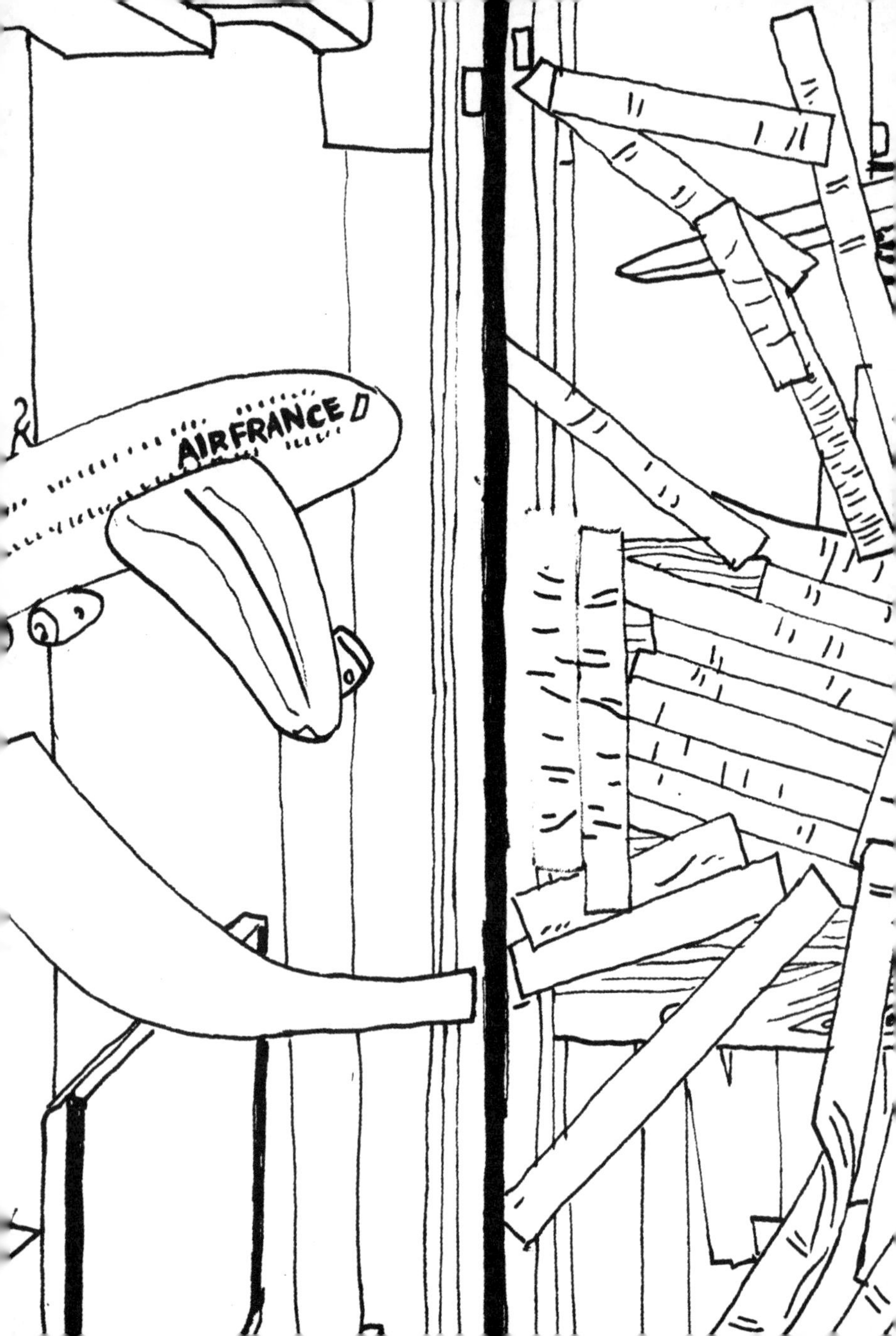
AIRFRANCE

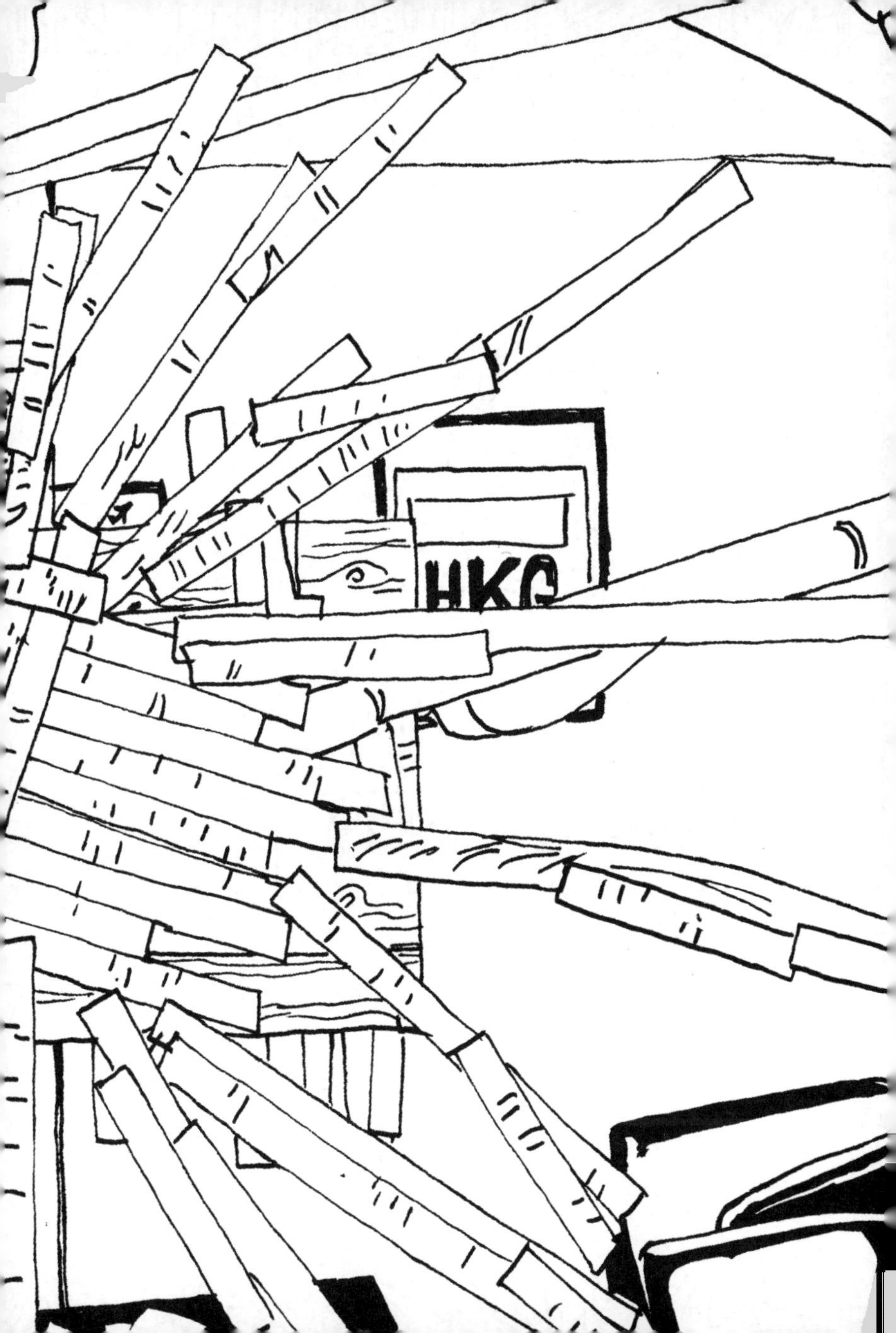
HKG

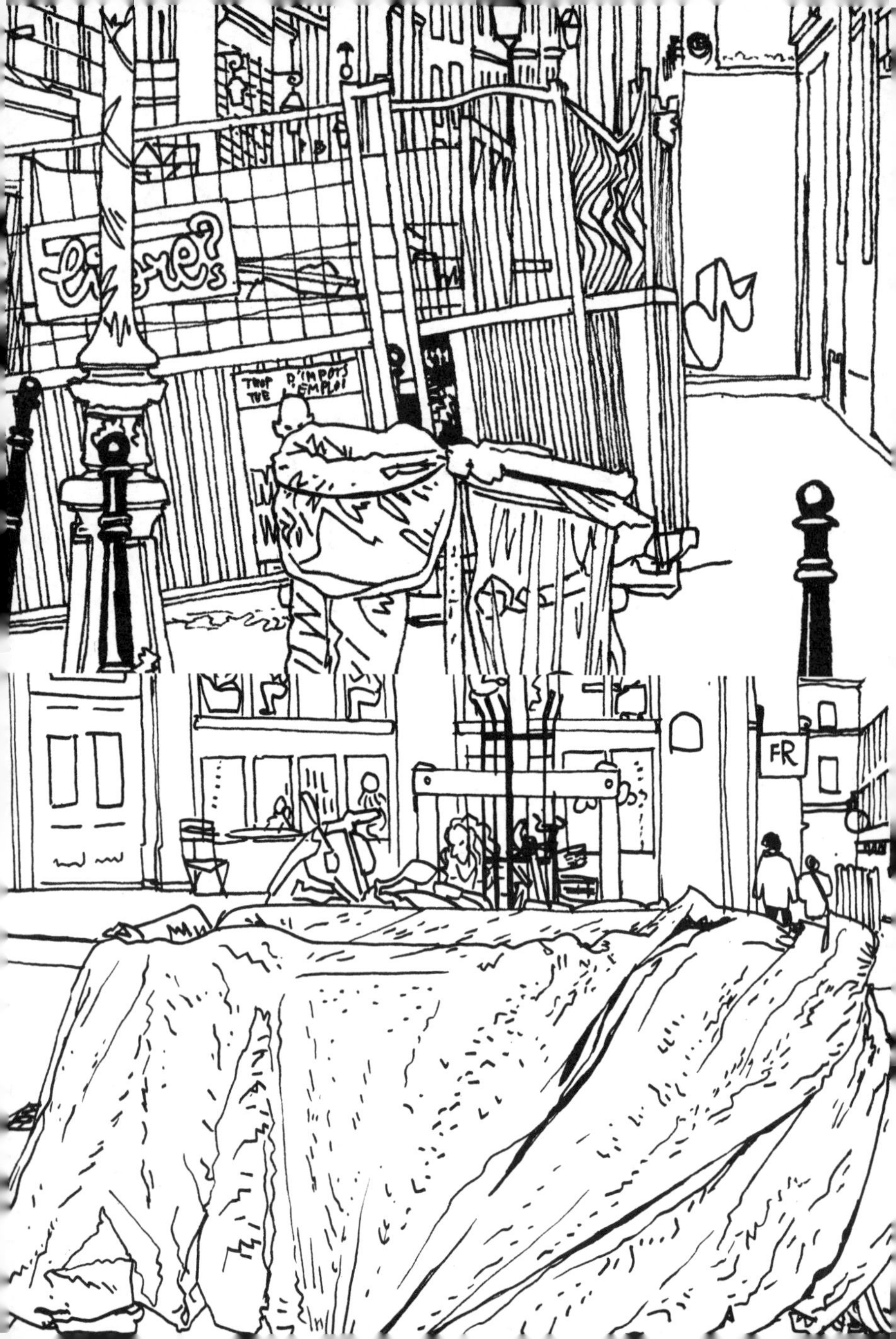
TROP D'IMPOTS
TUE
EMPLOI
FR

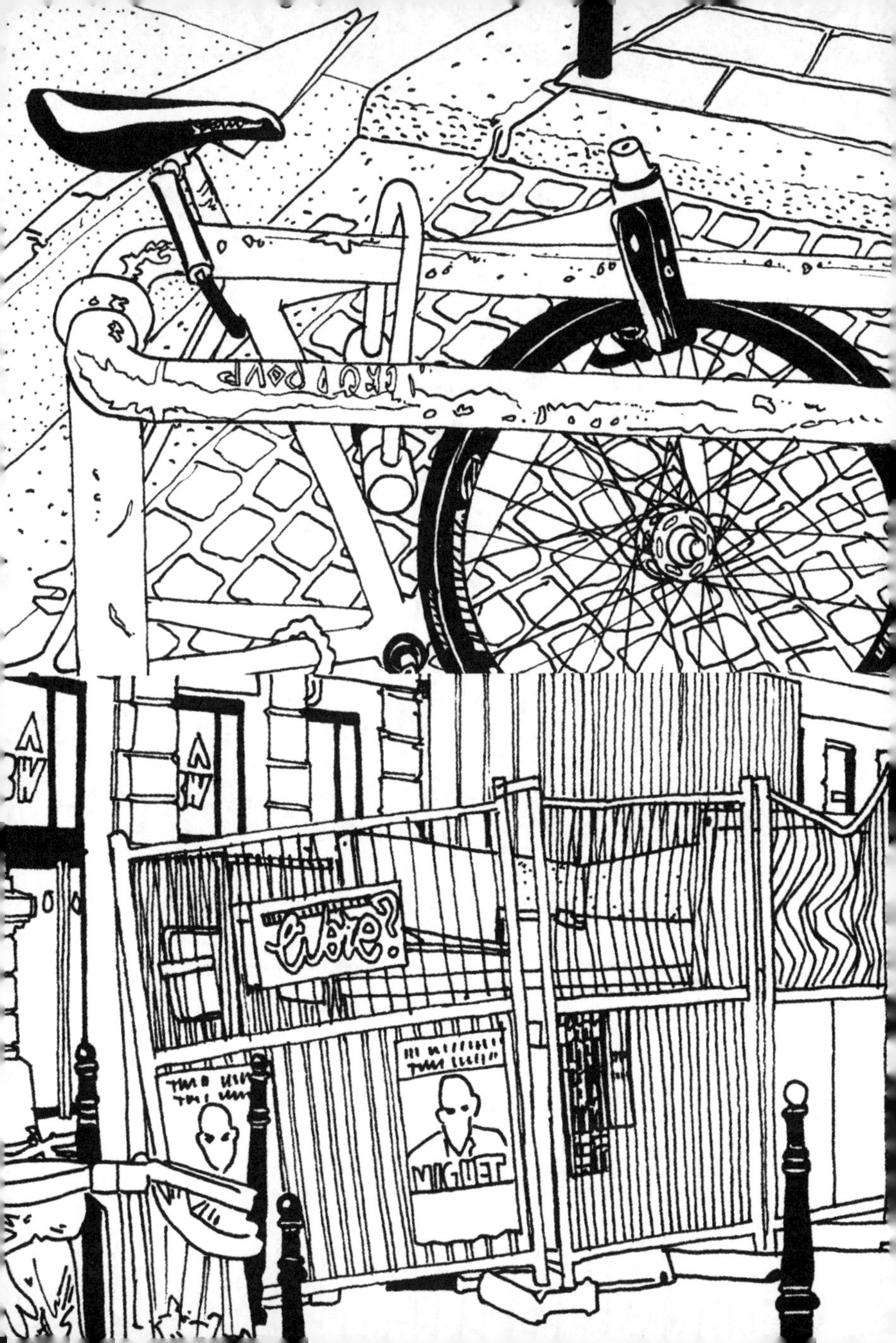
MIGUET

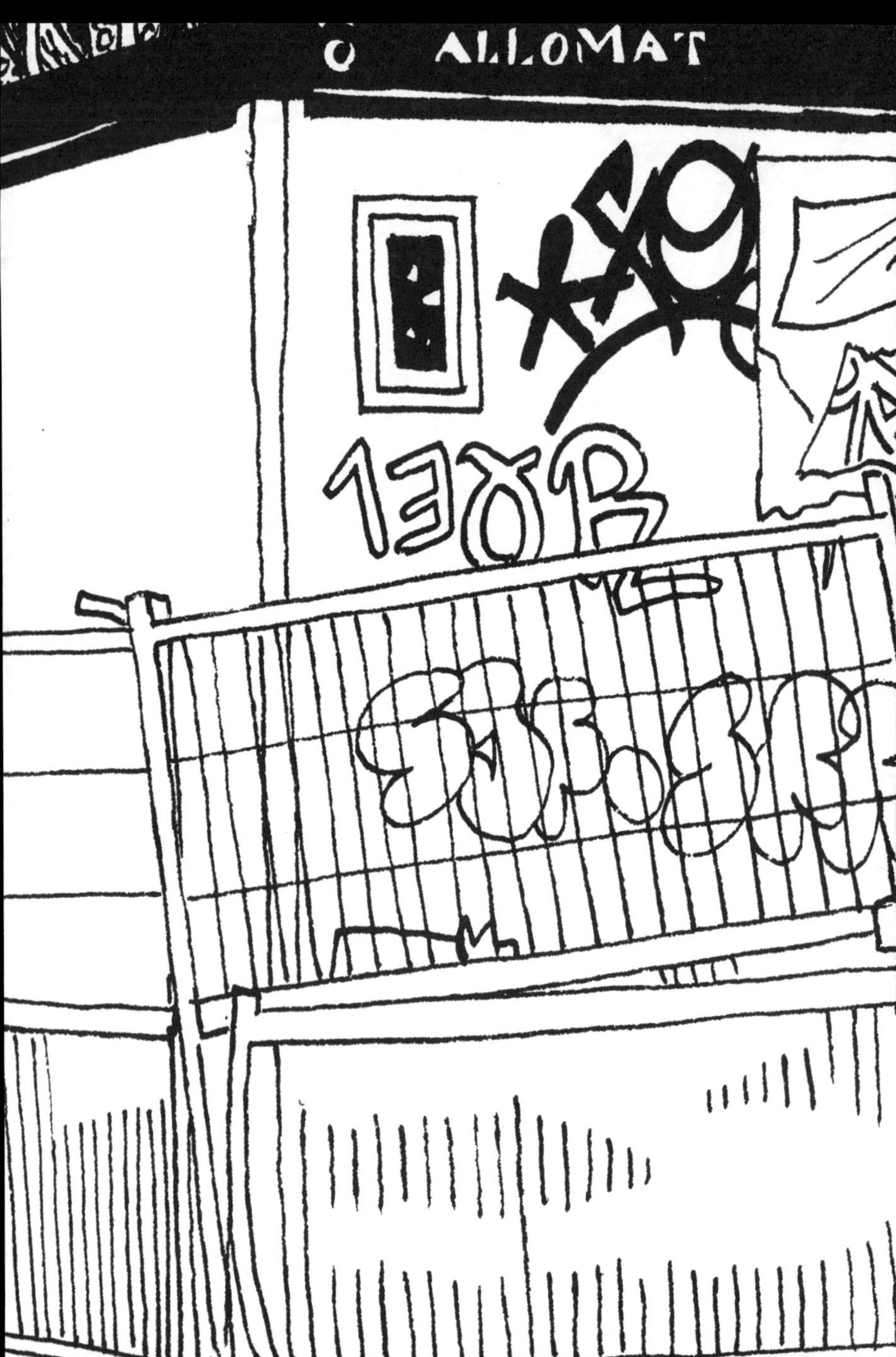
ALLOMAT

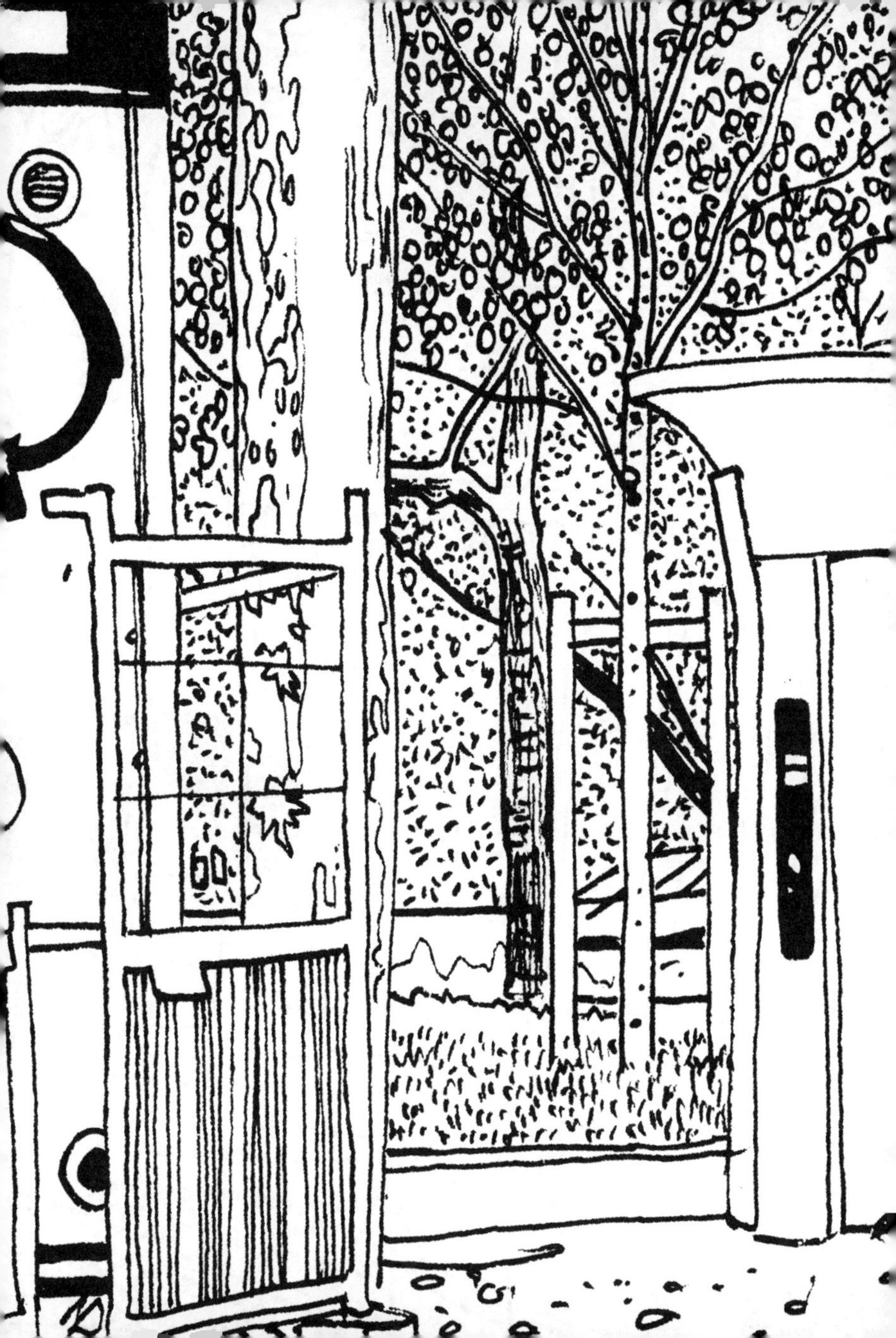

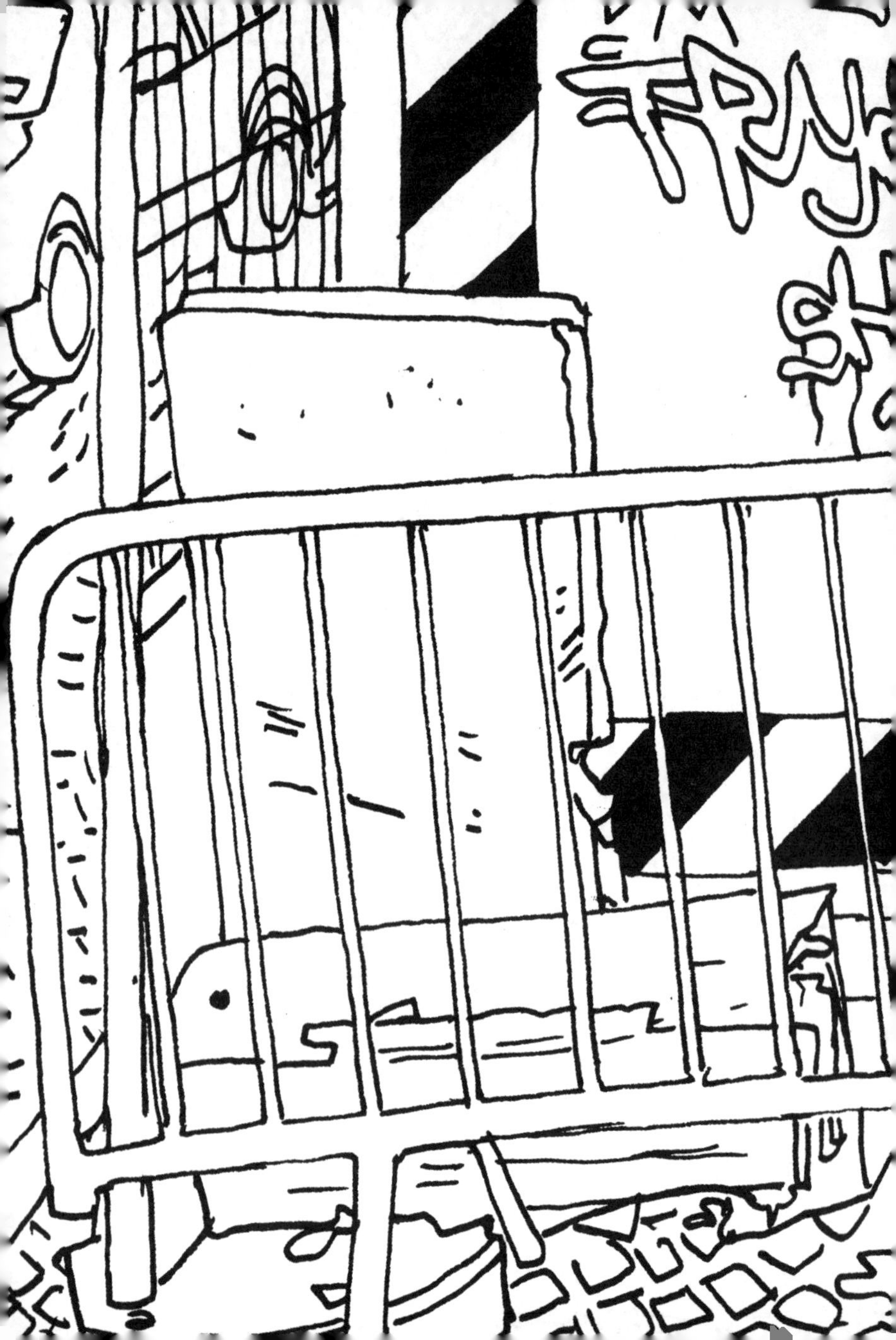

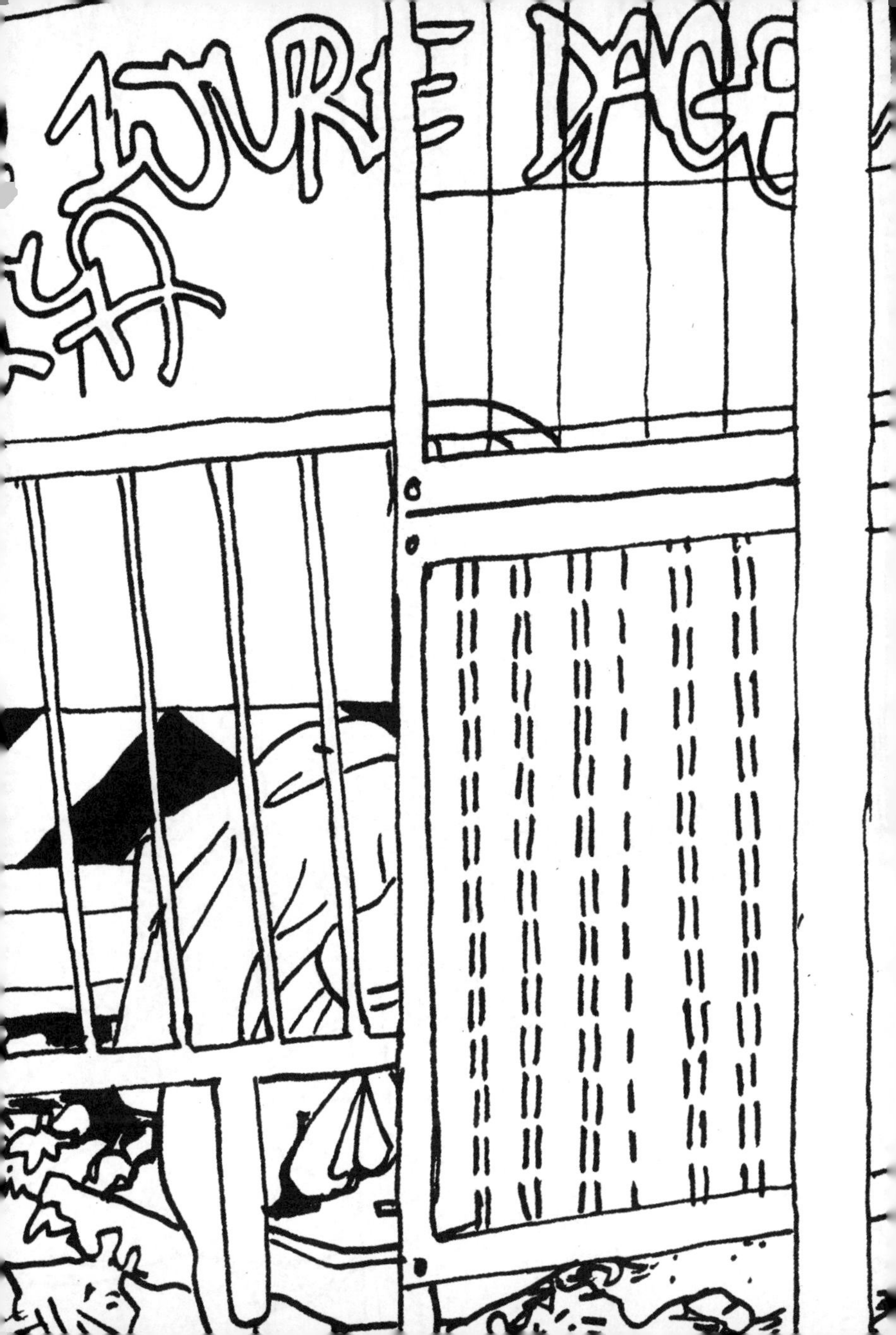

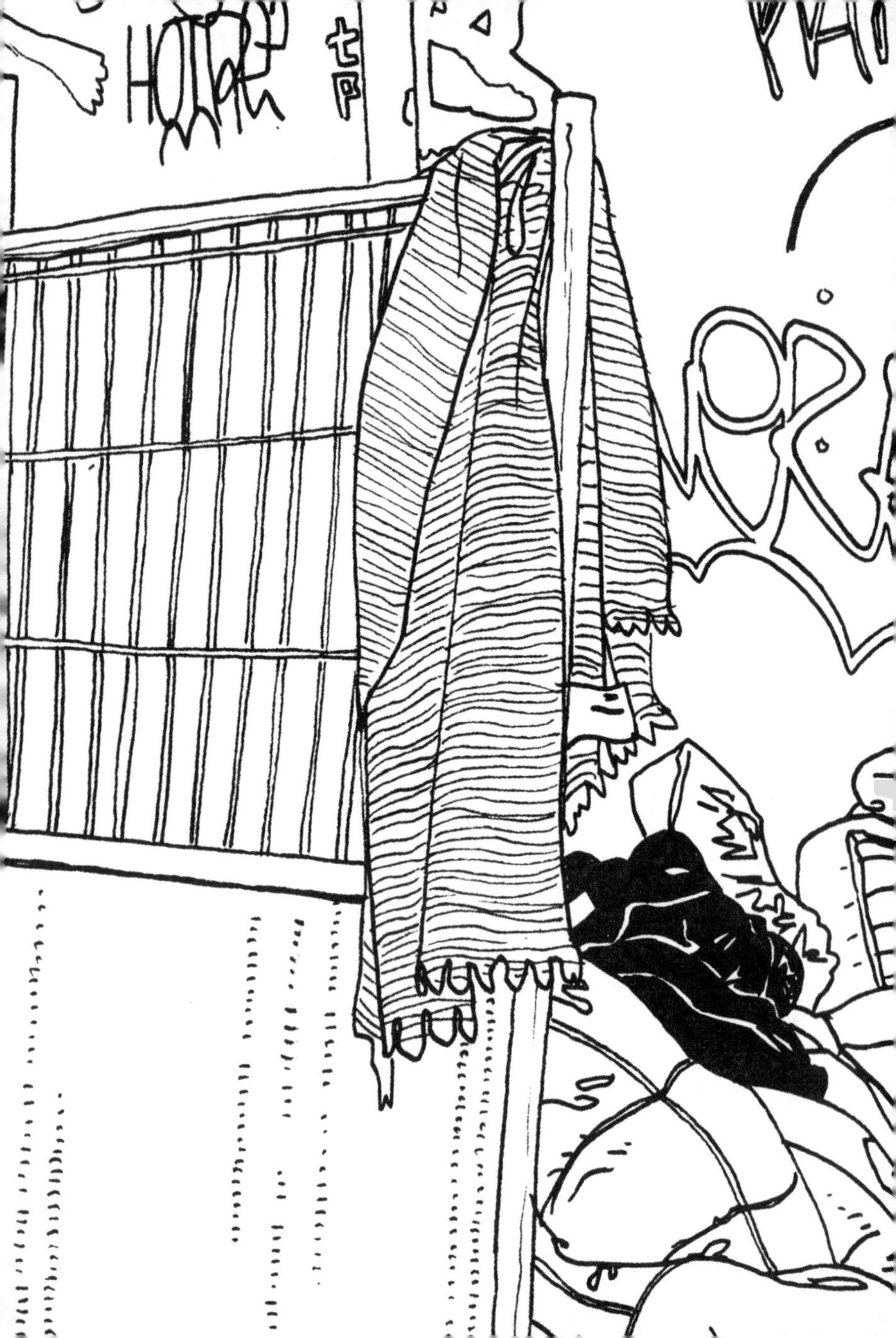

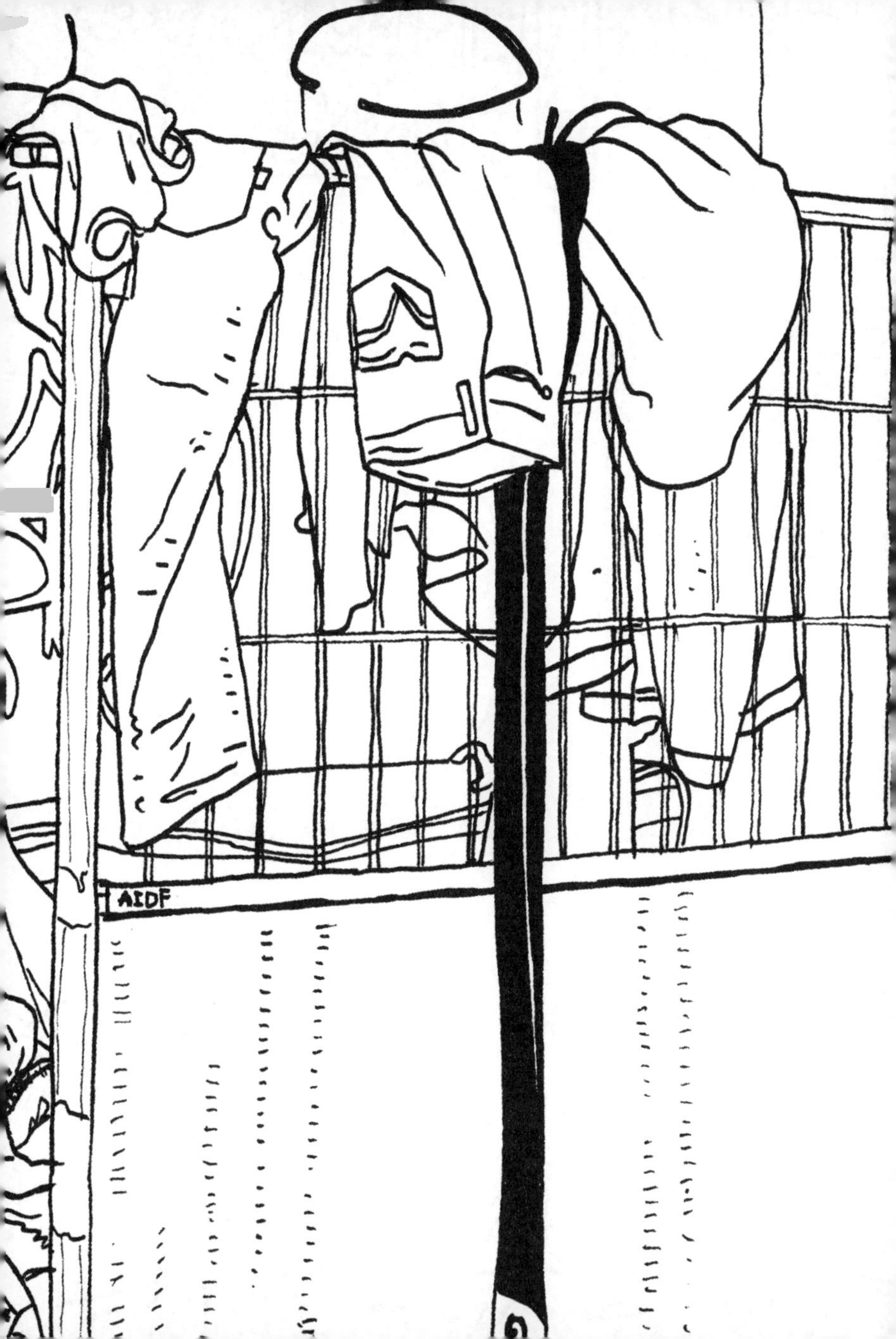
AIDF

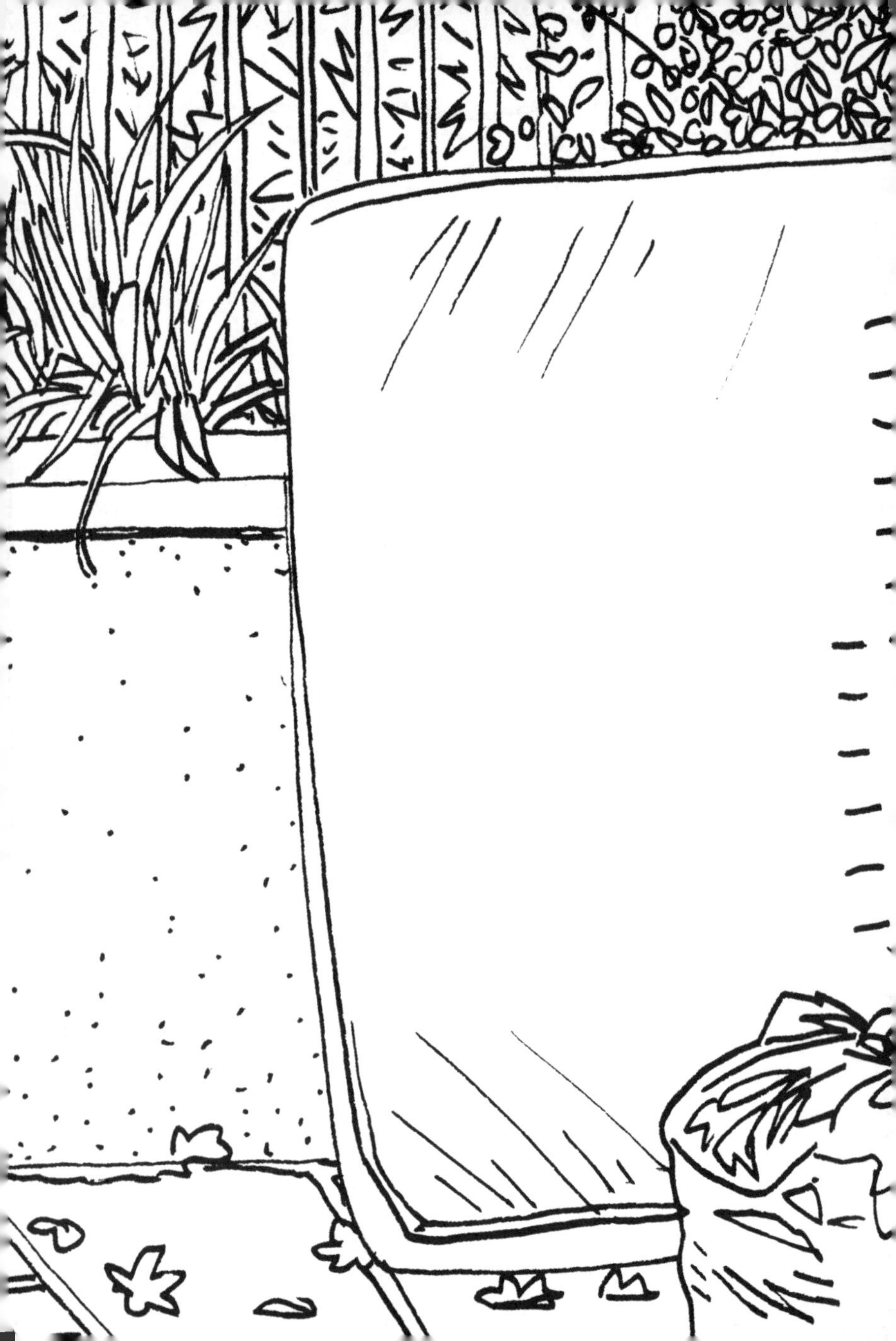

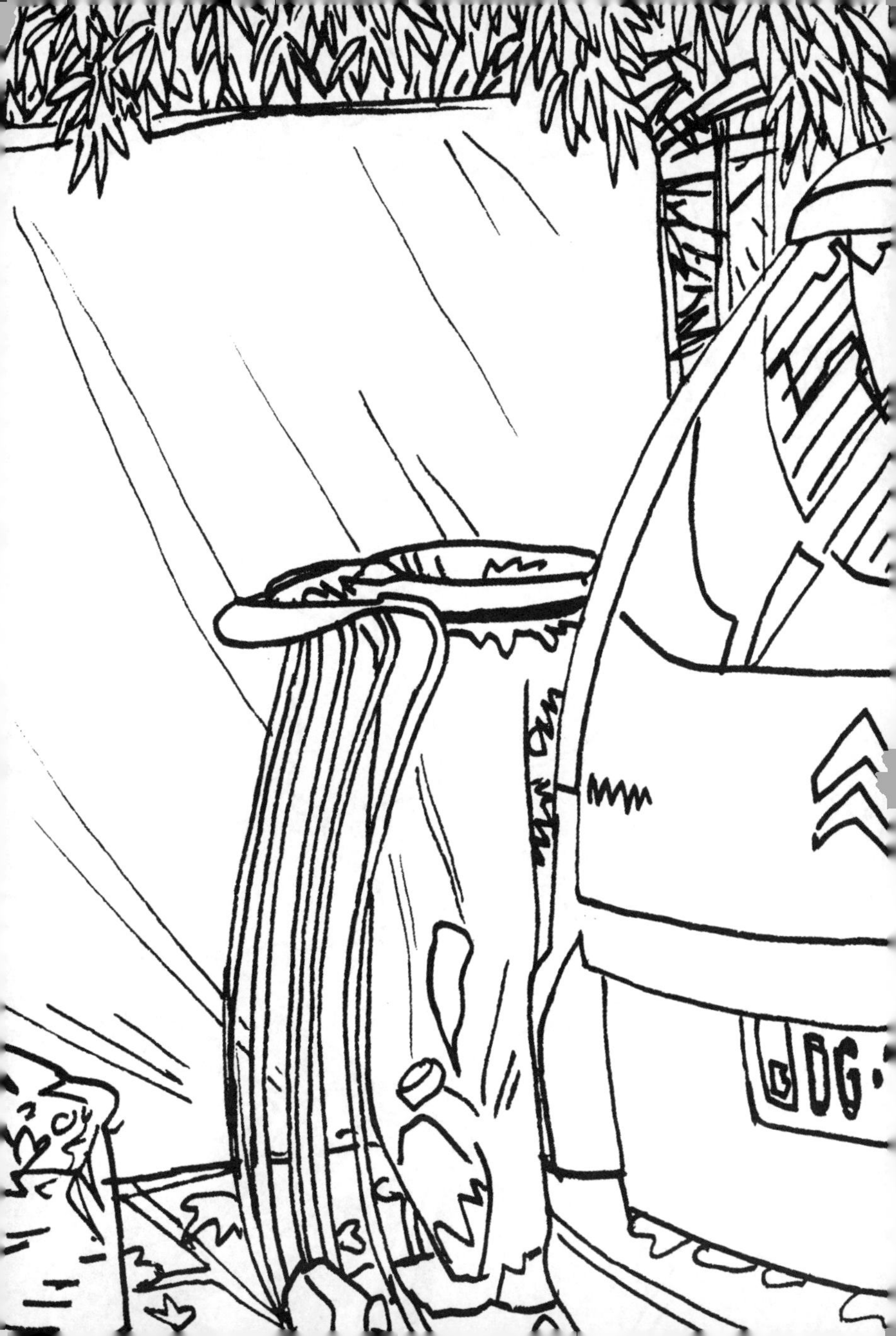

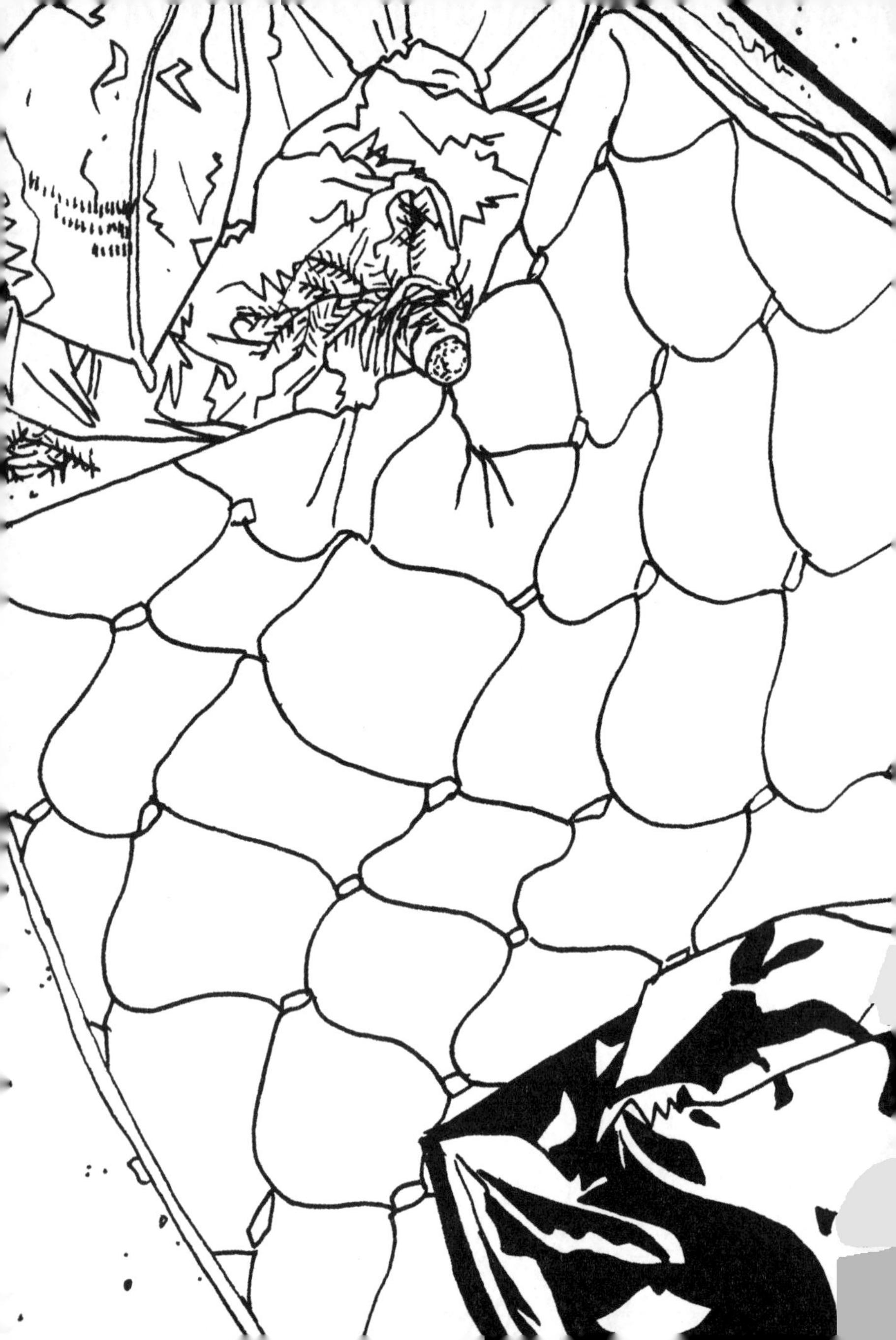

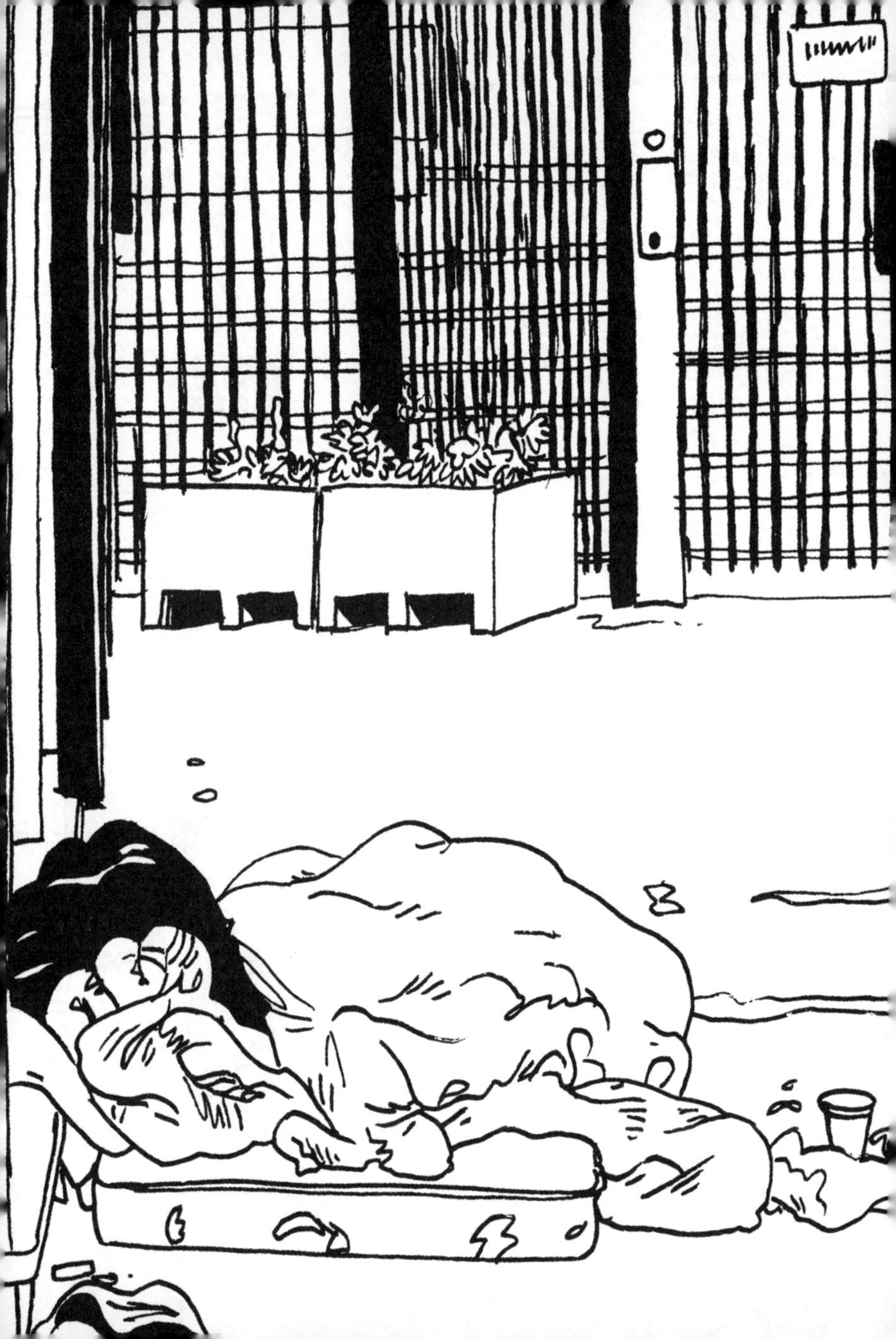

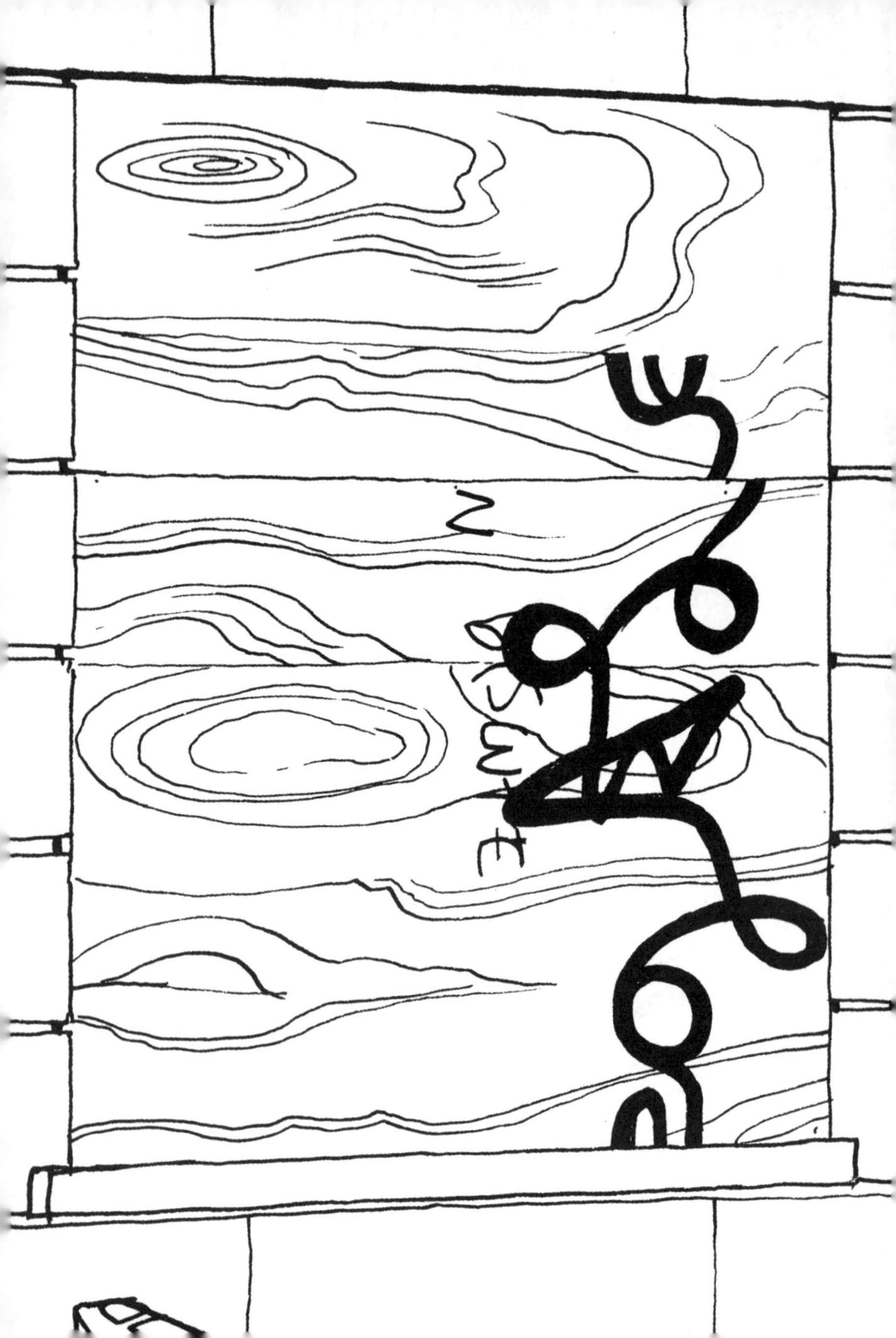

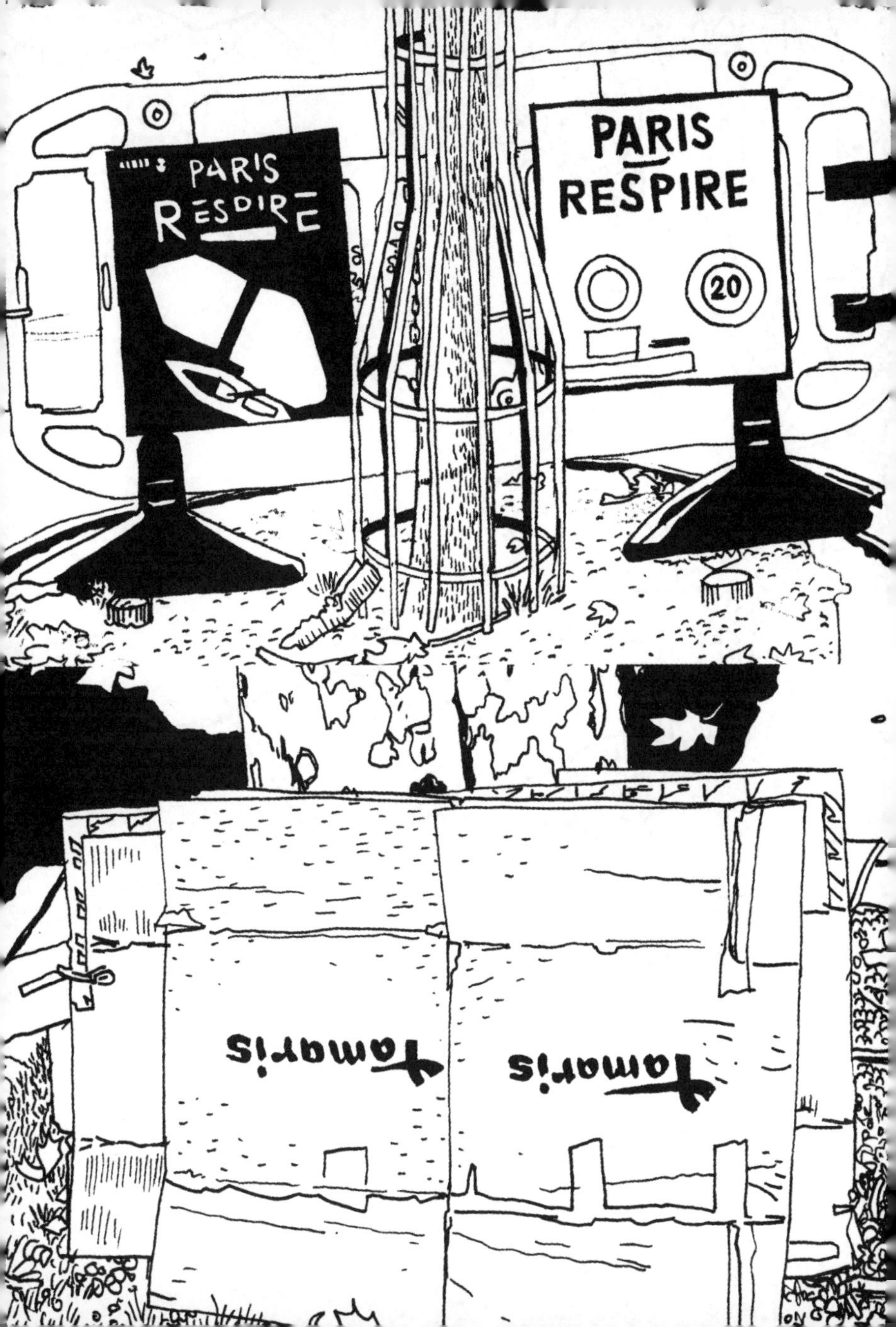
PARIS
RESPIRE
PARIS
RESPIRE
20
tamaris
tamaris

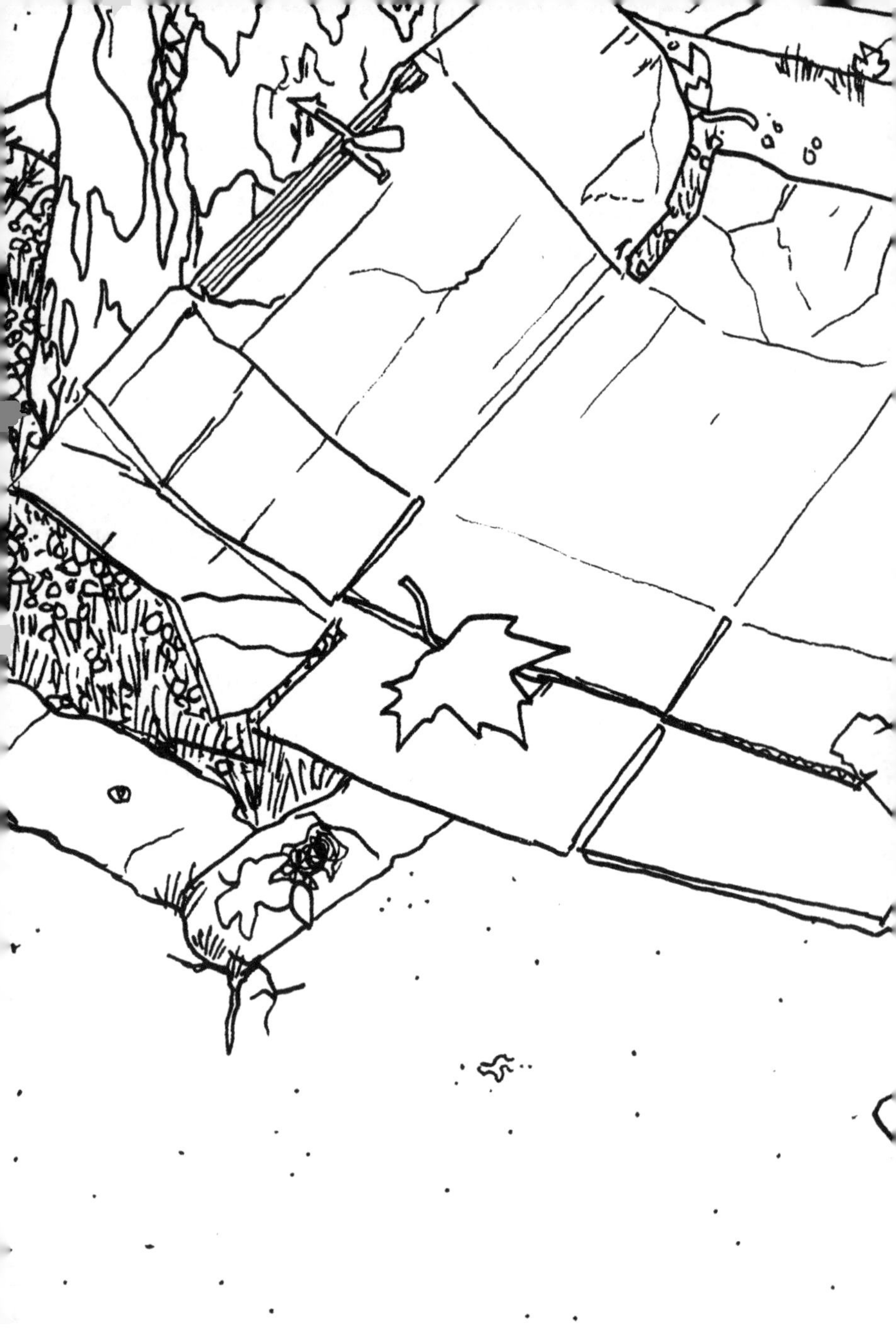

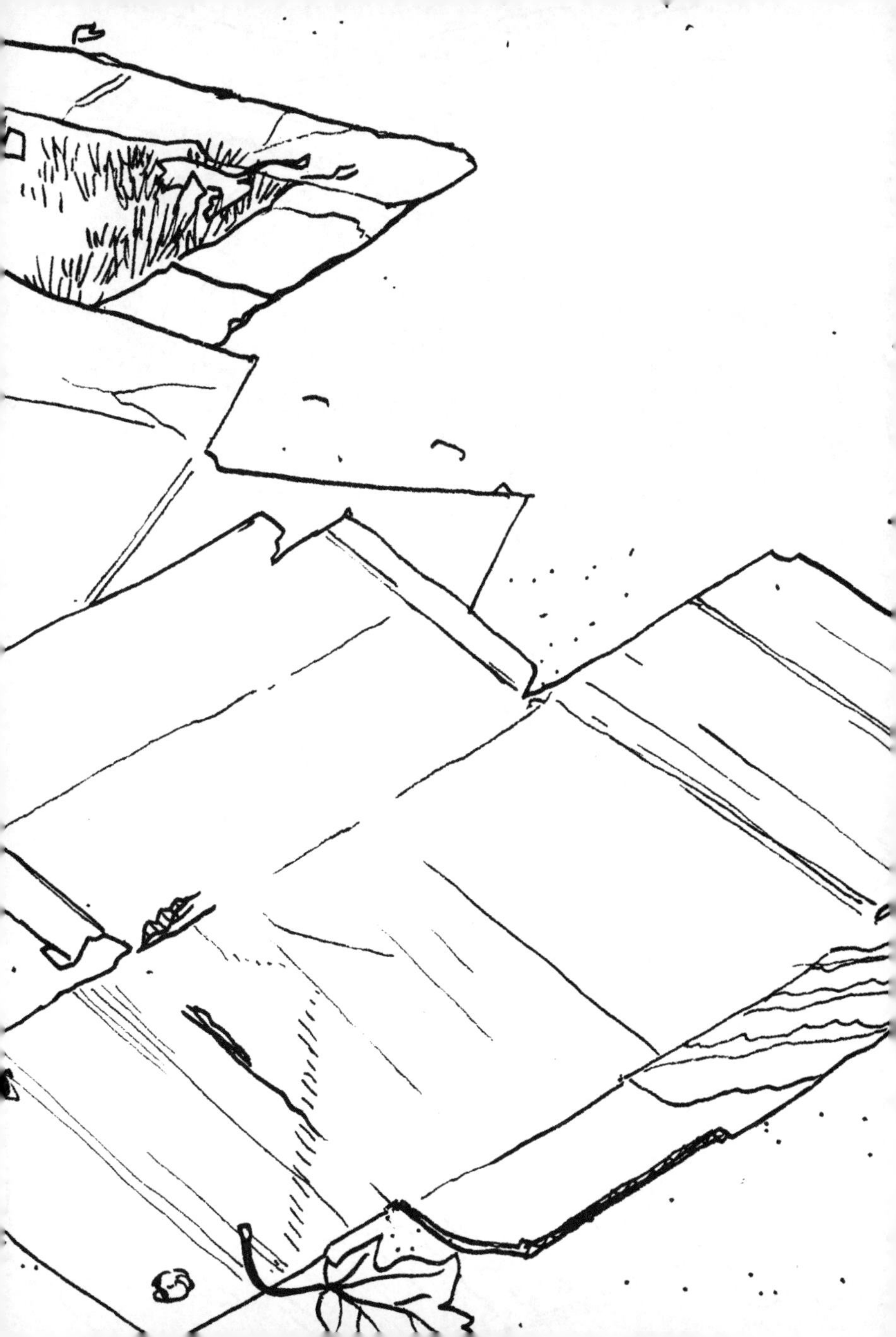

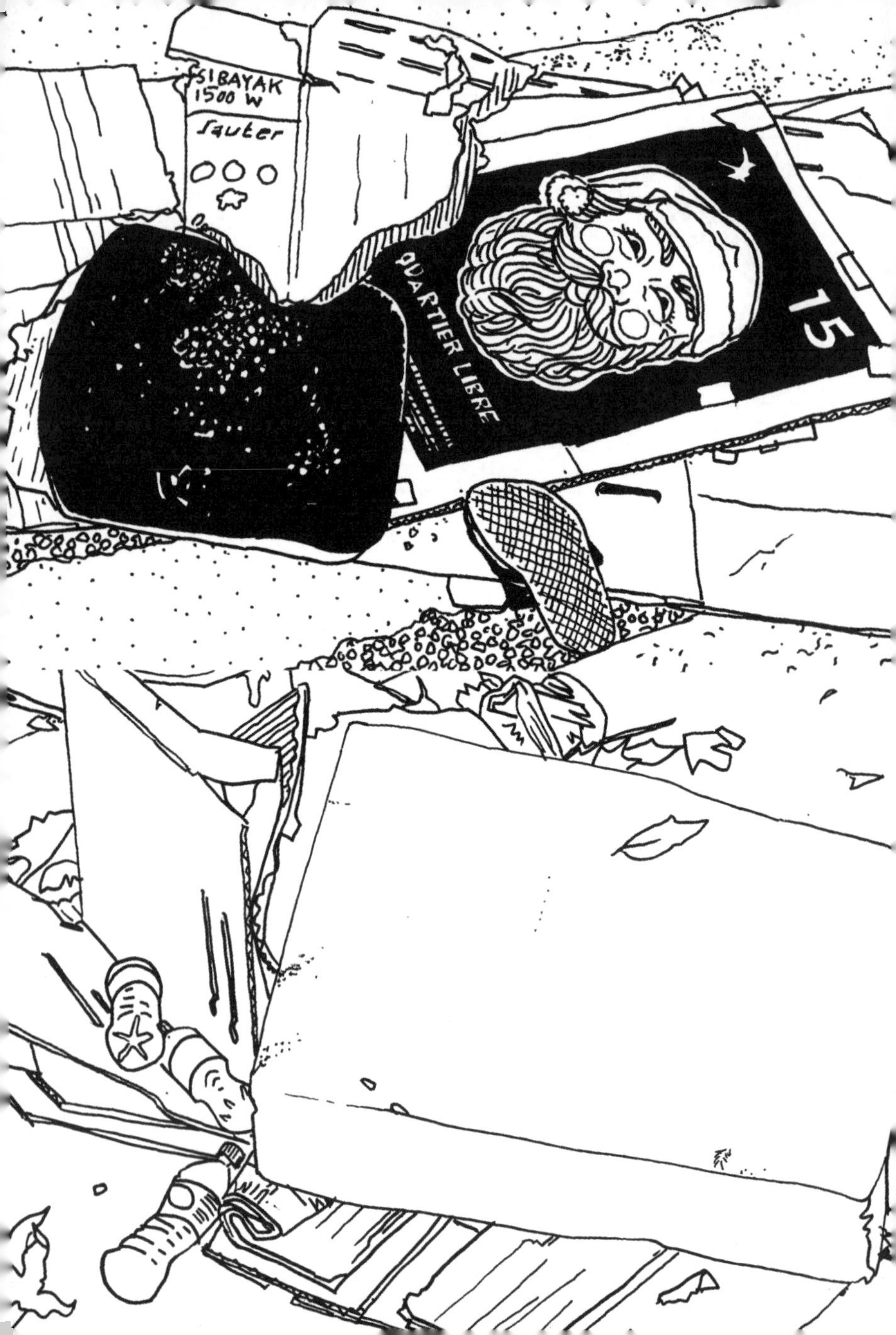
SIBAYAK
1500 W
Sauter
QUARTIER LIBRE
15

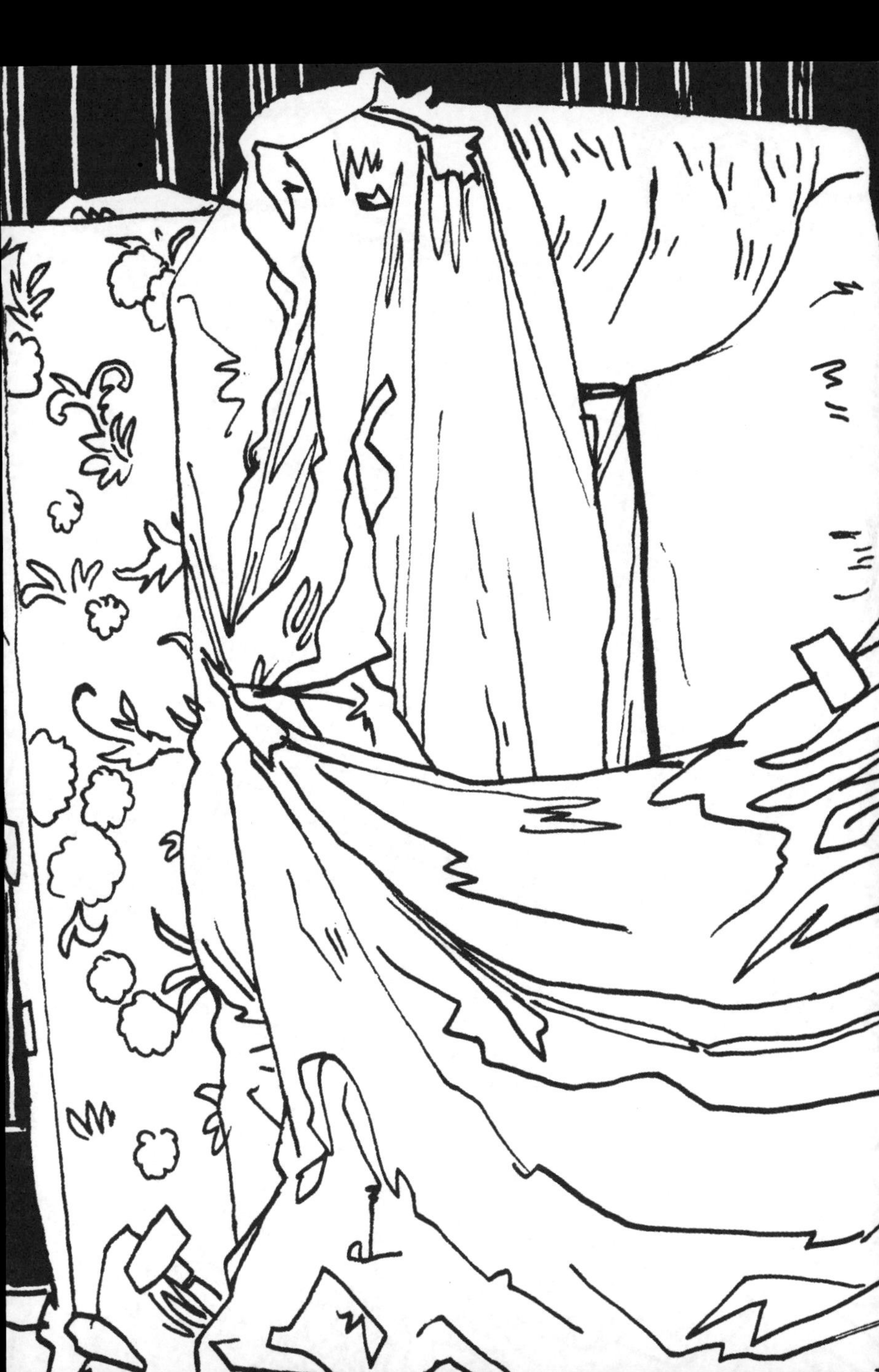

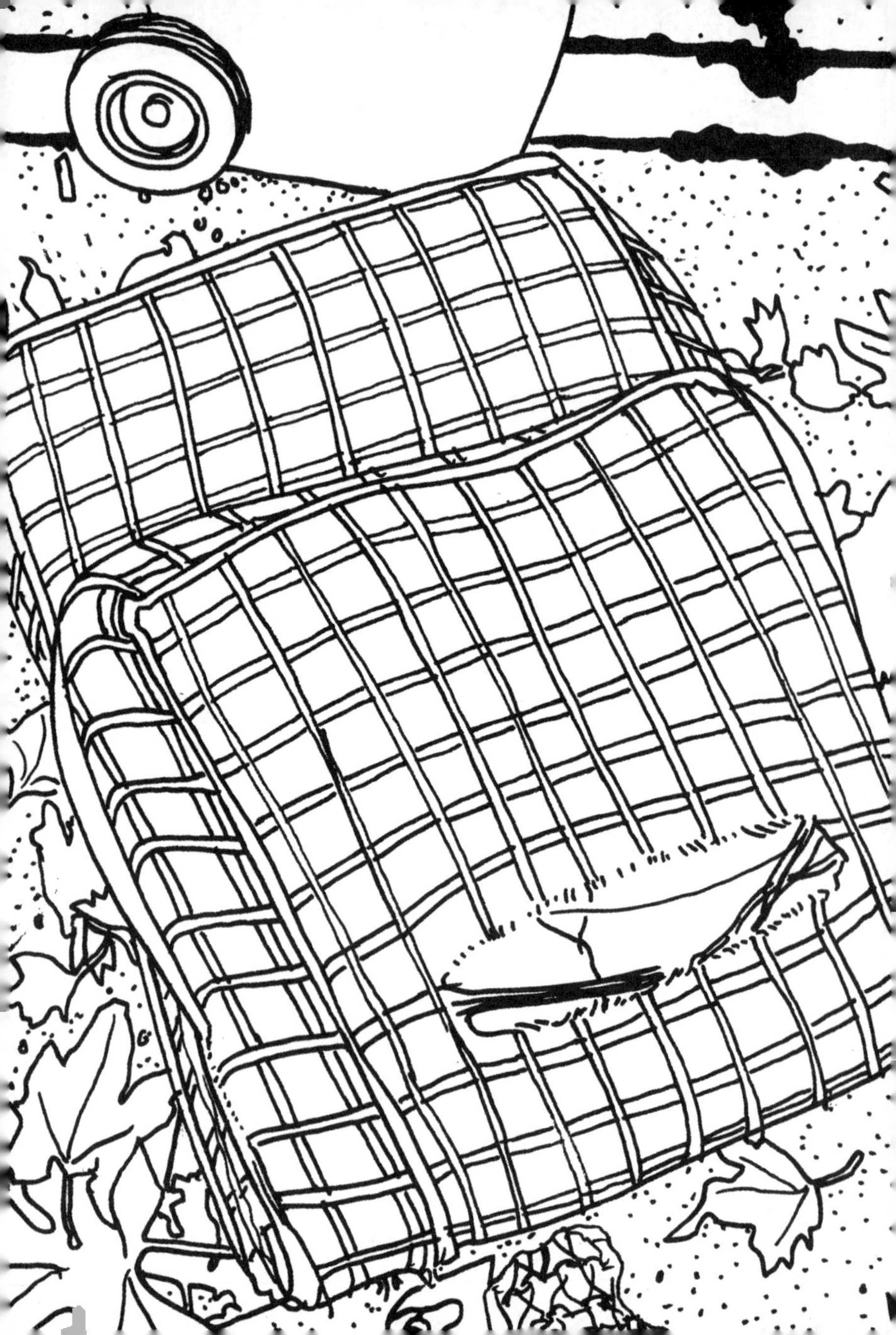

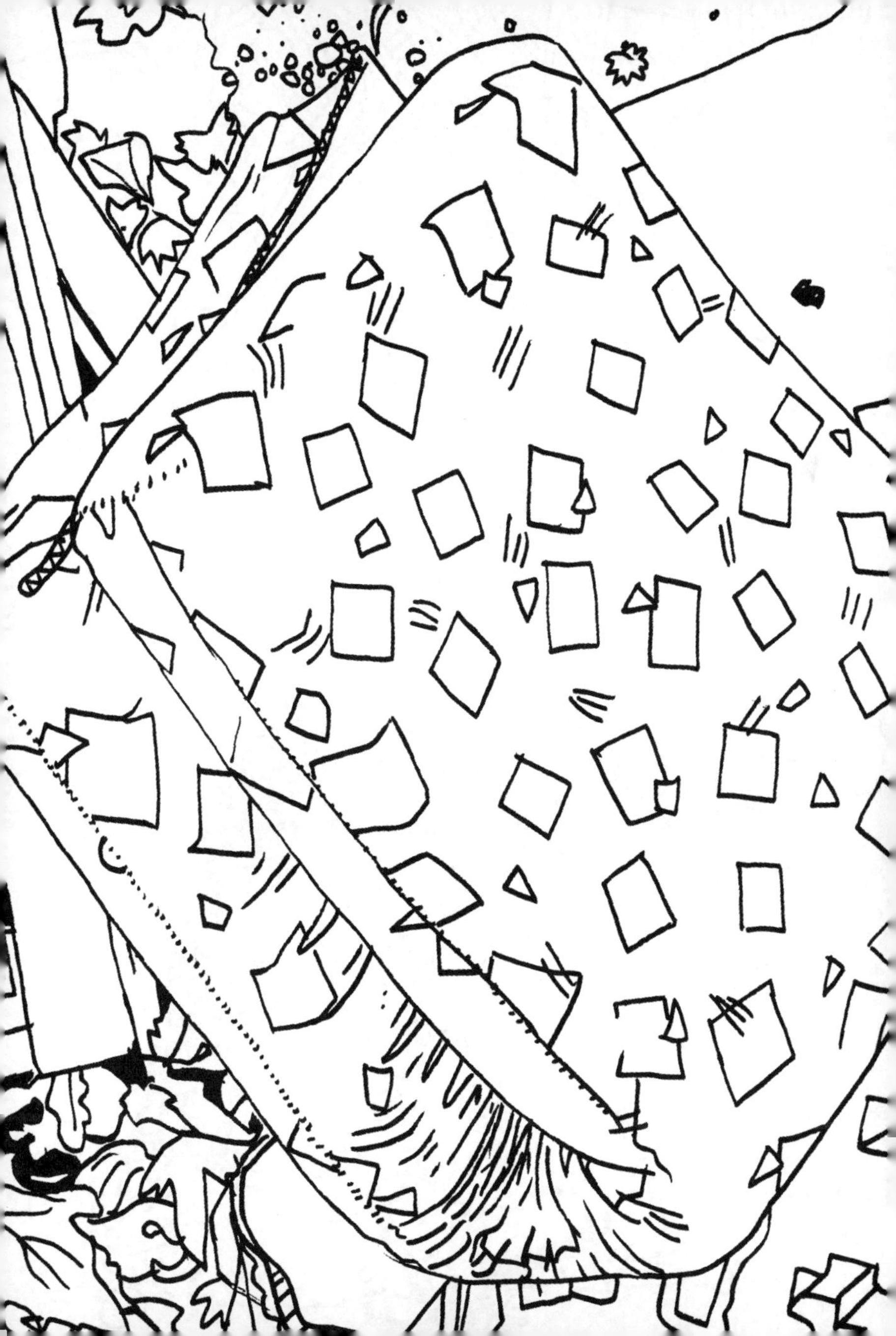

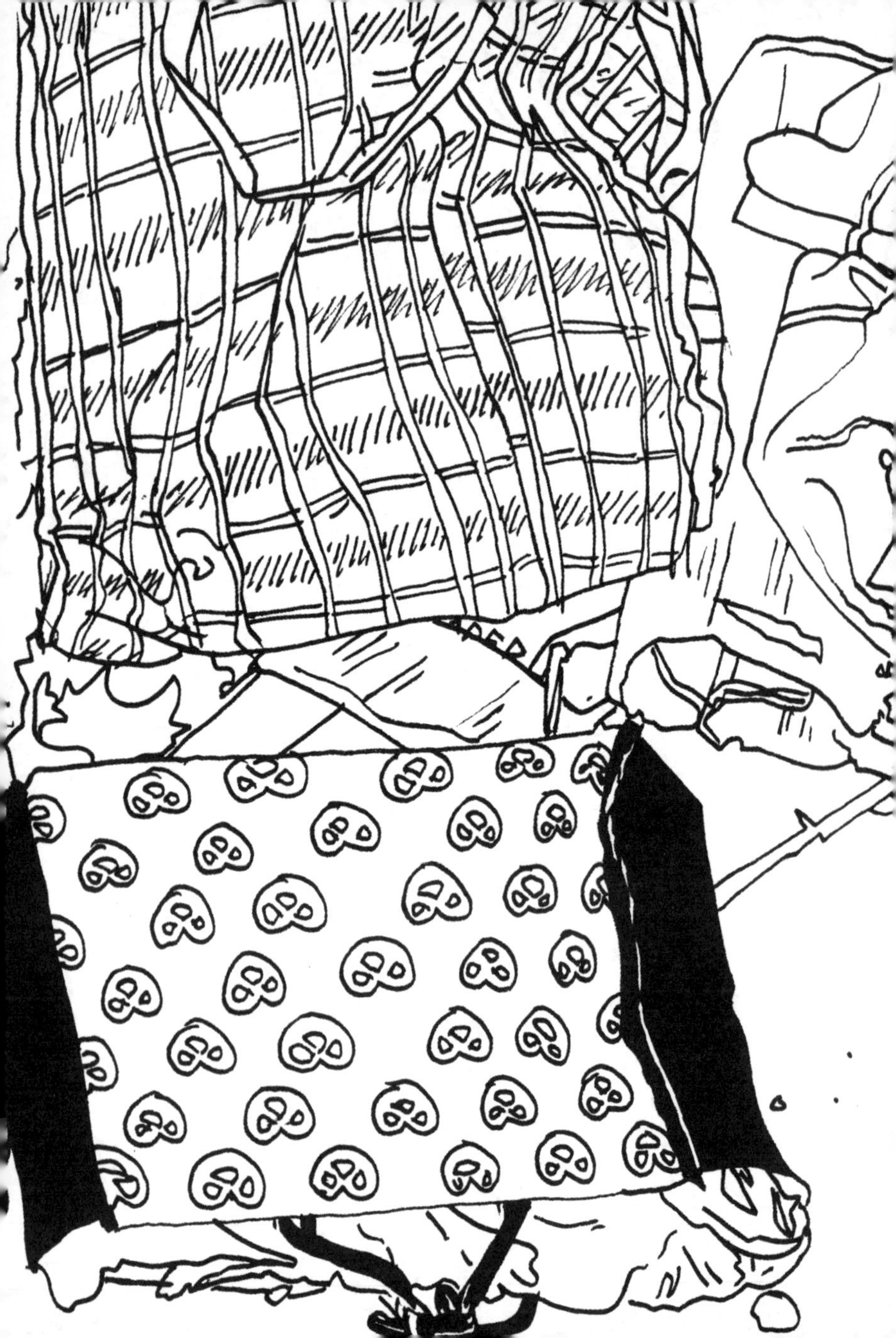

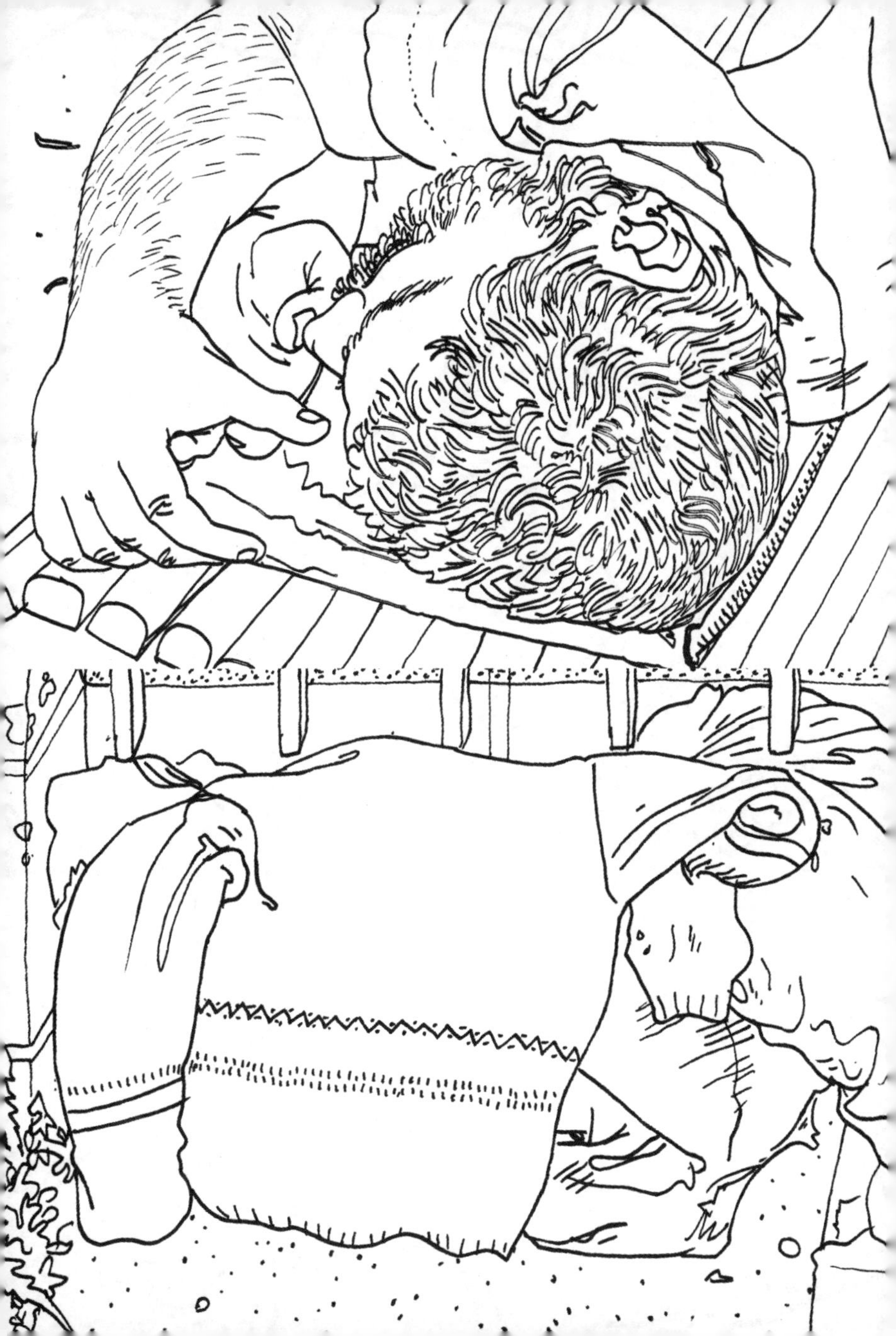

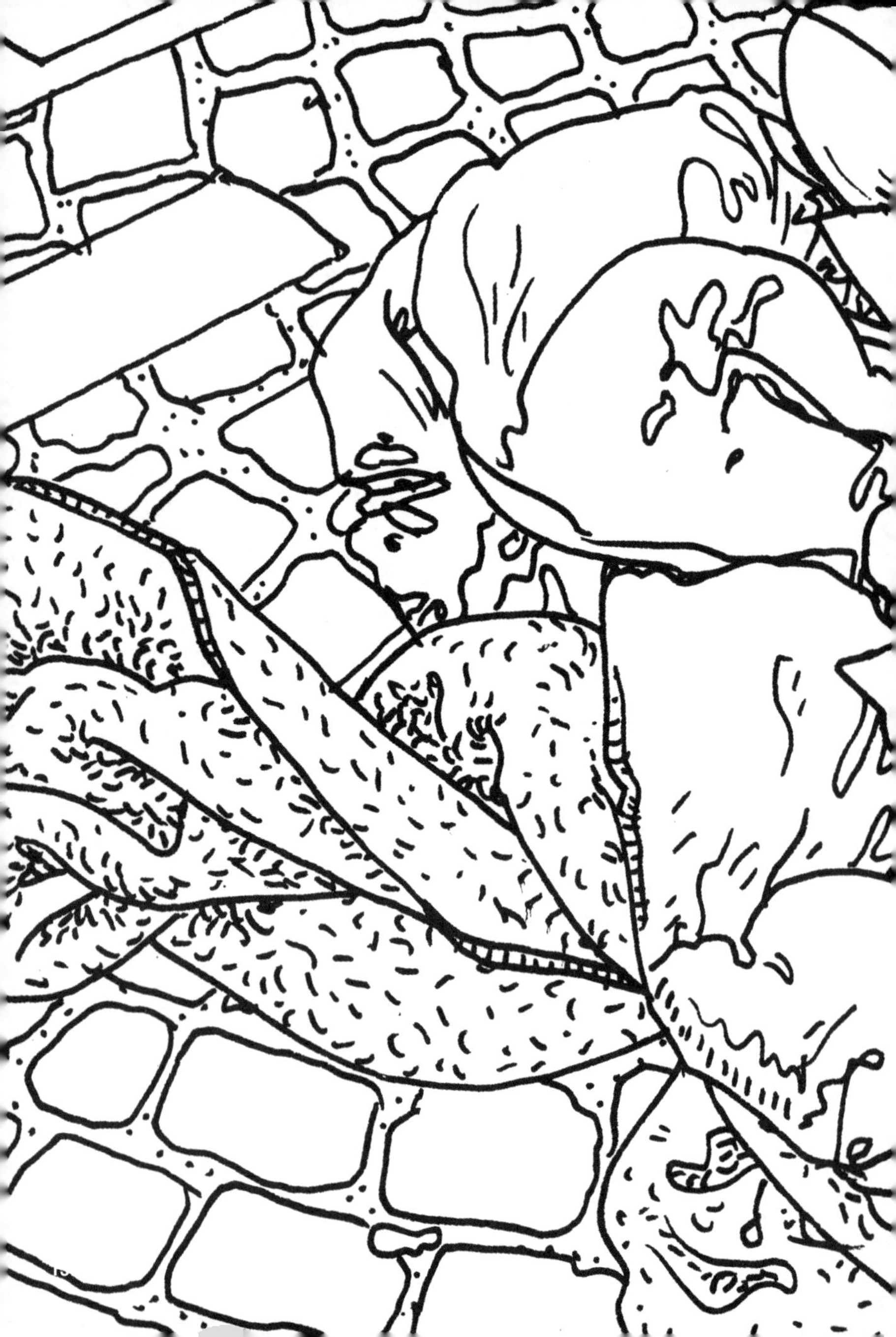

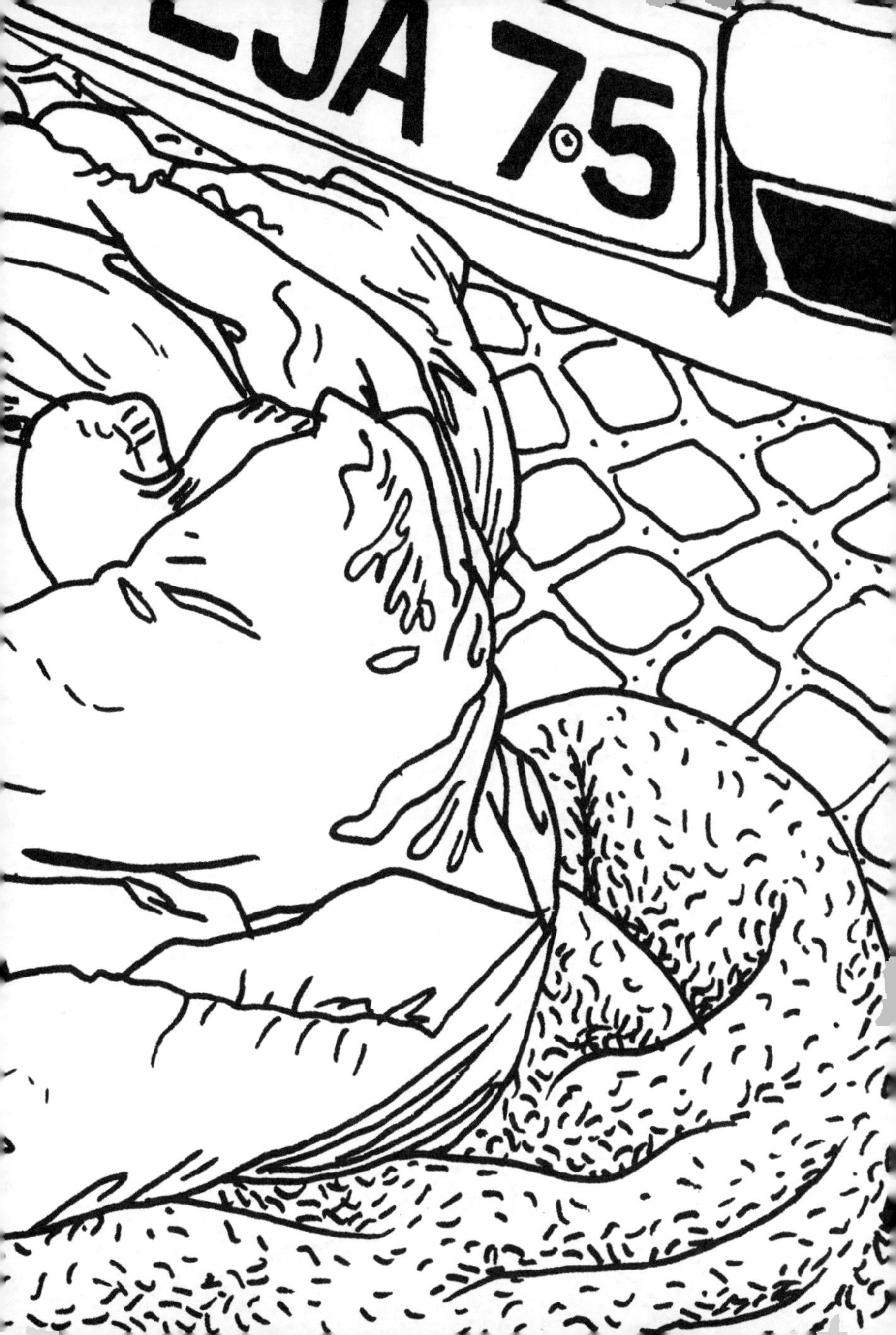
JA 75

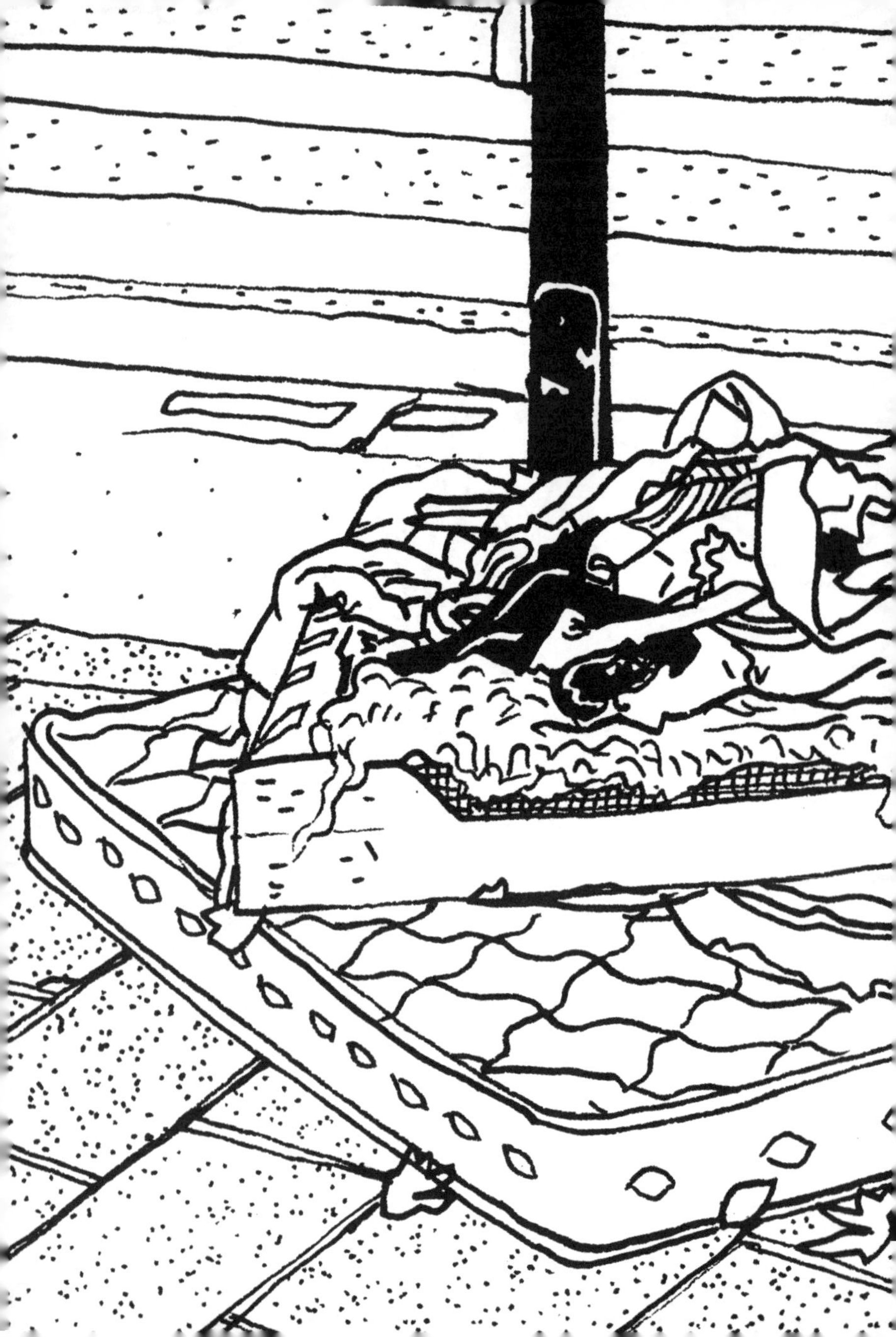

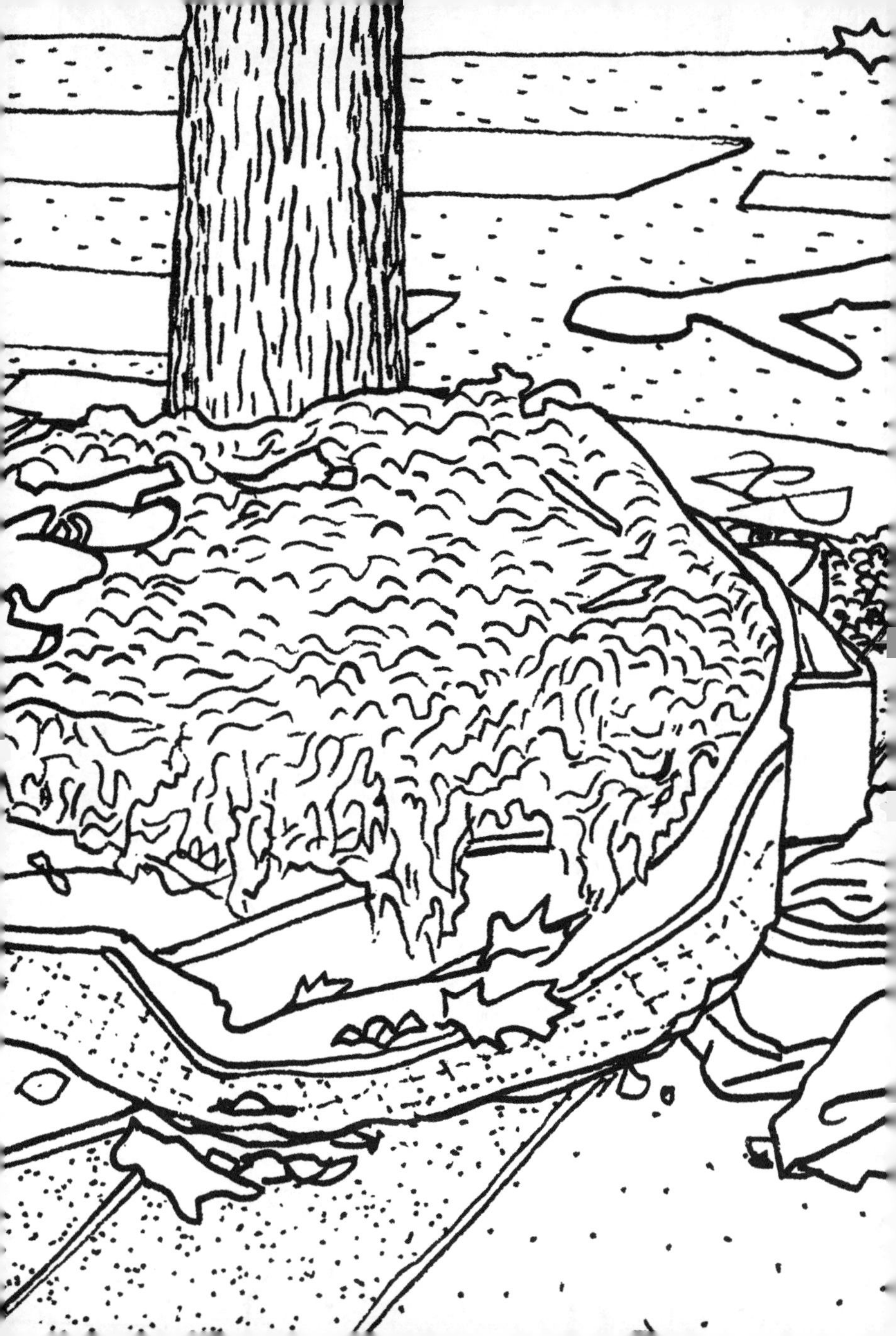

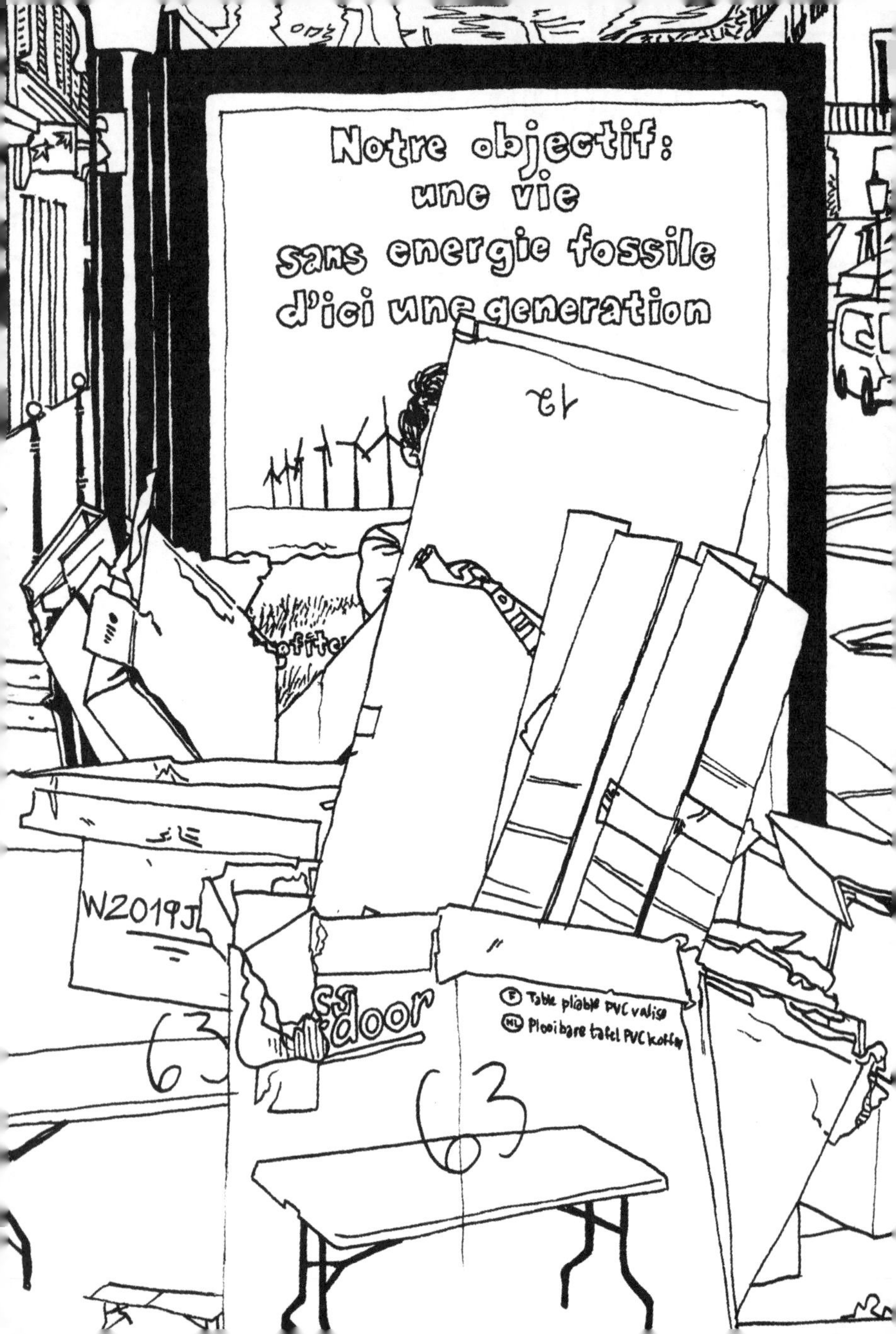
Notre objectif:
une vie
sans energie fossile
d'ici une generation
W2019J
door
Table pliable PVC valise
Plooibare tafel PVC koffer
63

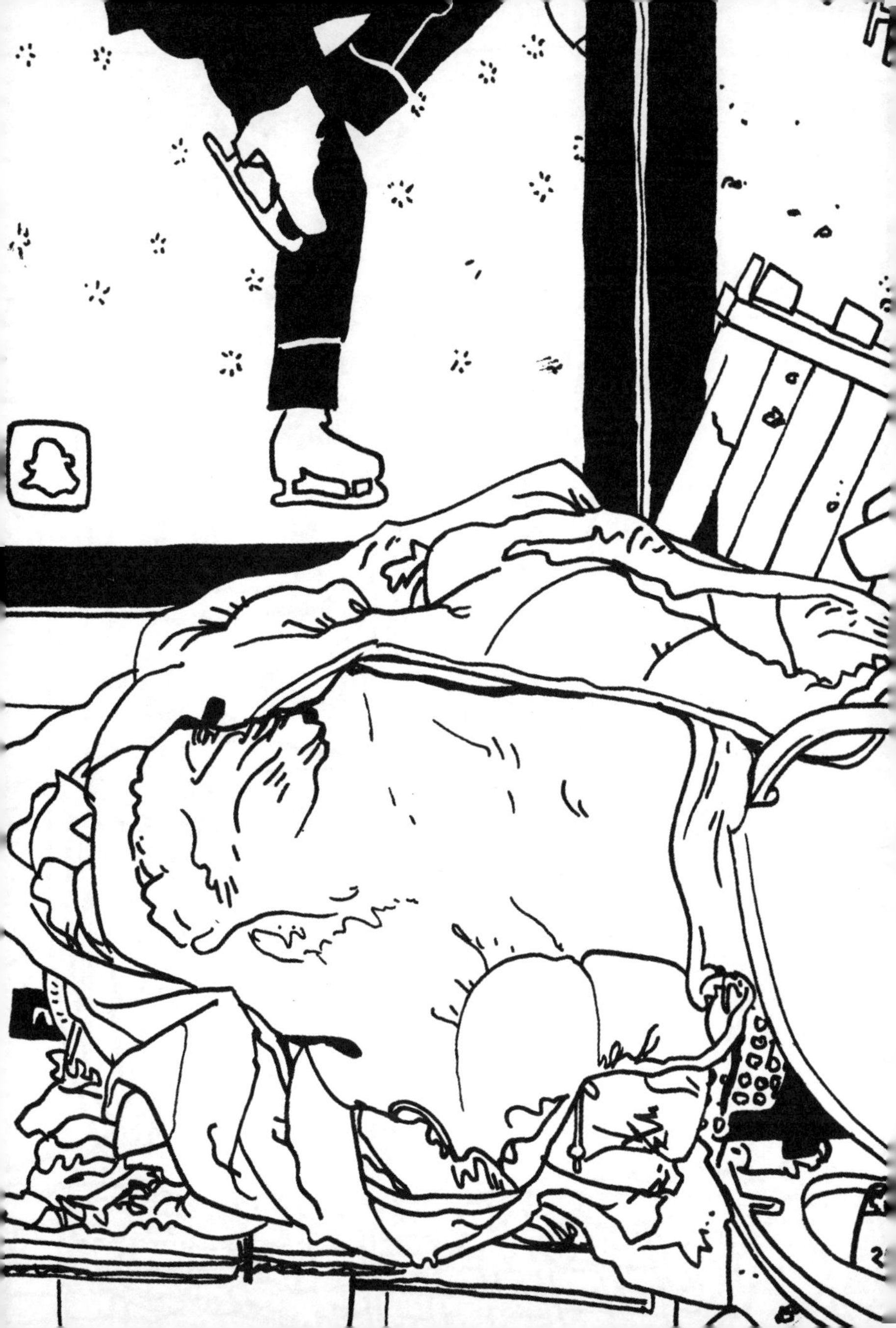

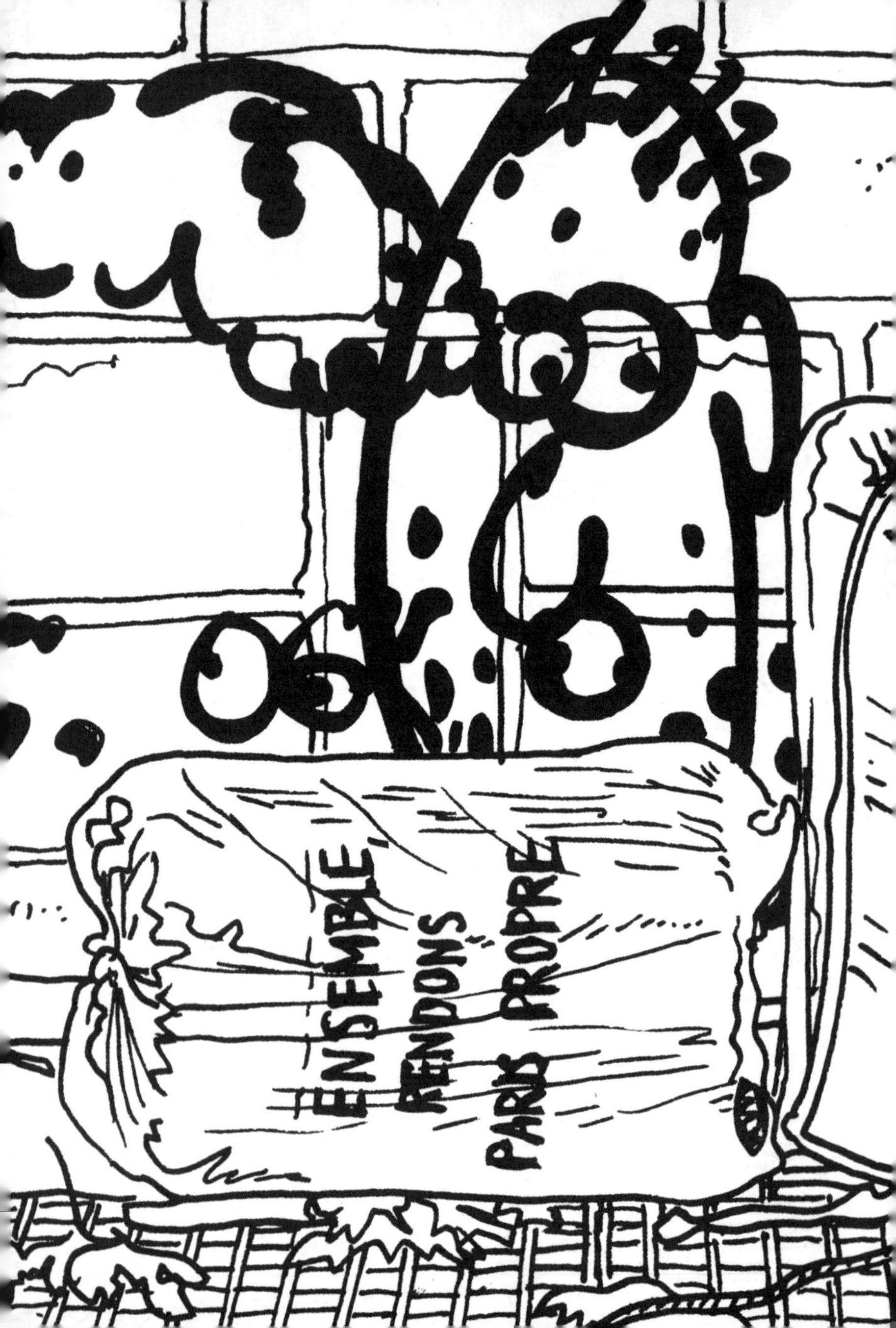
ENSEMBLE
RENDONS
PARIS PROPRE

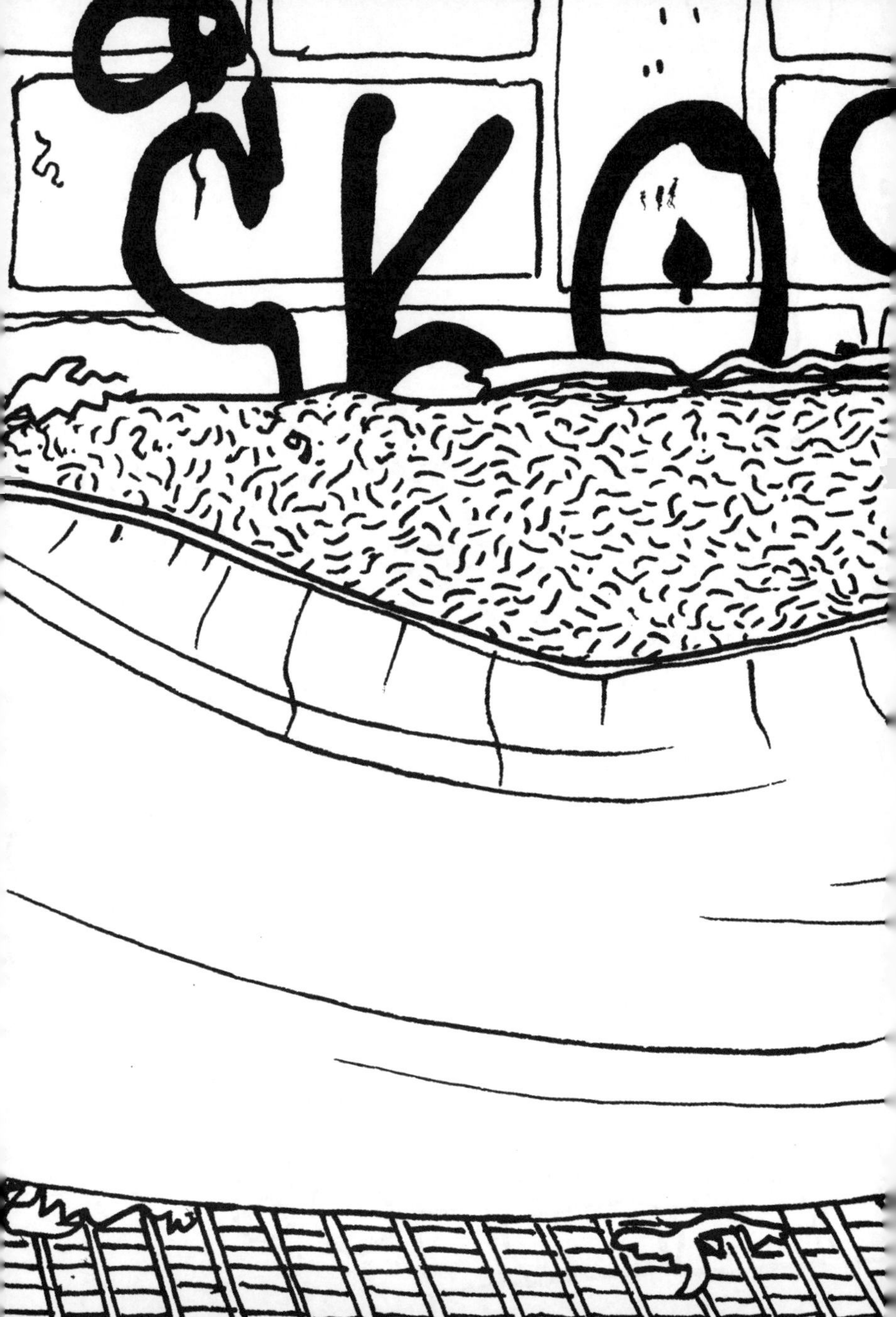

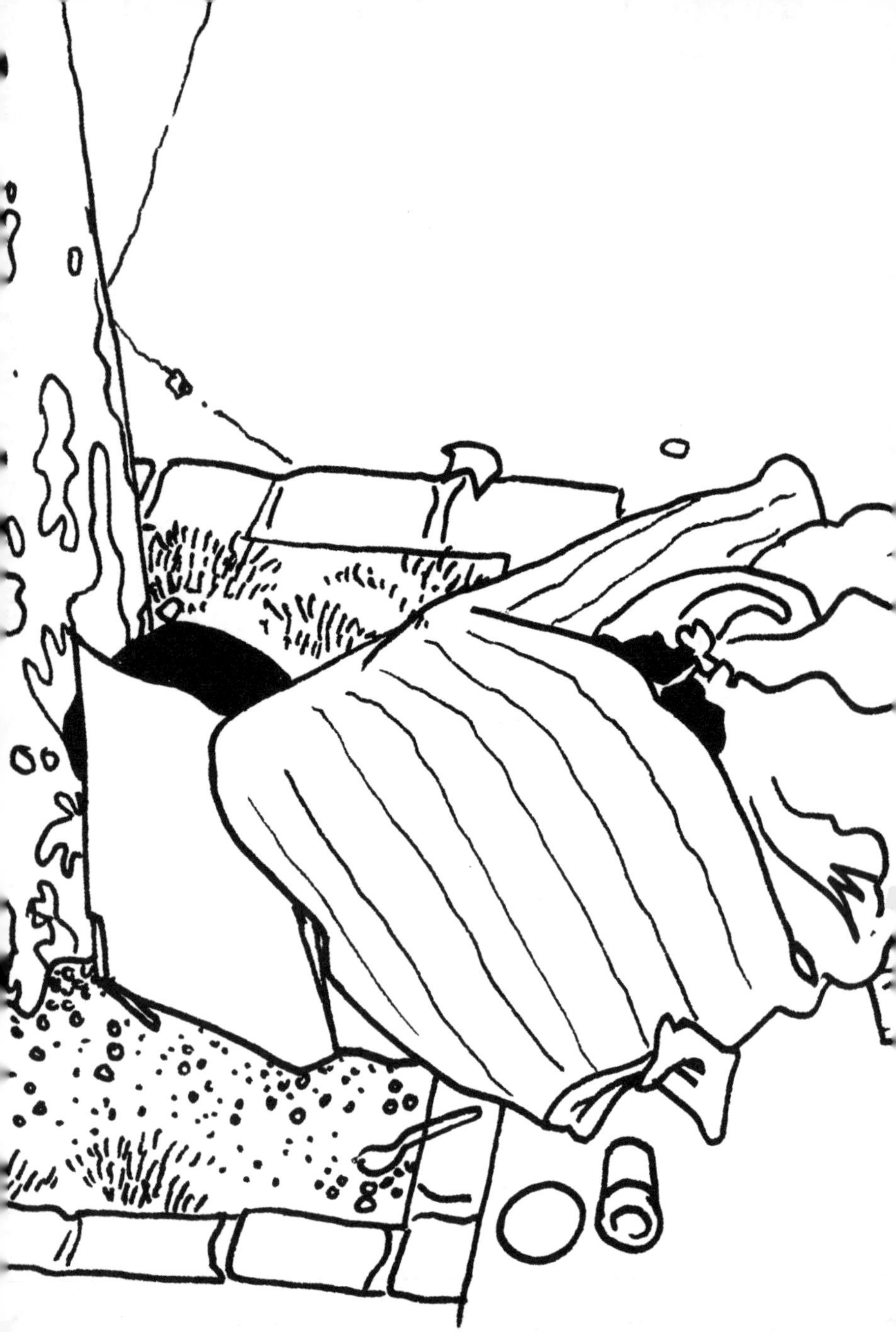

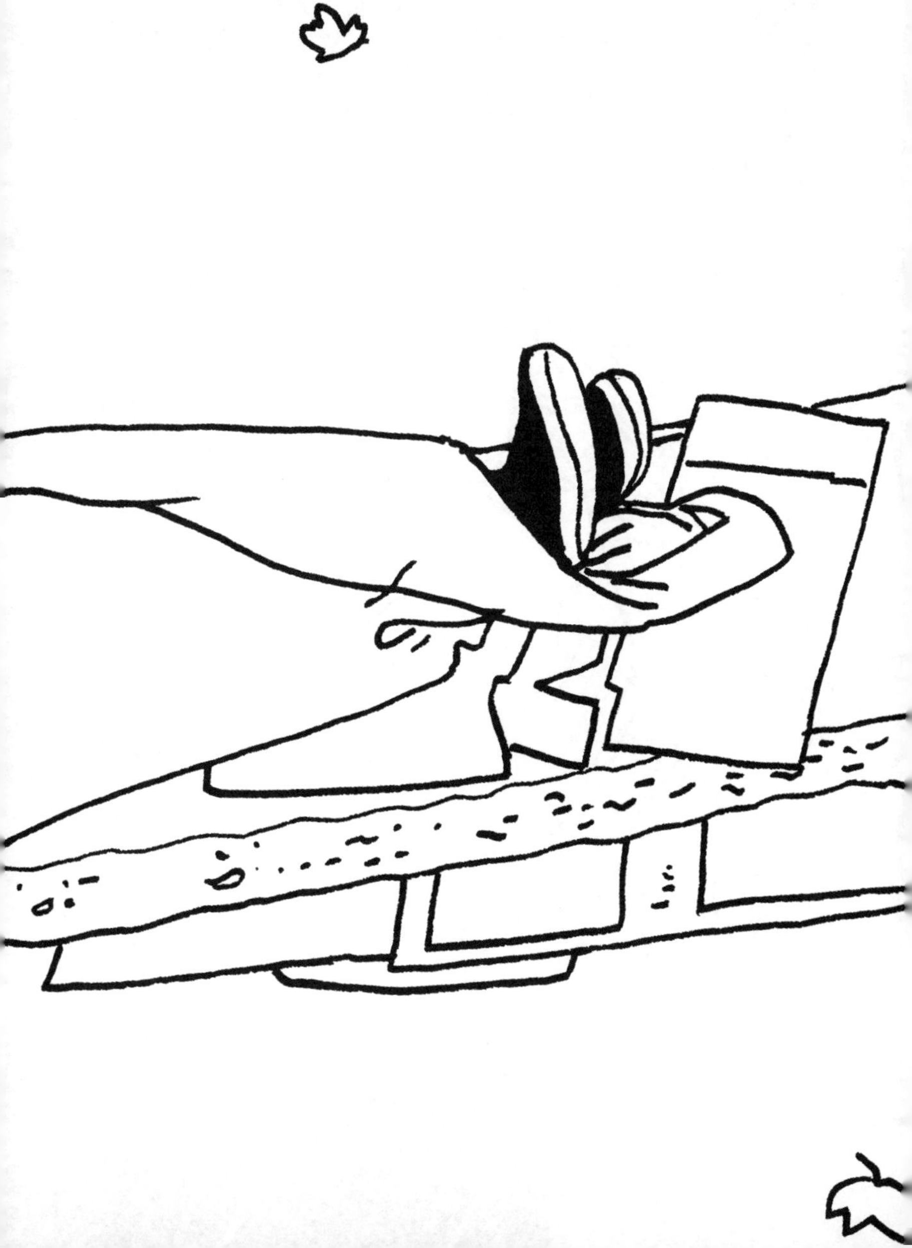

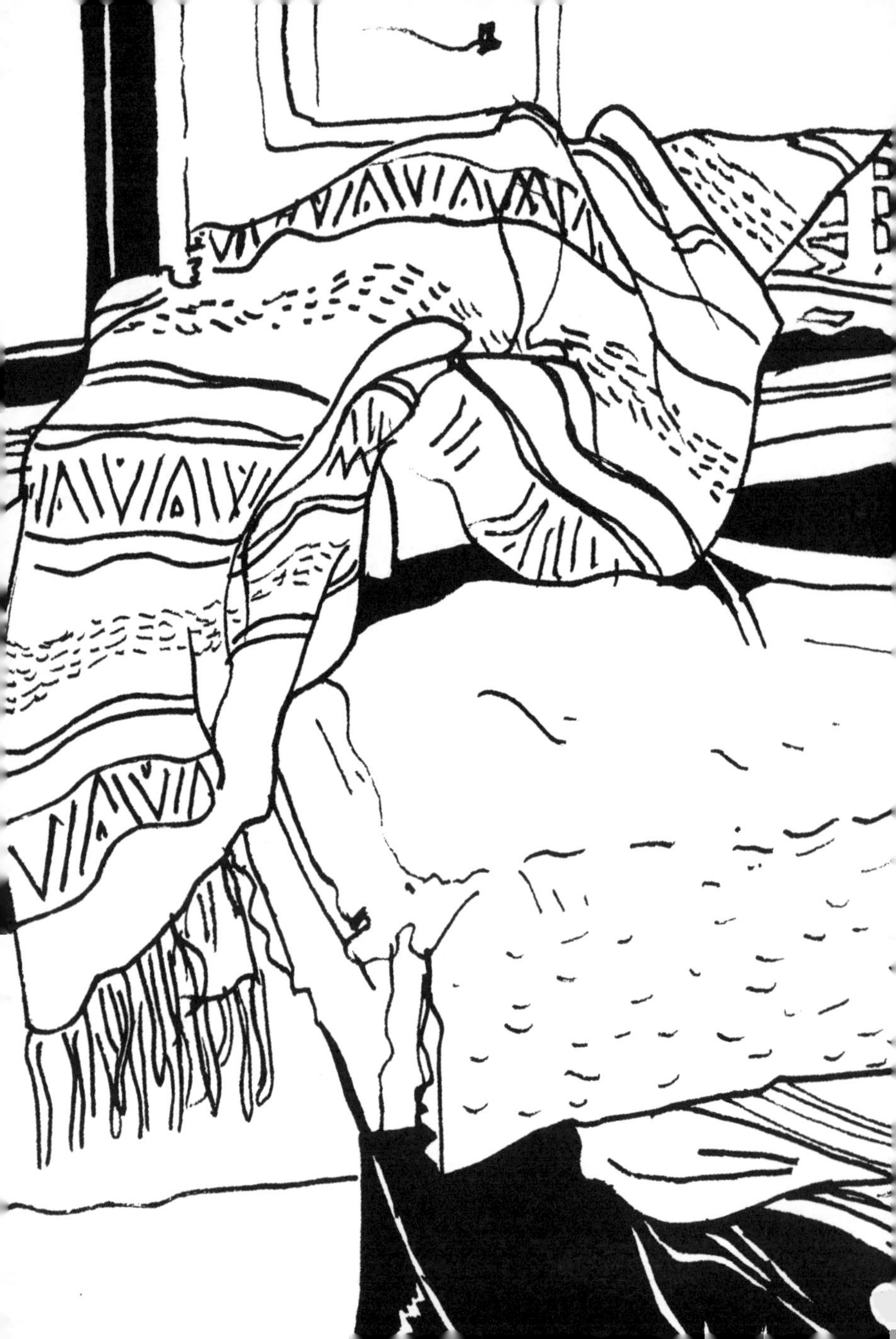

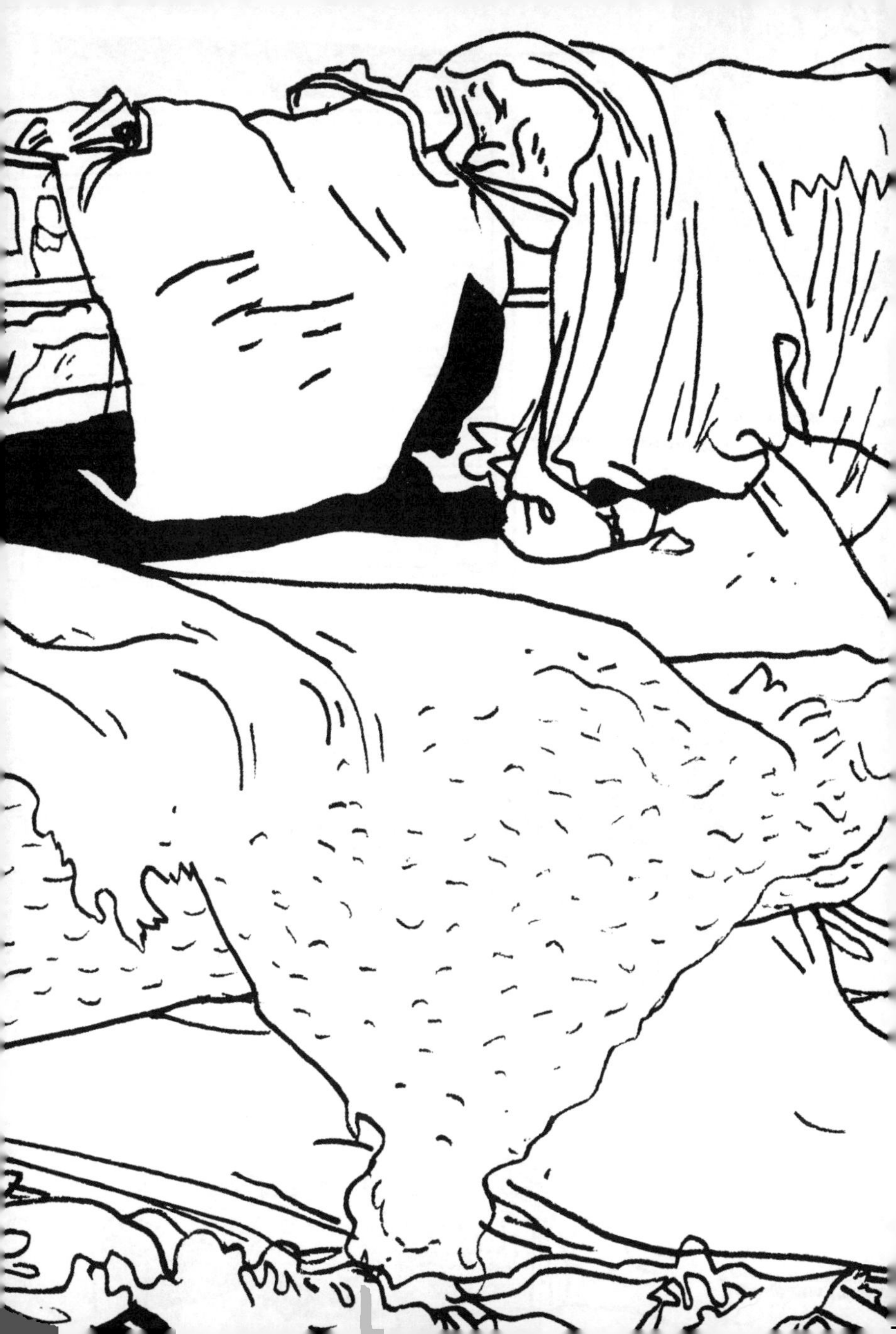

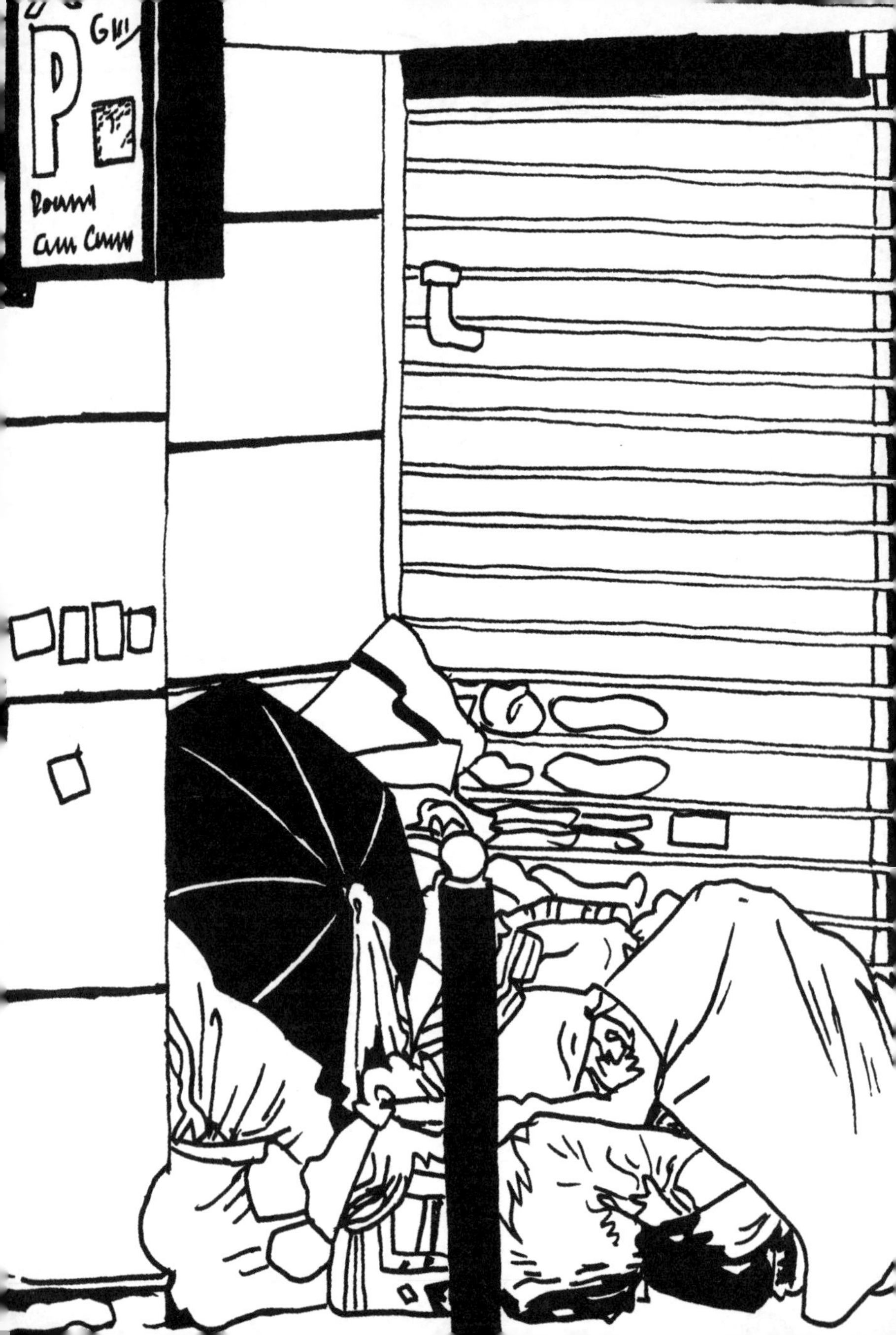

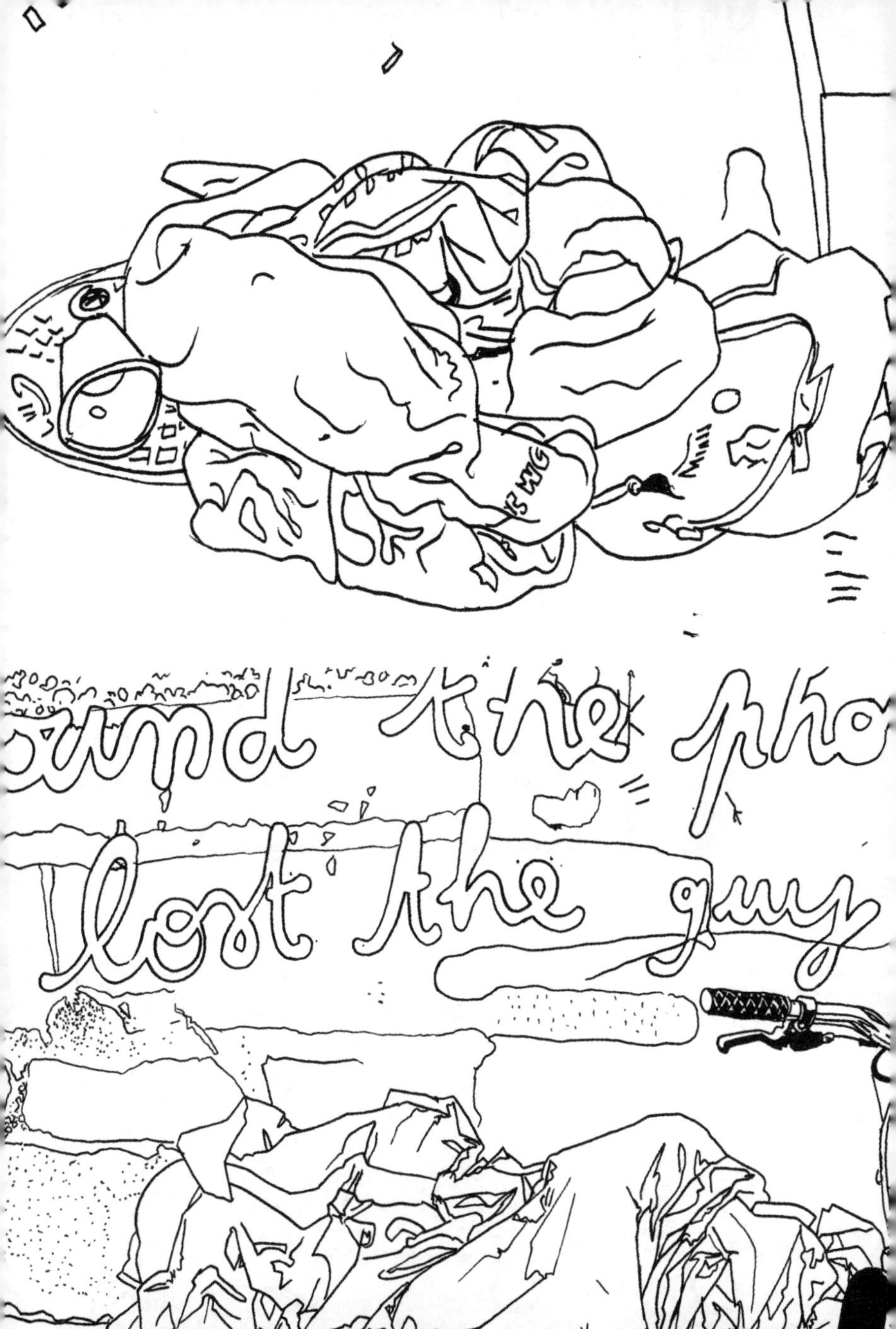

und the pho
lost the guy

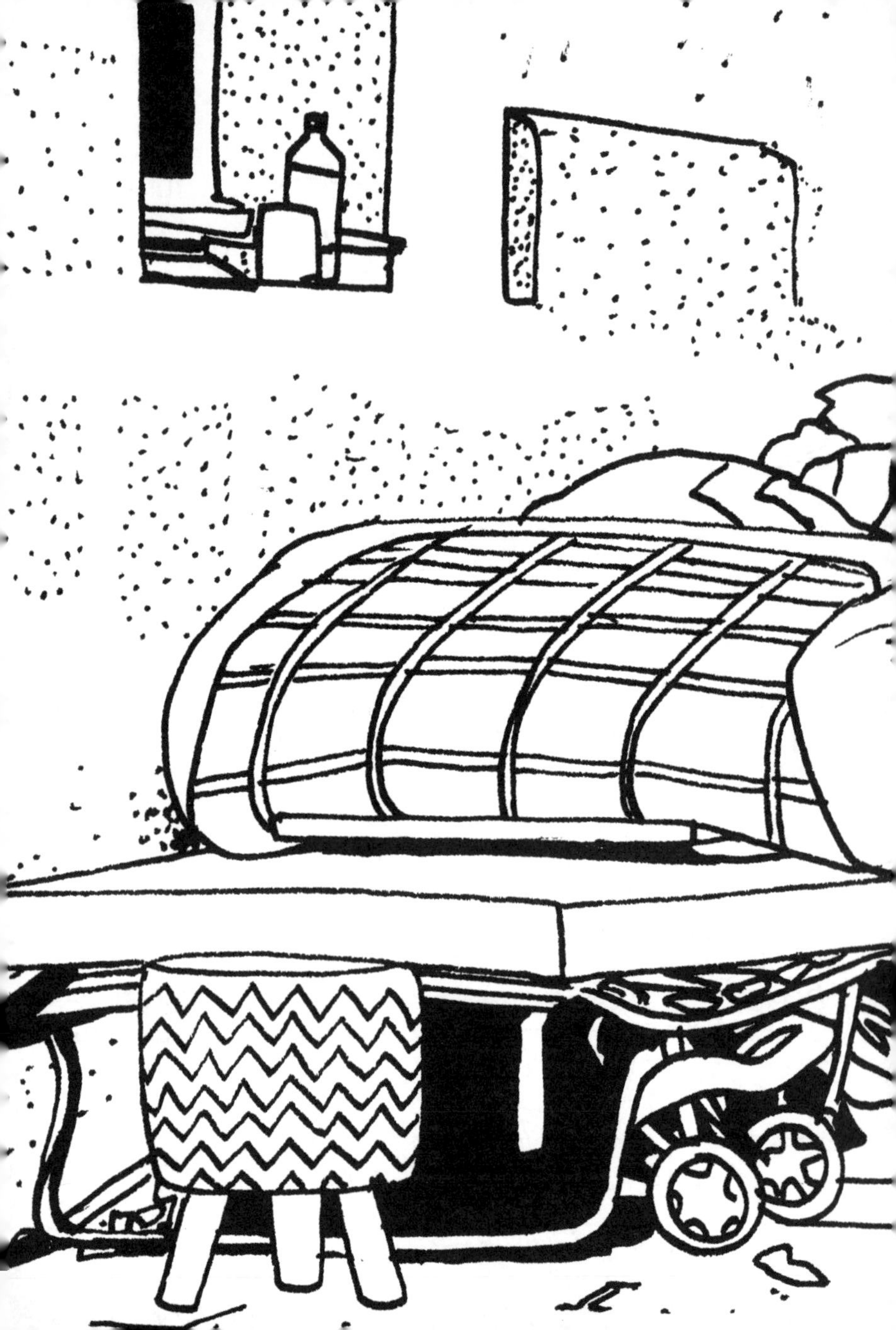

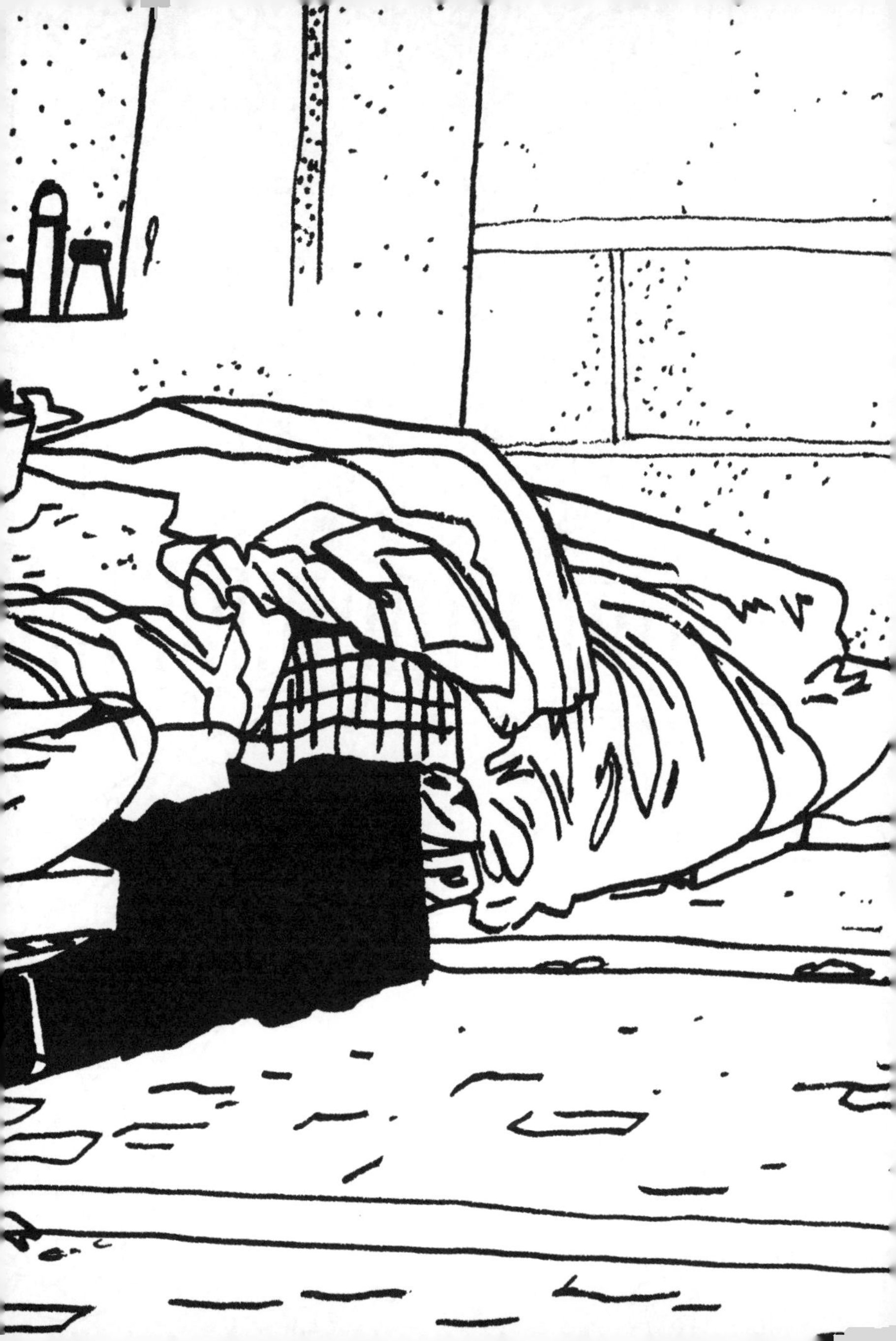

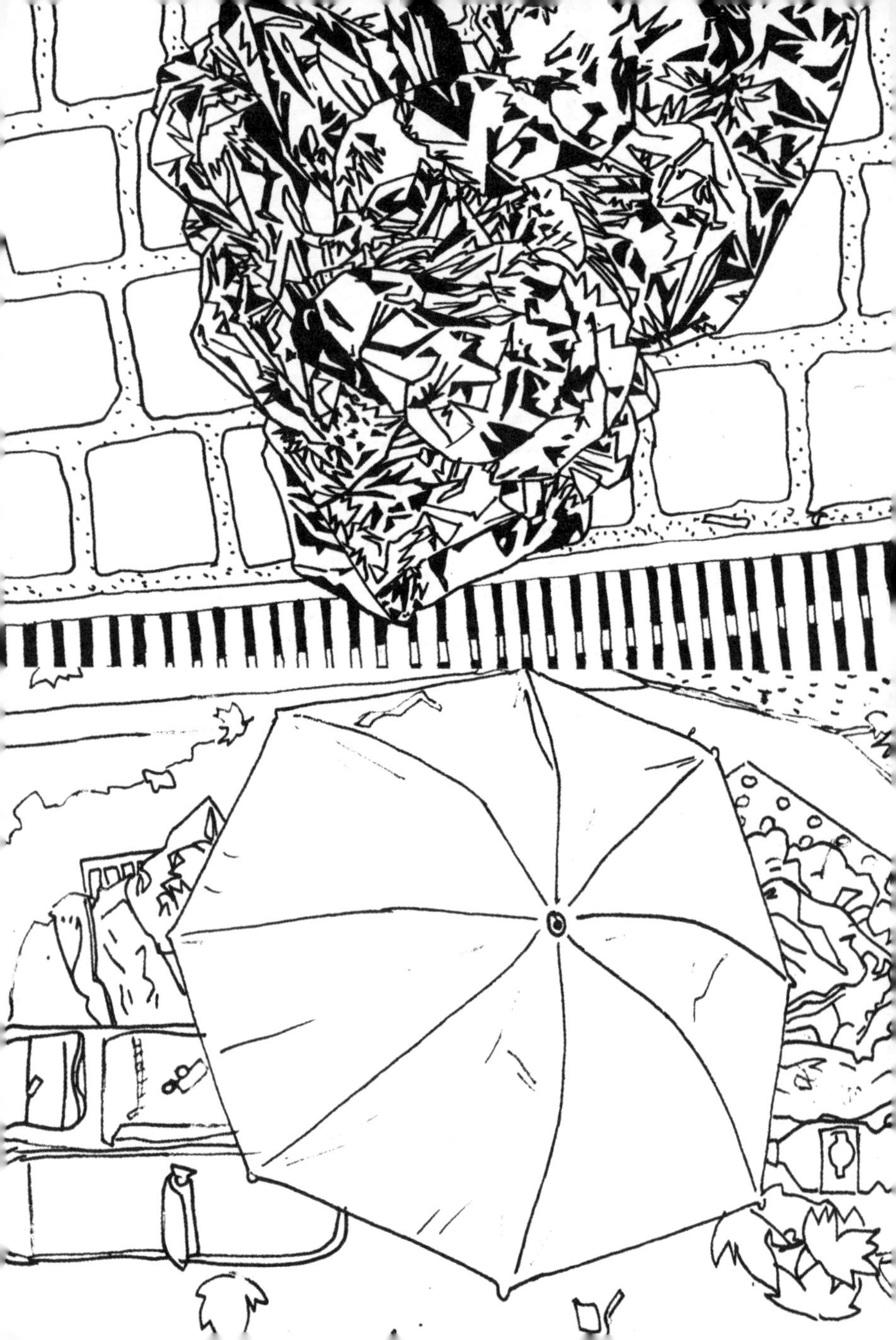

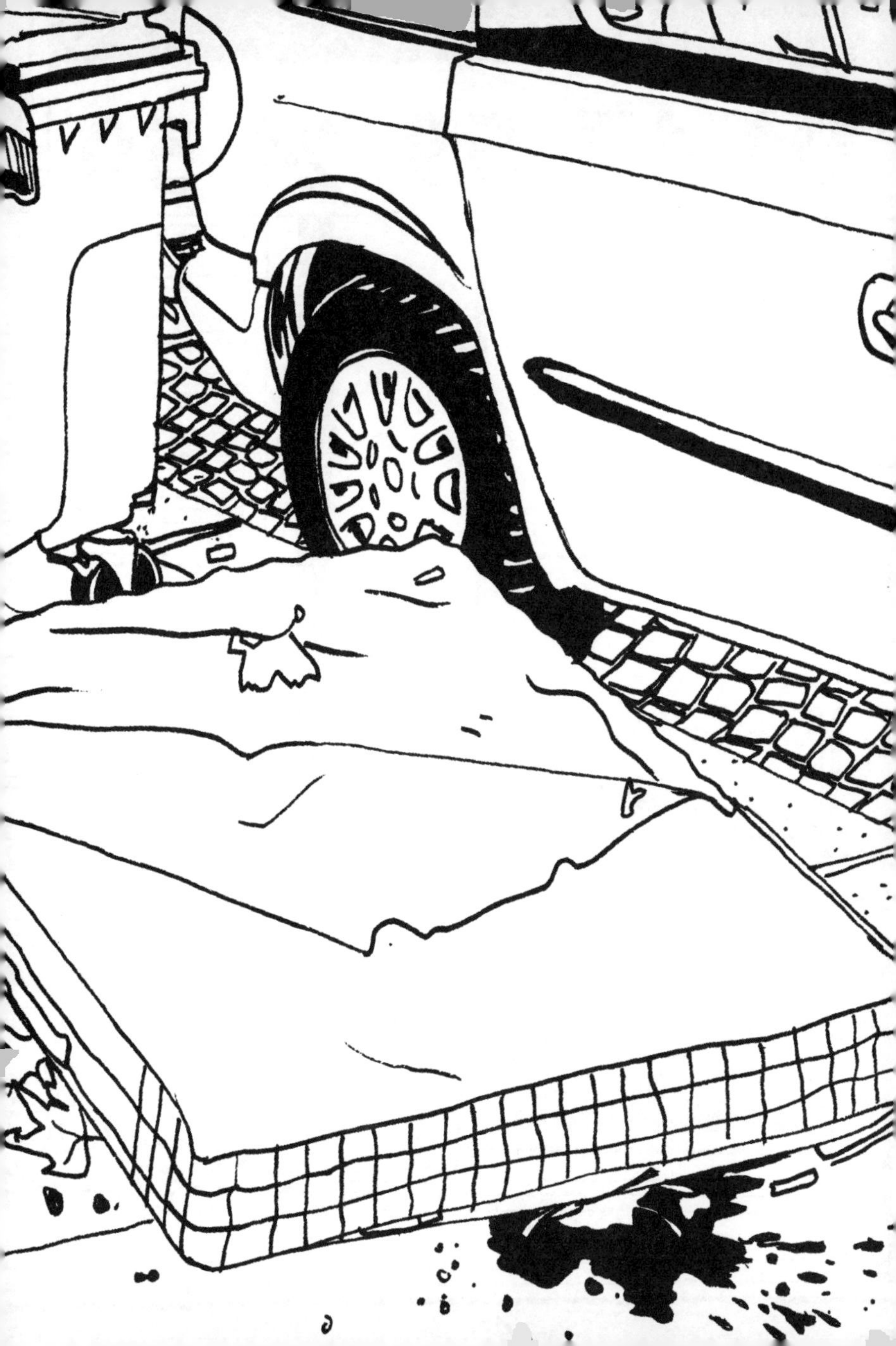

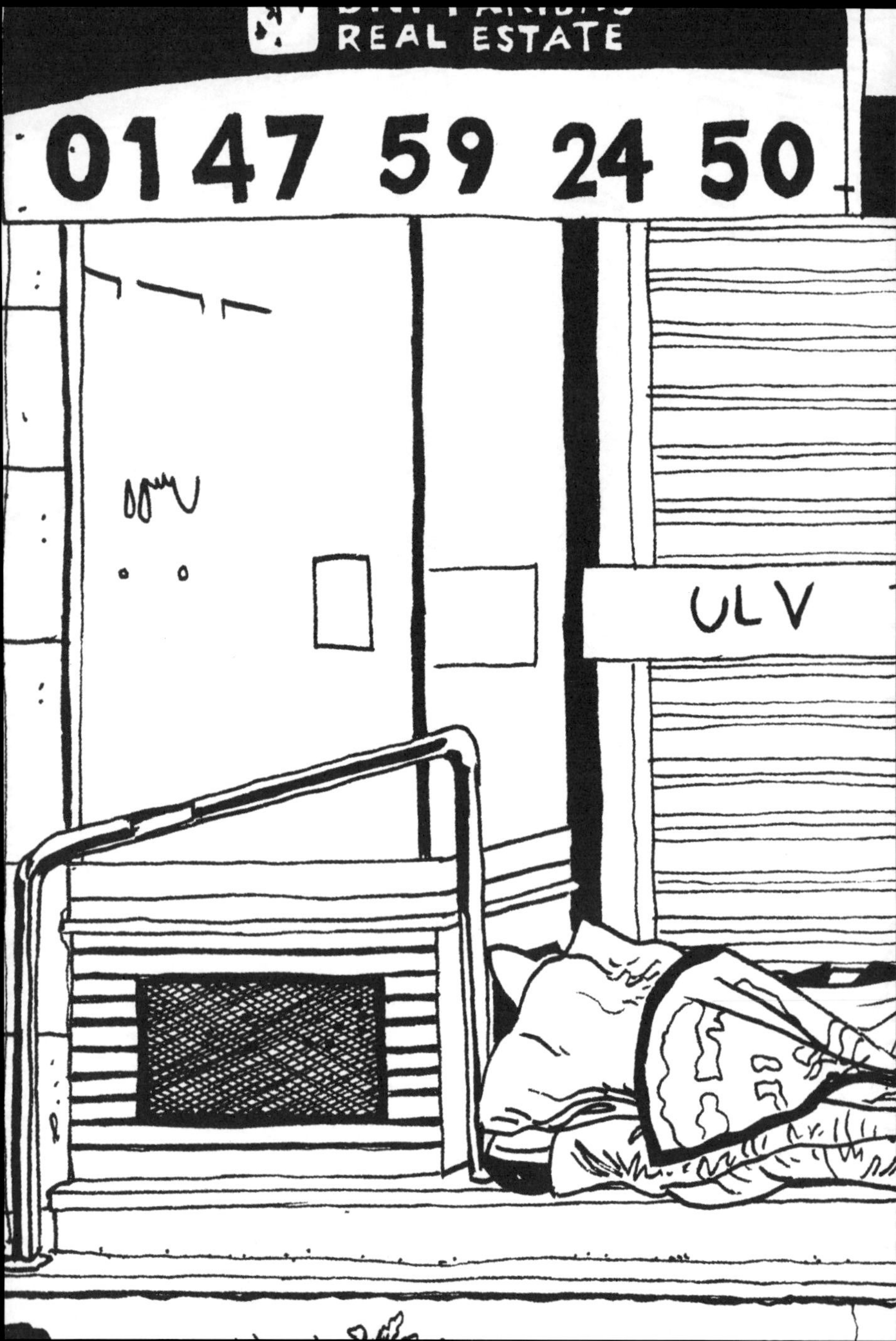

REAL ESTATE
01 47 59 24 50
ULV

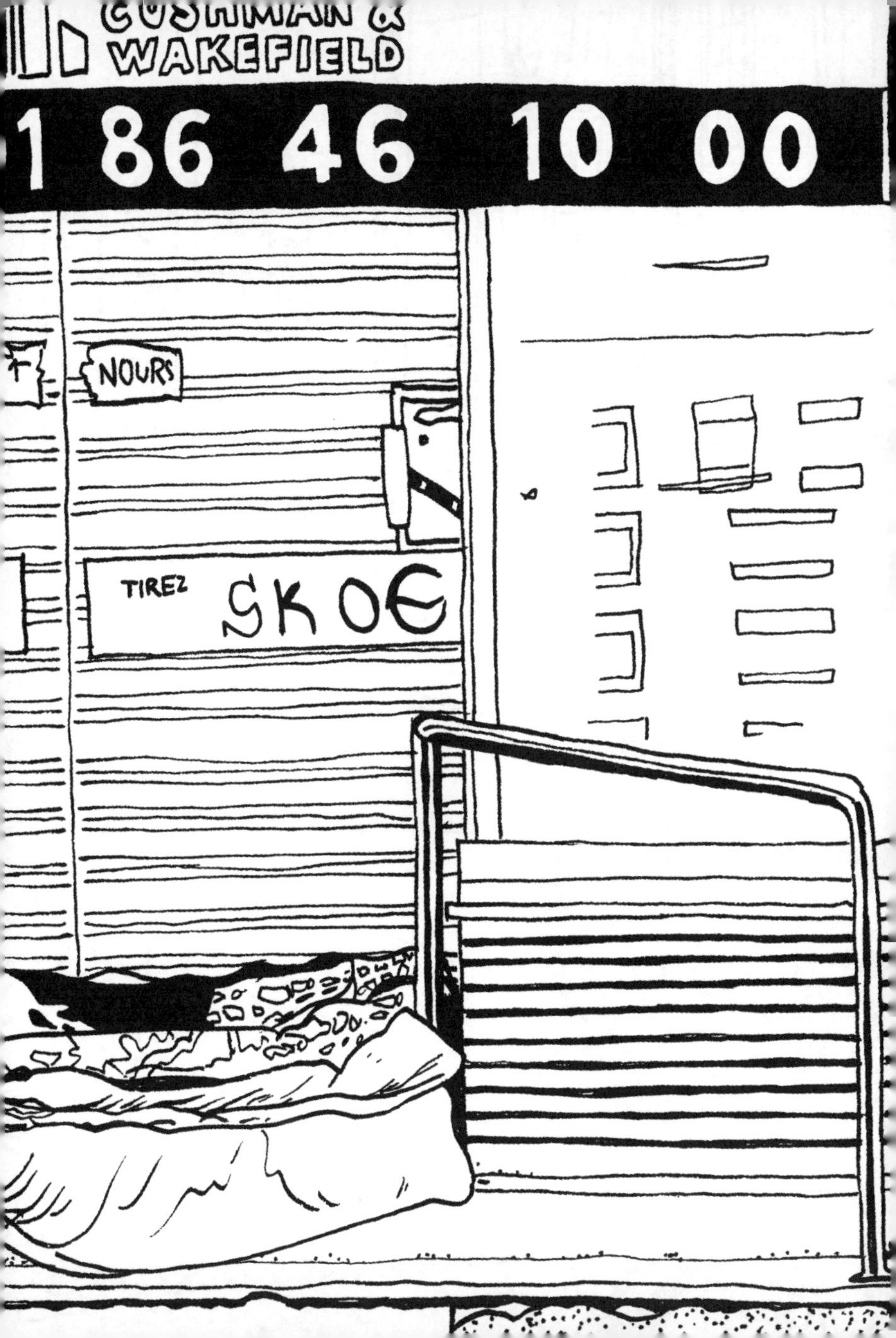

CUSHMAN &
WAKEFIELD
1 86 46 10 00
NOURS
TIREZ
SKOE

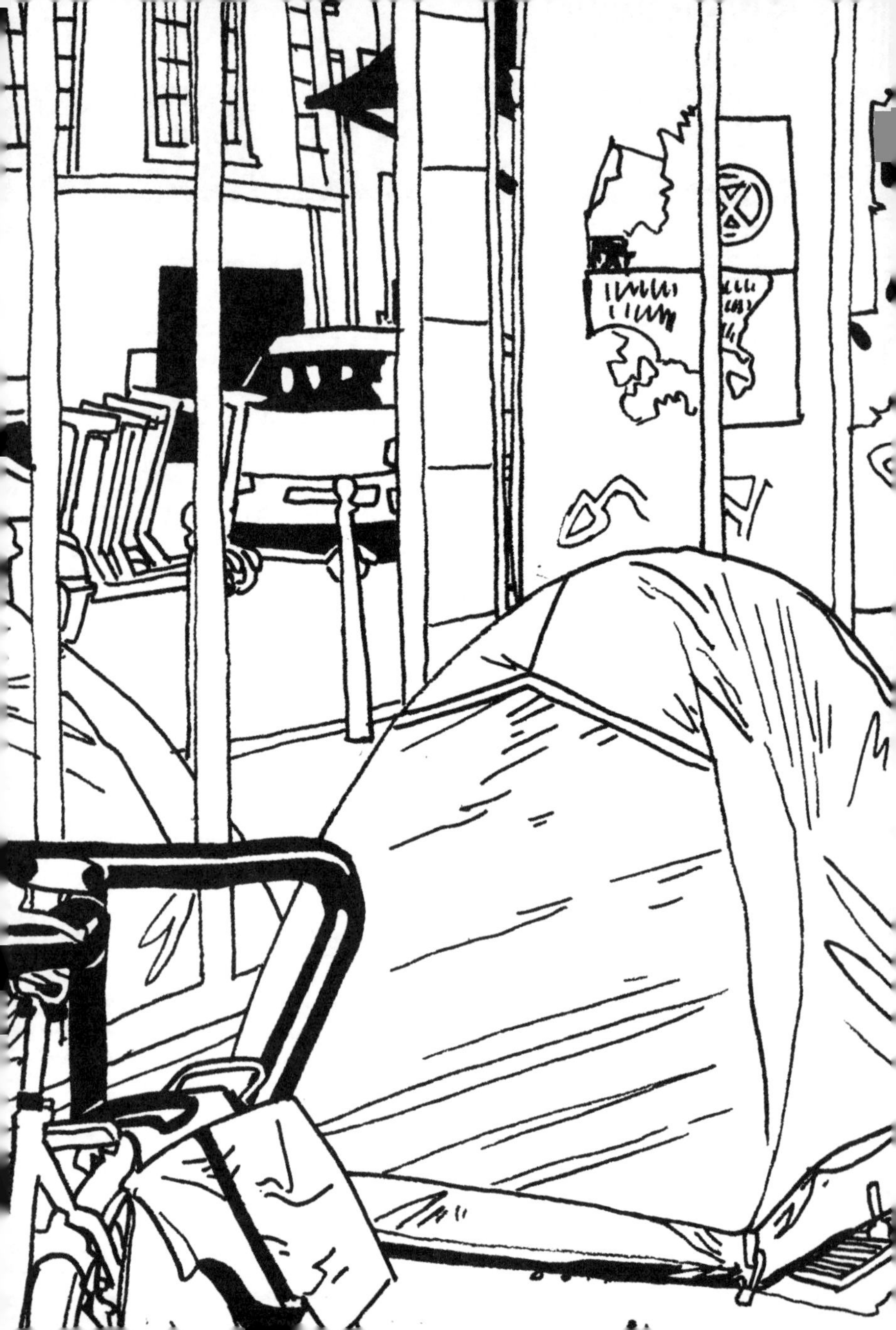

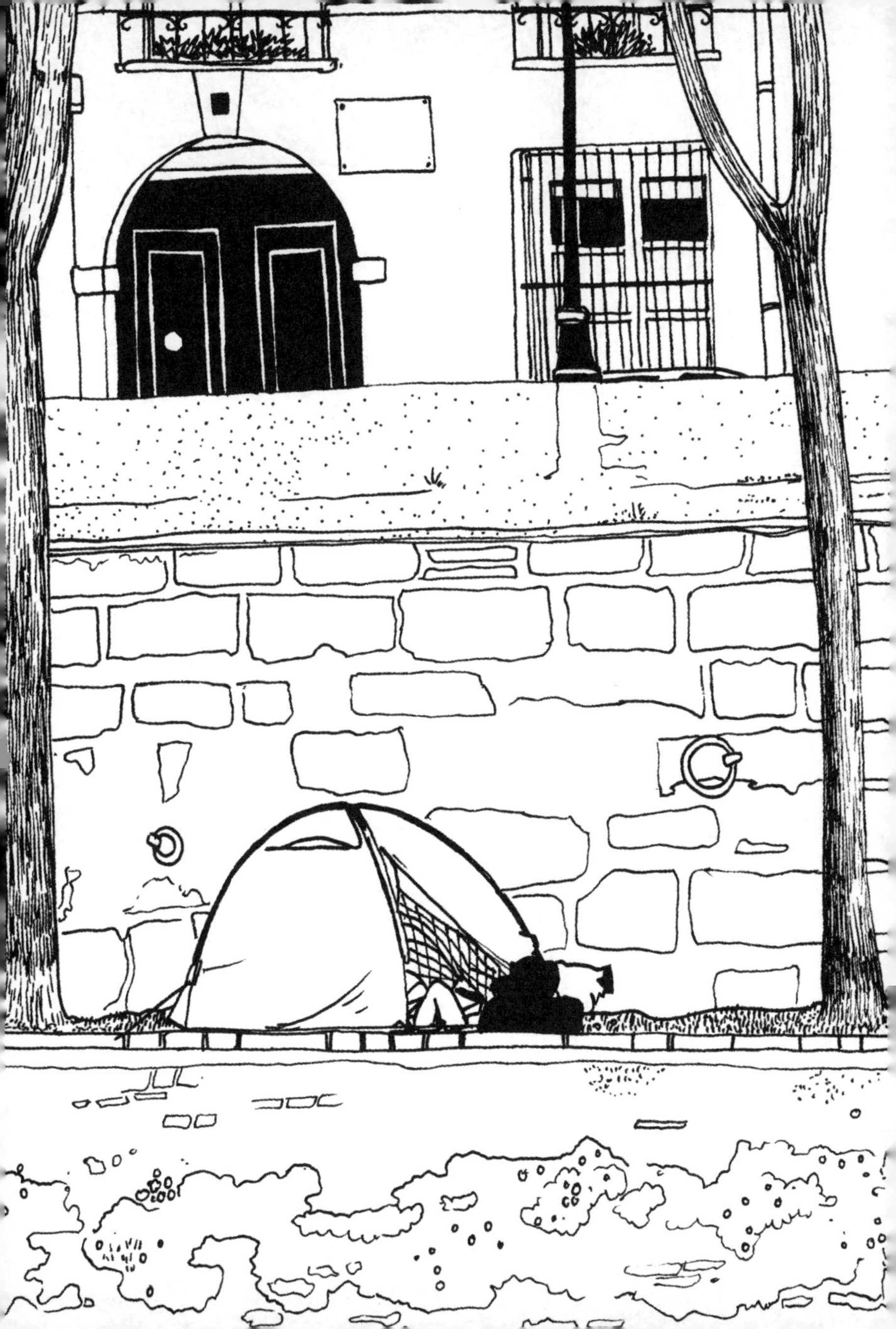

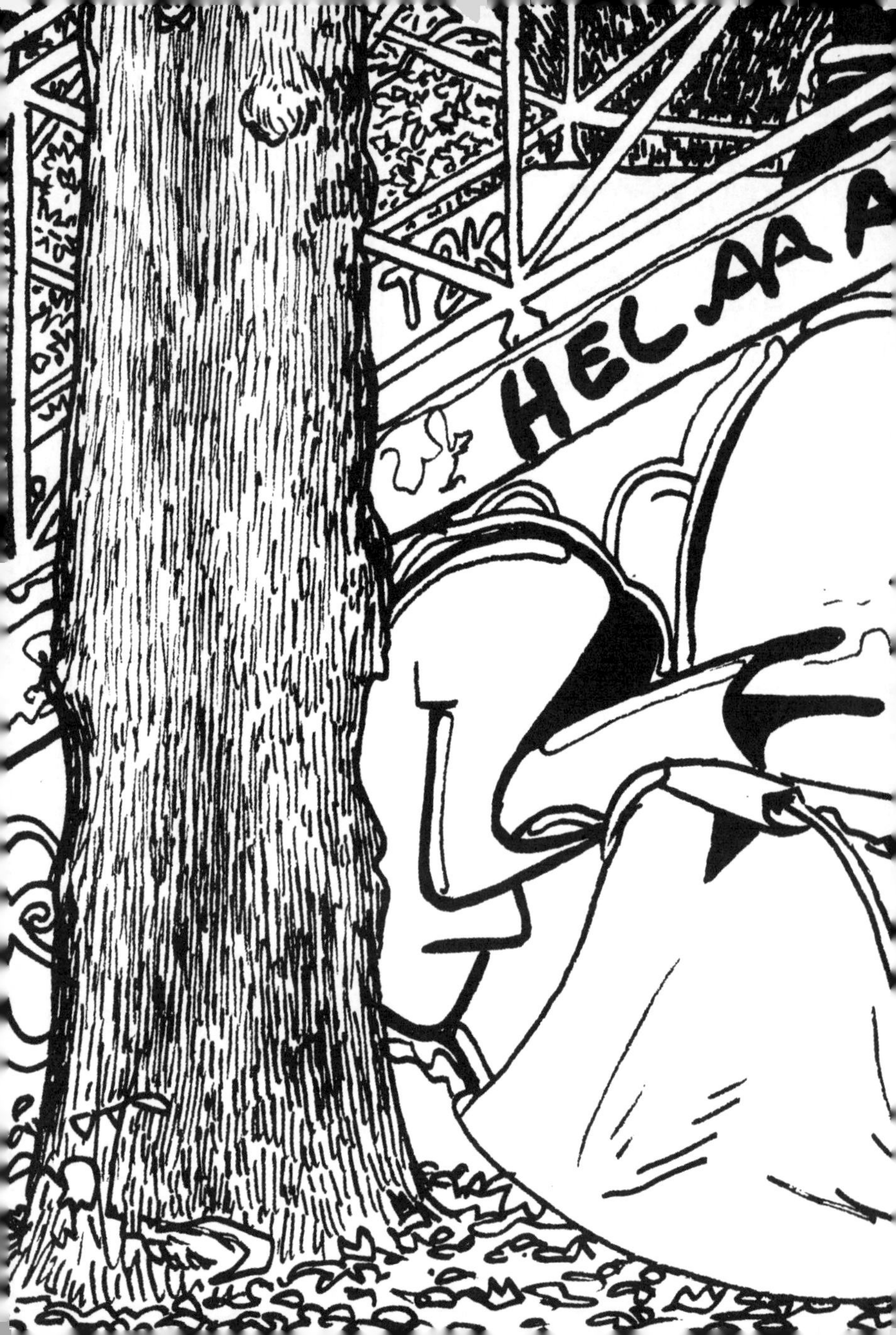
HEL.AAA

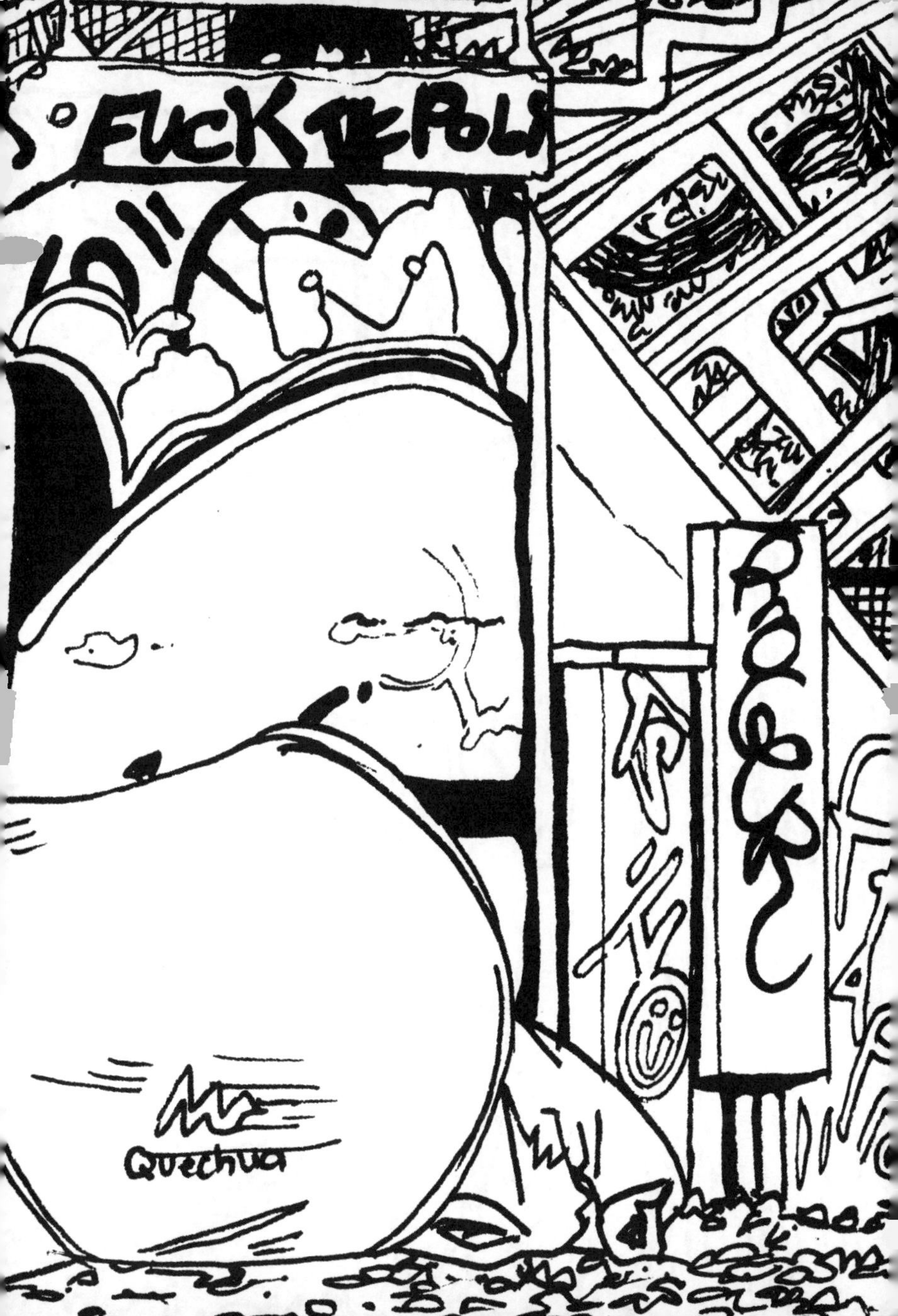
FUCK DE POLI
Quechua

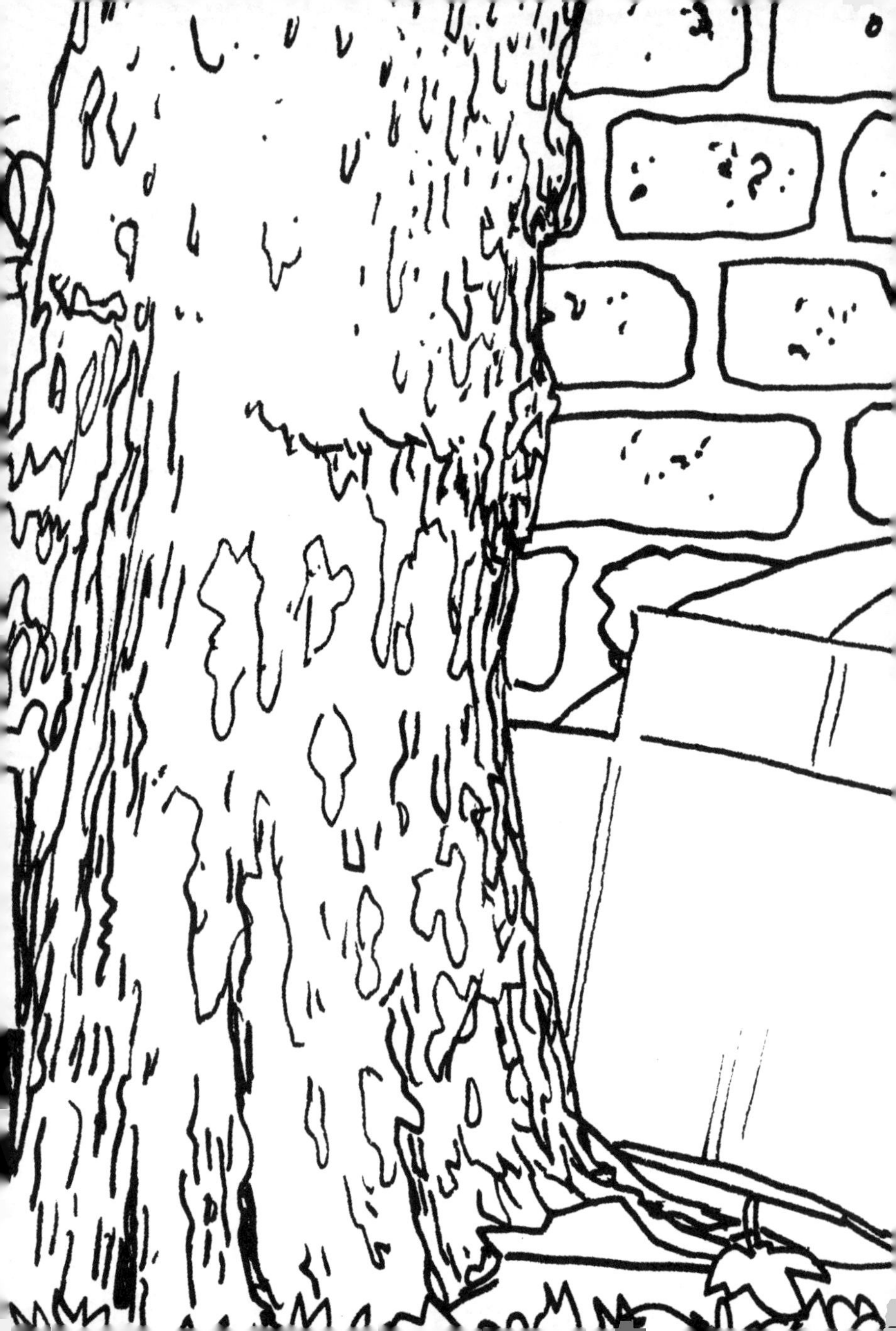

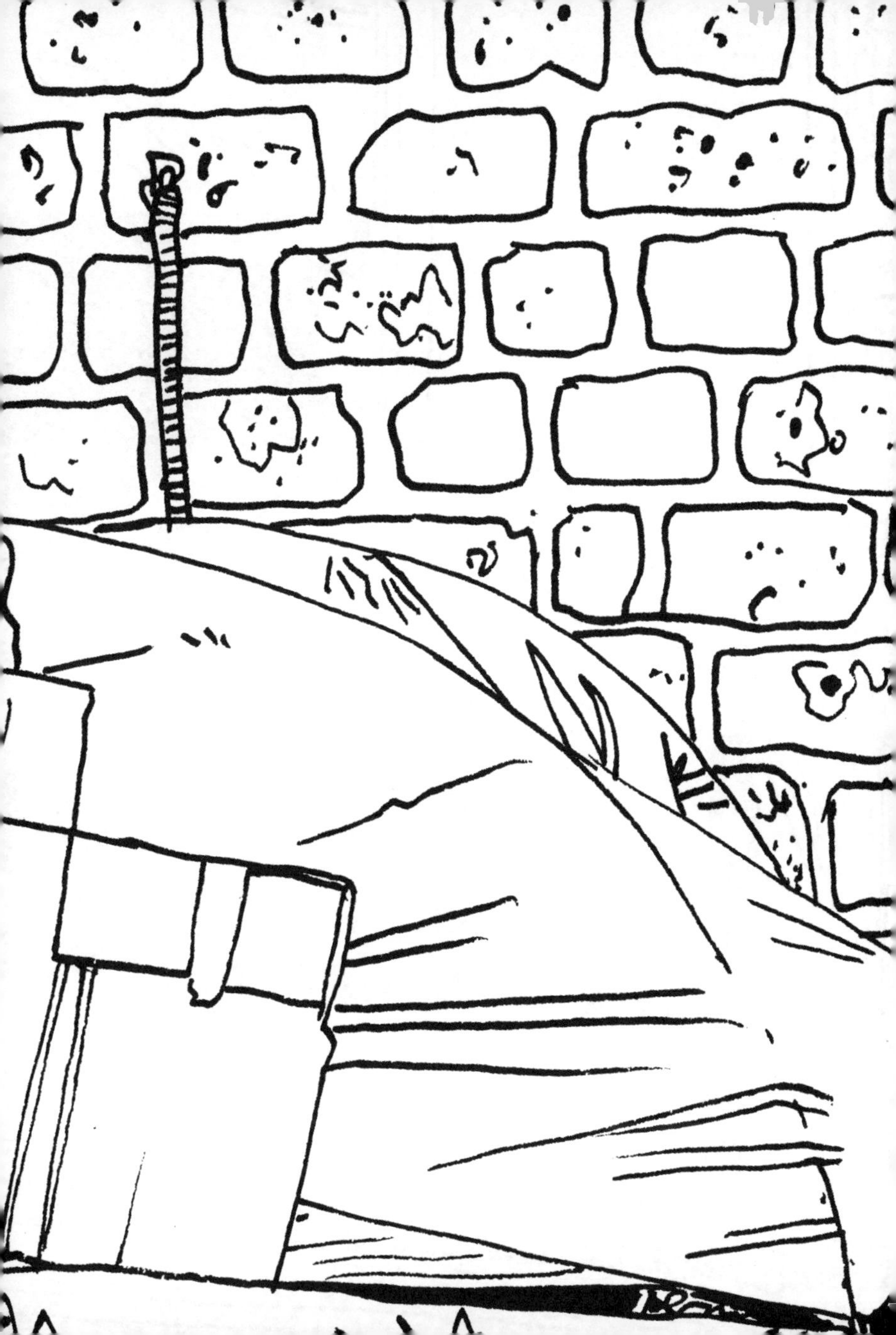

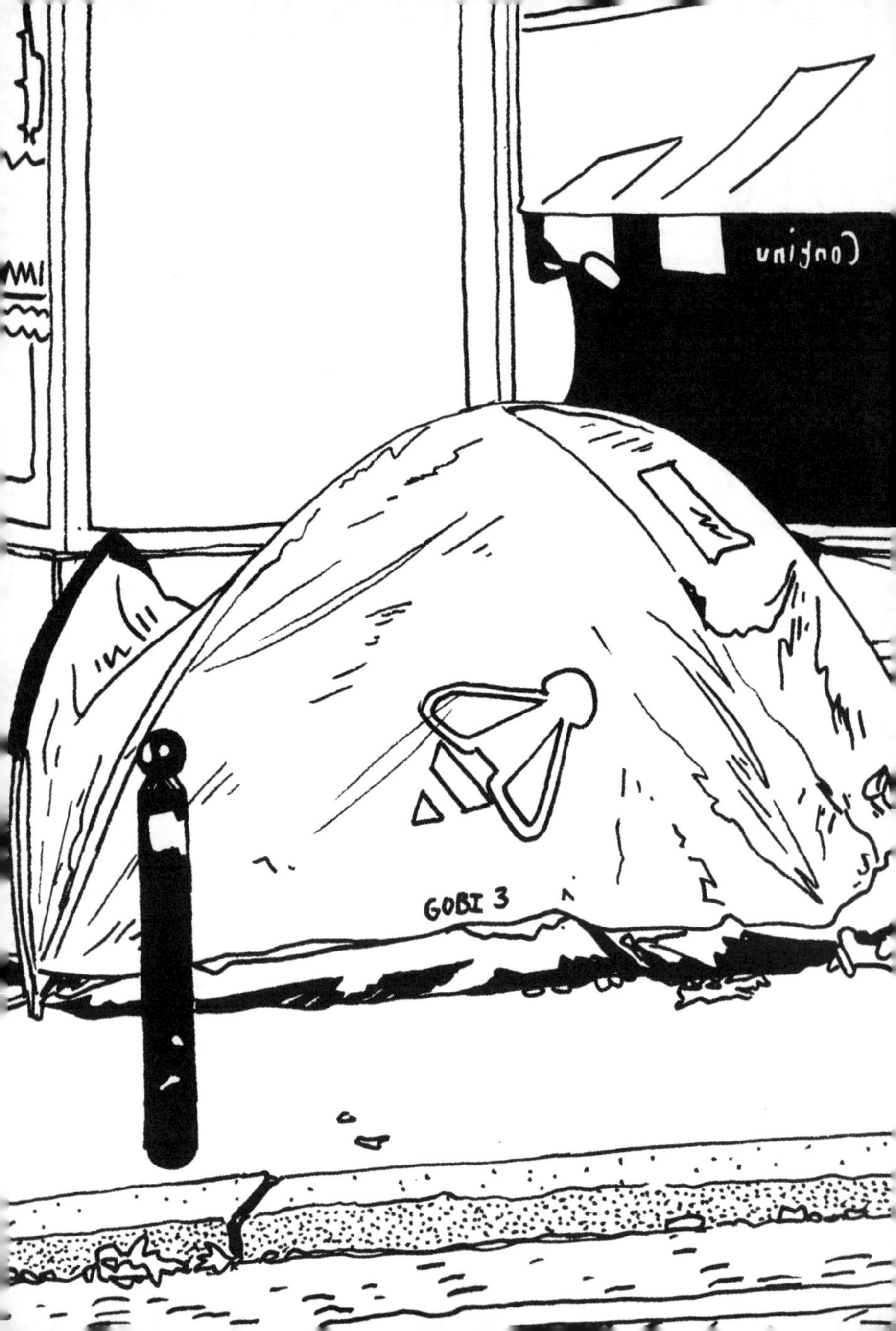
GOBI 3

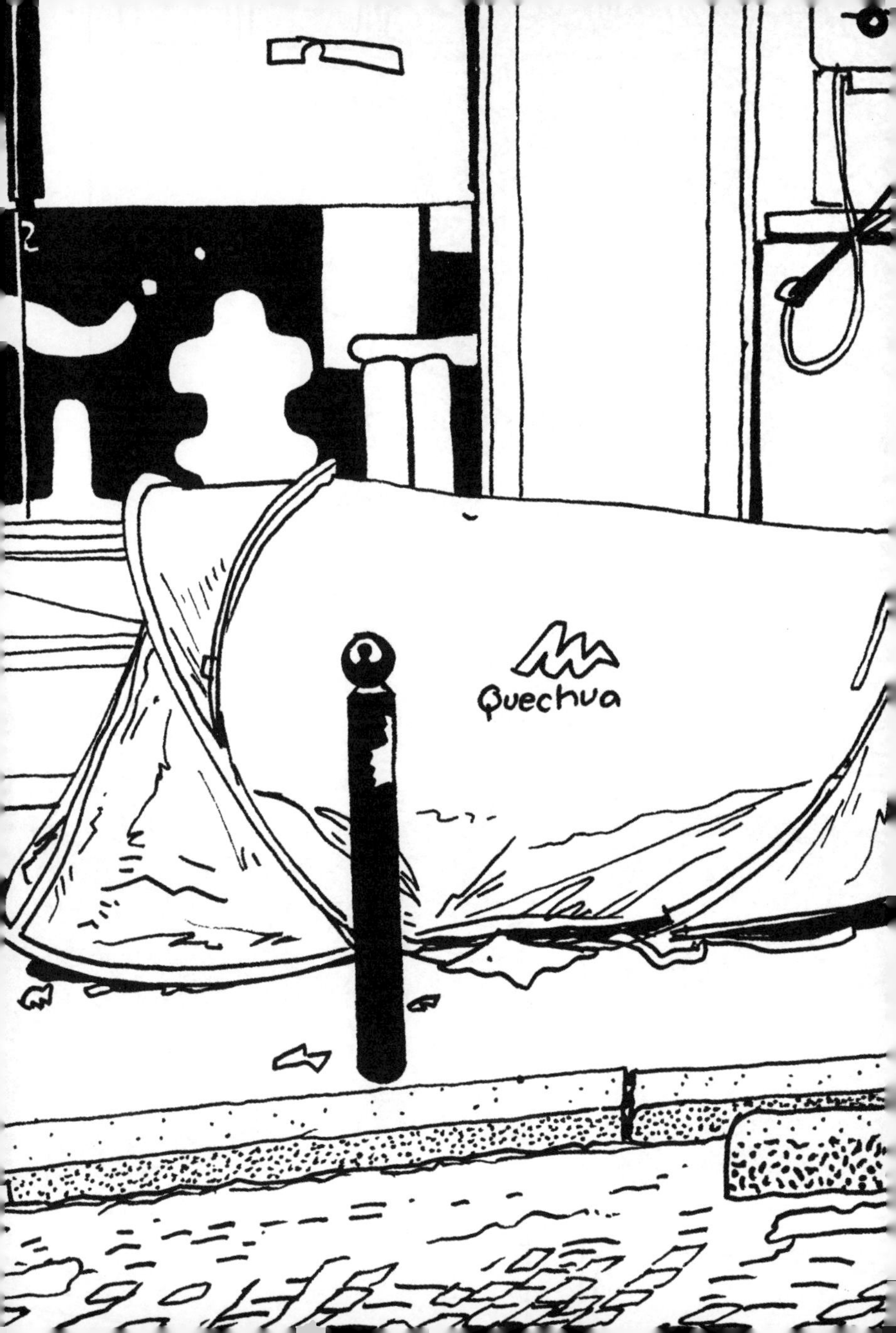
Quechua

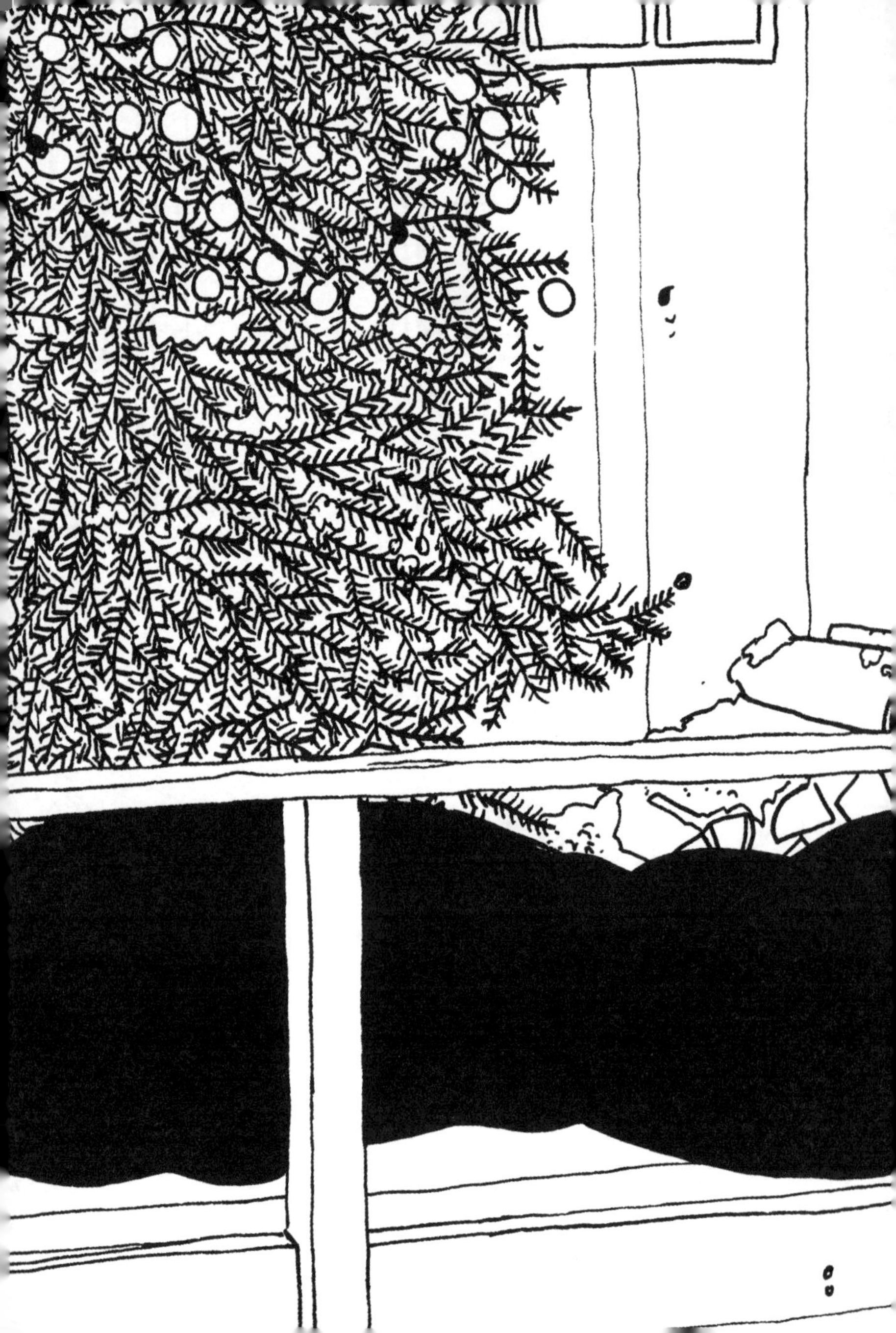

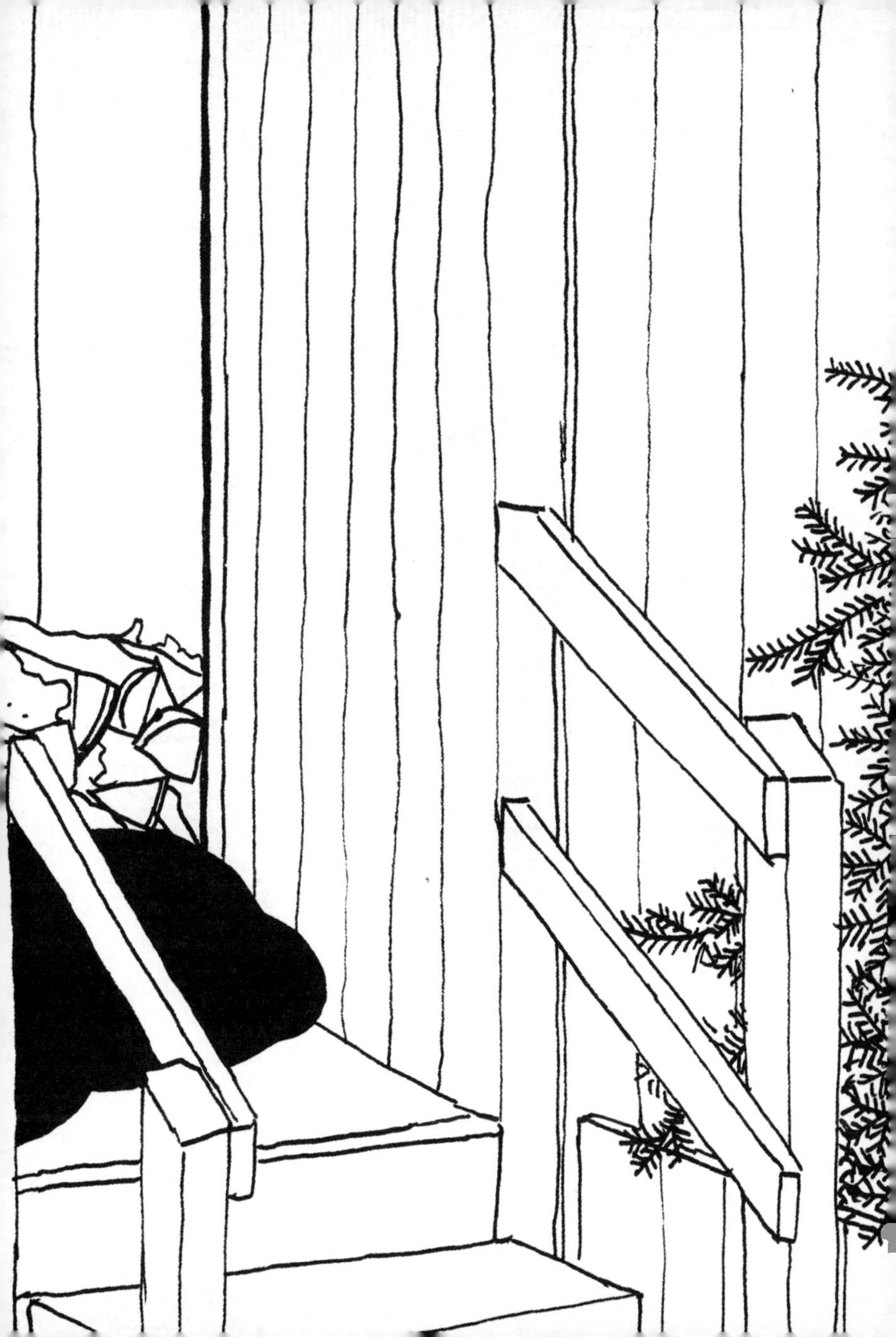

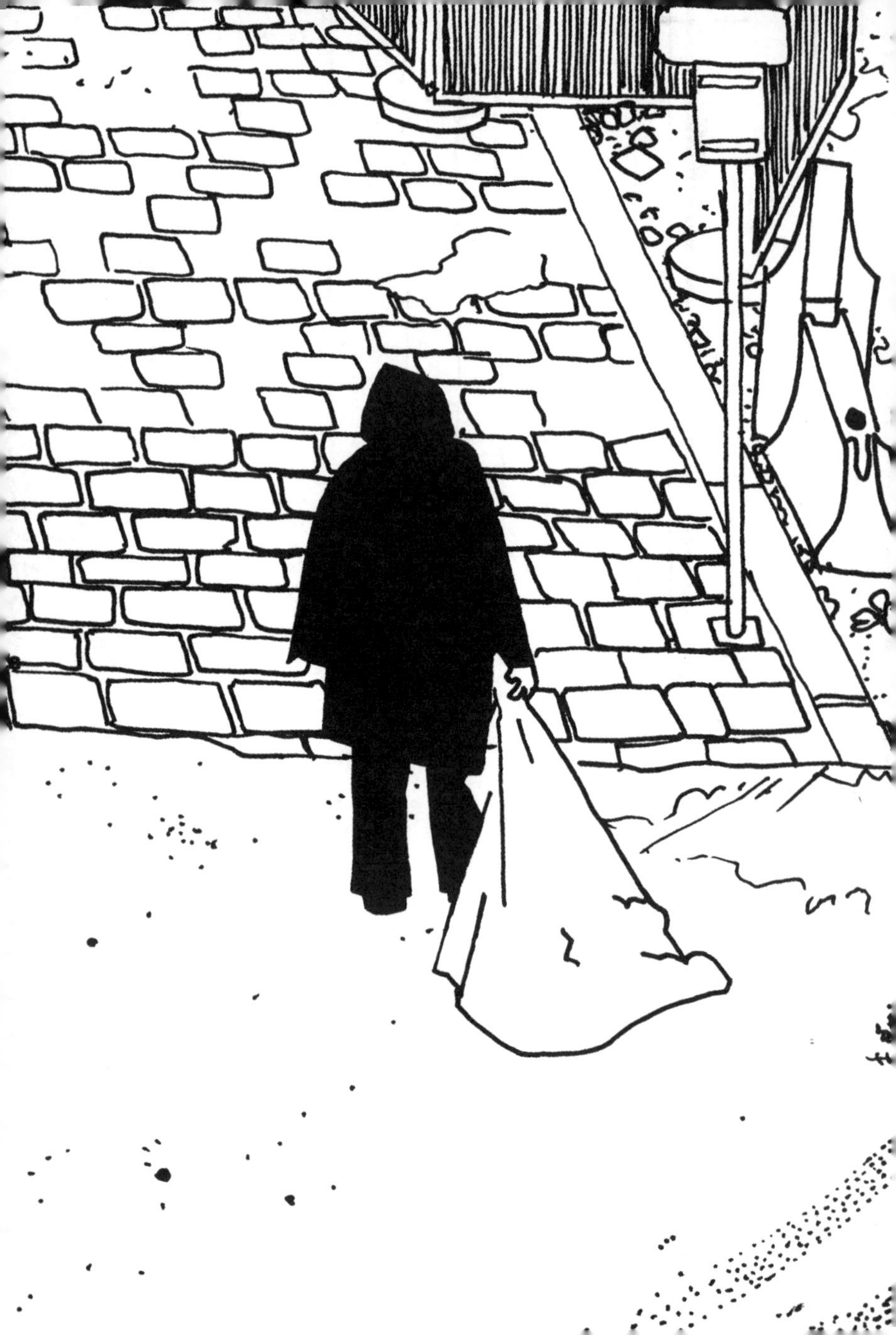